THOREAU
MYSTIC
PROPHET
ECOLOGIST

BOOKS BY WILLIAM J. WOLF

Man's Knowledge of God

No Cross, No Crown:
A Study of the Atonement

Lincoln's Religion

A Plan of Church Union

The Recovery of Unity:
The Thought of Frederick D. Maurice
(with John Porter)

THOREAU
MYSTIC
PROPHET
ECOLOGIST

WILLIAM J. WOLF

A PILGRIM PRESS BOOK

from United Church Press, Philadelphia

1997

Library of Congress Cataloging in Publication Data

Wolf, William J
  Thoreau: mystic, prophet, ecologist.

  "A Pilgrim Press book."
  Bibliography: p.
  1. Thoreau, Henry David, 1817–1862—Religion and
ethics. I. Title.
PS3057.R4W6   818'.3'09   73-22368
ISBN 0-8298-0269-X

Biblical quotations marked NEB are from *The New English
Bible,* © The Delegates of the Oxford University Press
and the Syndics of the Cambridge University Press, 1961.
Reprinted by permission.

United Church Press, 1505 Race Street,
Philadelphia, Pennsylvania 19102

TO
MY MOTHER AND FATHER
AND
THE FRIENDS
WHO HAVE
HELPED

CONTENTS

THOREAU CHRONOLOGY

1817 Born July 12 in Concord.

1833 Entered Harvard.

1837 Graduated from Harvard. Friendship with Emerson began. Started *Journal*. Taught short period in public school in Concord.

1838 Conducted a private school with his brother John. Lectured first time at Concord Lyceum.

1839 Ellen Sewall visited Thoreaus. Trip with John on Concord and Merrimack rivers.

1840 Published first essay and first poem in *Dial*. Wrote *The Service*.

1841 Signed off from First Parish. Went to live with Emersons for two years.

1842 Brother John died January 11.

1843 Helped Emerson edit *Dial*. Tutored children of William Emerson on Staten Island from May to December.

1844 Returned home and made pencils. Trip to Saddleback (Greylock).

1845 Built house at Walden and moved in July 4 for two years.

1846 Jailed overnight (July) for not paying poll taxes. Expedition to Katahdin.

1847 Left Walden (September) for a year at Emerson's house when latter lectured abroad.

1848 Delivered "The Rights and Duties of the Individual in

Relation to Government" ("Civil Disobedience") before Concord Lyceum. Published "Ktaadn and the Maine Woods" in *Union Magazine.*

1849 Published *A Week on the Concord and Merrimack Rivers.* "Resistance to Civil Government" ("Civil Disobedience") appeared in *Aesthetic Papers.* Met H. G. O. Blake of Worcester. First trip to Cape Cod (with Ellery Channing).

1850 Second trip to Cape Cod. Excursion to Canada (with Channing).

1851 Helped fugitive slave escape to Canada, one of many such occasions.

1853 Second trip to Maine woods. Published "A Yankee in Canada" in *Putnam's Monthly Magazine. Journal* entry about Association for Advancement of Science.

1854 Delivered "Slavery in Massachusetts" at abolitionist meeting in Framingham. Published *Walden* (August). Met Daniel Ricketson in New Bedford.

1855 Received gift of Oriental books from Thomas Cholmondeley. Third trip to Cape Cod.

1856 Surveyed at "Eagleswood," Perth Amboy. Met Walt Whitman.

1857 Fourth visit to Cape Cod. With Edward Hoar took third trip to Maine woods. Met John Brown in Concord.

1858 Published "Chesuncook" in *Atlantic Monthly.* Visited White Mountains.

1859 Father died February 3. Delivered "A Plea for Captain John Brown" immediately after Harpers Ferry.

1860 Last camping trip to Monadnock (with Channing). Delivered "The Succession of the Forest Trees." Caught cold that led to his death.

1861 Trip for health to Minnesota with Horace Mann, Jr. Began revision of his manuscripts.

1862 Died on May 6 of tuberculosis. Buried (now) in Sleepy Hollow Cemetery.

INTRODUCTION

Ever since Odell Shepard started me reading Thoreau's *Journal* at Trinity College, I have been increasingly interested in trying to solve some mysteries about Thoreau's religion. What, for example, did he really believe about God? How did he hold together his nature mysticism and his concern for social righteousness? And (more recently) how were his religion and ecology related to each other?

Having written on Lincoln's religion, I was naturally fascinated when Odell Shepard wrote in a preface to the Dover paperback of his *Heart of Thoreau's Journals* (p. x): "They bring back alive a man who, with all his extravagances, perversities, and fierce denunciations of much that America now stands for, is as quintessentially American as Abraham Lincoln. He comes, moreover, as great men are wont to do, in a time of great need." Next, the appearance of Walter Harding's *The Days of Henry Thoreau* spurred me on, because with it as the definitive biographical guide I could reread Thoreau chronologically to mark the development of his religious orientation. The third catalyst was a grant from the Fund for Theological Writing that made possible a year's absence from teaching duties at The Episcopal Theological School. I am very grateful to the donors of the Fund, not only for the grant but for a friendship of many years.

The place chosen to do the writing was our "summer place," two thousand feet high in Western Massachusetts, where the northwest winds blast the hill from which can be seen four of Thoreau's mountains: Greylock, Hoosac, Monadnock, and Wachusett. A relative of the Rice who put Thoreau up overnight on his 1844 walk over the Mohawk Trail to Saddleback helped me gravel a new road to our house that could be kept open when fifteen-foot drifts sealed off the old town road.

Special thanks are due my wife, Eleanor, who wanted to type the manuscript, and to our three sons, Edwin, John, and Stephen, who from their college and university libraries kept sending me needed books and articles.

In particular, I want to thank the following friends and scholars who have helped: Henry Bird, Larry Bothell, Robert and Sydney Brown, William Clark, John Coburn, Esther Dickinson, Edith Gleason, Harvey Guthrie, Anne McGrath, John and Pat Maines, Lloyd Patterson, Esther Phillips, John and Nelle Porter, Phil and Joan Porter, David Scott, Walter Sobol, Owen Thomas, Brendan Whittaker, and George Williams. I am especially grateful to Walter Harding, who read the manuscript and made valuable suggestions and comments.

1

THOREAU, HIS INTERPRETERS, HIS RELIGION

The incident recorded by Henry Thoreau in his *Journal* for March 5, 1853, explains his religious orientation as he himself understood it a little beyond midpoint in his writing years. The entry shows the complexity of his position and his awareness of the difficulty of communicating it to others. The confession of faith which it evoked, for that is what it really is, or as near to one as Thoreau would come, will be a useful guide in marking shifts in emphasis and developments in his religion up to May 1862, the date of his death.

The secretary of the (American) Association for the Advancement of Science, who had met Thoreau previously on a trip to Concord, wrote him, inviting him to become a member and to fill in a questionnaire about the branch of science that most interested him.

Now, though I could state to a select few that department of human enquiry which engages me, and should be rejoiced at an opportunity to do so, I felt that it would be to make myself the laughing-stock of the scientific community to describe or attempt to describe to them that branch of science which specially interests me, inasmuch as they do not believe in a science which deals with the higher law. So I was obliged to speak to their condition and describe to them that poor part of me which alone they can understand. *The fact is I am a mystic, a transcendentalist, and a natural philosopher to boot.* . . . Now I think of it, I should have told them at once that I was a transcendentalist. That would have been the shortest way of telling them that they would not understand my explanations.

How absurd that, though I probably stand as near to nature as any of them, and am by constitution as good an observer as most, yet a true account of my relation to nature should excite their ridicule only![1]

Thoreau's problem of self-understanding and communication appears manageable and somewhat within focus by contrast with the conflicting interpretations of his contemporaries and later critics. Broadly speaking, the basic divergence is between the naturalists and the humanists. Some of his disciples, more the heirs of Rousseau than the Thoreau they have canonized, advocate the cult of nature either as a solid good in its own right or as an escape from the problems of society and history. Others seem only to have read "Civil Disobedience" and, in defiance of the *Journal* of a lifetime, picture him as turning his back on nature to engage in radical politics and reform. Both camps have solid ground for their affirmations, but only a quaking bog for their denials. Both aspects are in Thoreau, but they are held by him in a dialectical unity that was seeking a deeper understanding of oneness in a religious dimension of experience and thought. The interpretation of Thoreau's religion which will be developed in this book owes much to the impressive body of Thoreau criticism that pours from the presses in accelerating volume; it seeks not so much to debate the major points of conflict between them as to complement their positions by pointing to the religious dimension so long neglected and yet so fruitful in interpretation. Thoreau enjoyed climbing mountains on his trips away from home and sauntering up his native Nawshawtuct Hill on his daily Concord walks, for the perspective it gave him on the countryside. The contention of this study is that the religious dimension provides a needed perspective in Thoreau scholarship and while it cannot, and should not, be offered as reconciling all divergence, it yet illuminates remaining points of opposition. Thoreau himself called for such an analysis when he wrote in his essay on Carlyle, "We want to hear more of his inmost life; his hymn and prayer more."[2]

Another polarity in interpreting Thoreau is between those who emphasize the details of his life and those who simply want to regard him as a writer, subject only to aesthetic.

canons of interpretation. The divorce is an unnatural one for any human being who takes up a pen, but it is especially so with respect to Thoreau, in whom integrity of life and of expression is interwoven in a rare and rich texture. Thoreau himself was aware of the problem when he wrote:

> My life has been the poem I would have writ,
> But I could not both live and utter it.[3]

Biographers of Thoreau have, in general, been slow to analyze their subject in terms of psychoanalytic theory, particularly in Freudian categories. Raymond Gozzi's *Tropes and Figures: A Psychological Study of Henry David Thoreau*[4] does just this, with special emphasis upon Thoreau's dominant mother and rather weak father, which he sees as leading to an unresolved Oedipus complex. Gozzi concludes that Thoreau's love of nature stemmed from unconscious mother fixation and his hostility to the state expressed repressed feelings of hate toward his family. He believes that Thoreau brought about his own death subconsciously through feelings of guilt and remorse after the death of his father. There is obviously rich pasture here for both measured and wild conclusions. There may be some viable explanation about his religious orientation, some way of accounting for his dislike of the excessively male terminology in Old Testament descriptions of God and his preference for certain Hindu ways. Any mystic is bound to use images which are erotic to describe his ultimate yearnings. What is plainly needed as an enrichment to the study of Thoreau would be an analysis of him by someone like Erik Erikson, who combined clinical experience in psychiatry, literary gifts, and imaginative insight into religious perspectives in his studies of Martin Luther and Gandhi.

Any study of Thoreau's religion which aims to be more than a catalog of religious terms and phrases must explore the experiential basis of his faith. Technical theological issues were almost never discussed by him, but this does not mean that specific experiences and crises in his life did not give rise to careful and exploratory thought. The difficulty is that his *Journal* is not primarily a diary of the events of the day or of self-analysis, but the recording in tranquil recollection and often in polished literary form of thoughts long after their initial stimuli had passed. Sometimes the original situation that gave the entries birth can be recovered from earlier passages in the *Journal.* Sometimes the use of Walter Harding's *The Days of Henry Thoreau,* a masterpiece of biographical research, will identify the context, but it is often a very uncertain enterprise. The journals of his friends Ralph Waldo Emerson, William Ellery Channing, and Bronson Alcott sometimes provide the needed clue. There have been brilliant analyses of the literary craftsmanship of *Walden,* but with a few exceptions they usually shy away from discussing Thoreau's religious orientation that helped to shape the literary energy displayed through at least eight revisions. He was not simply polishing his Damascus steel, but sharpening a weapon for the battle. Or, to paraphrase the quotation given about scientists, Thoreau might have said that there are critics who do not believe in a *criticism* which deals with the higher law.

The purpose of this analysis is not to establish a privileged sanctuary for the theologian by an imperialist rejection of other professional approaches to Thoreau, but simply to bid for equal time or minority representation in a crowded field of contenders. The theological community, indeed, has been strangely silent about Thoreau, quick to rebuke what without real study of his writings it assumed was "nature at the expense of people." It has been slow also to grasp the prophetic and biblical elements in his writings on social issues, often led back to him for the first time by later followers of some of his ideas, like Gandhi or Martin Luther King. The reasons for this neglect are many and cannot be analyzed here, except to point out that Thoreau's criticism of the churches of his day evoked a defensive attitude from offended orthodoxy that probably was inherited unconsciously by the contemporary religious community long after it or its fathers had accepted many of the points behind Thoreau's criticism and contempt. To a fellow boarder in the town of Haverhill, where he was surveying some sixty house lots, Thoreau prophesied, "Fifty years from now the majority of people will believe as I do now."[5] He was accurate as to the trend but overoptimistic about the time span and his electoral pluralities.

It is time to focus the conflict in interpretations more concretely on some religious questions. Joseph Wood Krutch, one of the most discerning and articulate writers on Thoreau, has not hesitated to face the religious issue. He reached the conclusion "that observation on the one hand, and a kind of pantheism much less humanistic than

Emerson's on the other," tended to become "more and more important parts of his activity and of his thought."[6] An equally discerning and able critic, Paul Elmer More, takes an opposite stand. He contrasts Shelley and Wordsworth with Thoreau. "But the deepest and most essential difference is the lack of pantheistic reverie in Thoreau."[7] The question of whether or not Thoreau was a pantheist remains a fascinating challenge for this study and will be discussed in the concluding chapter by way of evaluation after the evidence has been examined throughout his life and writings. The word pantheism itself is notoriously difficult to define: there is a much greater willingness today to discuss the issue without regarding the term as a derogatory epithet, but it was often used by the orthodox in Thoreau's time as a stick with which to beat him. When Horace Greeley, the editor of the New York *Tribune*, reviewed Thoreau's first book, *A Week on the Concord and Merrimack Rivers*, he praised it as a "fresh, original, thoughtful work" but added:

His philosophy, which is the Pantheistic egotism vaguely characterized as Transcendental, does *not* delight us. It seems secondhand, imitative, often exaggerated—a bad specimen of a dubious and dangerous school. . . . May we not hope that he will reconsider his too rashly expressed notions on this head?[8]

It remains to be seen whether Thoreau accepted any of this advice. Considering his resistance to criticism and his prized independence, it would seem most unlikely, but the evidence itself must be examined.

The conflict between interpreters of Thoreau can be driven back to the source. There are a number of unresolved parodoxes concerning his religious orientation that Thoreau was apparently quite willing to live with. Joseph Wood Krutch has ferreted out one which it is useful to analyze at this stage of investigation. "Like many of his contemporaries Thoreau had cast off institutional Christianity easily enough and, indeed, he cast off Christianity itself almost as easily—so far at least as it was specifically distinguished from the Oriental religions which he would put above it."[9] But within a page of further discussion Krutch senses a contradiction within Thoreau on this issue.

Thoreau could hardly have failed to be aware of the fact that the sermon which he spent his whole life preaching was on a text from that Bible, a book he professed to believe too exclusively emphasized, if not exactly overrated. "What is a man profited, if he shall gain the whole world, and lose his own soul?"[10]

It is quite possible that this apparent contradiction may be a key to understanding Thoreau. "Oriental religions" is in itself a very large order, since there are major points of difference between Hinduism in its myriad forms and Buddhism, for example, or even within Islam between the "orthodox" and the Sufi mystics whom he particularly admired. Obviously Thoreau selected within the Oriental religions certain elements of which he approved and rejected many features with which he was not in sympathy. This eclectic approach raises the question about the values from which he made his judgments and selections. The second quotation from Krutch supplies the answer. Unconsciously at most times, but occasionally rising to conscious awareness, Thoreau borrowed certain elements from the biblical tradition that had come to him through his Puritan inheritance, from the Christian training of his childhood, and from his biblical studies at Harvard. These biblical elements he played against what he called "the respectable Christianity" of his day, in much the same way that many of the biblical prophets and writers had done against the popular orthodoxies of their times. With this private selection of biblical values he pronounced contemporary Christianity deficient at times and from his highly selective reading of the Oriental religions saw them as superior. It will be a major task of this study to clarify Thoreau's biblical Puritan inheritance and to inquire whether the presupposed scale of values shifted with the years, resulting in changes of emphasis and evaluation. In short, did his enthusiasm for Eastern religions peak early? One of his major contributions to our day is his pioneering exploration of the riches of the world's religions, not his limited knowledge of them in an era before the comparative and anthropological study of religion had evolved. It can be more appreciated now in the Christian churches, as they more and more begin to enter that further phase of the ecumenical movement beyond just Christian reconciliation and commence live dialogue with representatives of the world's religions with a view to mutual understanding and respect and not as fodder for conversion. It is Thoreau's breaking out of the confined circle of Concord church life that still brings a liberation to many of his followers today who, like him, hunger for authentic religious experience for themselves and not the hand-me-downs of religious institutions and outmoded dogmas.

There is, of course, the danger of overinterpretation on the religious issue. One can mistake a casual reference to God as more dynamic for the whole of Thoreau's orientation than it really is. The method of symbolic interpretation, always an inviting one in studying Thoreau because he himself used it, can grow into a Frankenstein monster all on its own. One recent interpreter is resolved to find nearly every incident of the camping trip the brothers took in 1839 on the Concord and Merrimack rivers either a conscious or unconscious "nineteenth-century version of the Hindu itinerary of the divine journey (*devayana*) to spiritual liberation."[11] Thoreau described "the most constant and memorable sound of a summer's night," heard by the campers beside the stream, as "the barking of the house-dogs, . . . at first loud and rapid, then faint and slow, to be imitated only in a whisper; wow-wow-wow-wow—wo—wo—w—w."[12] Our interpreter sees and hears more.

But it is in the dissolution of "wow" into "wo," of "wo" into "w," and of the "w" into engulfing silence that he recaptures the essence of meditation on the mystical monosyllable *Om*. Adapting the sacred formula of deliverance to the New England scene, he prefigures his mastery of the technique of Indian *sanyama* (*sungyuma*). The union with *Brahman* implied in yoga is thus infused with the spirit of Concord harmony.[13]

Where everything becomes a symbol of something else, nothing retains meaning.

Thoreau, in many of the problems of philosophy and theology, remains the despair of a metaphysician determined on clarity and consistency, but on another level the very richness of his expression of unresolvable paradoxes or of viable alternatives brings to the reader the reassurance of integrity and of a ruthless honesty that will not give up the struggle in exchange for a philosophically tidy statement or a conventional religious platitude. But even here the difficulties are not ended. Sometimes the dryness of his humor has been lost on his commentators in such a way that a tongue-in-cheek comment by Thoreau, in which he implies the very opposite evaluation of what the words say, at least

on the first level of analysis, has been prosaically misinter-
preted by them to convey the very opposite of his meaning.
James Russell Lowell, for example, in a critical study that did
much to cause his contemporaries to ignore Thoreau's
genius, faulted him for a lack of humor. Lowell, with his
genially urbane humor, simply did not get Thoreau's point.
Another aspect of this problem is that Thoreau will often
say something in a rhetorical outburst that if quoted in
isolation will say the opposite of what he really means,
when, in the context of the whole passage, sentences before and after the telling remark provide the clue to the
meaning of the statement itself. At times he deliberately
exaggerates, and the reader is left to guess Thoreau's more
reasoned position. Many people have opinions about
Thoreau's religion that can be traced back to some quotation from him quoted by others that says almost the opposite of what he really meant when the original context is
reexamined. This study of Thoreau's religion will try scru-
pulously to avoid this pitfall of quotation out of context,
but since it does not aim at encyclopedic coverage of the
topic but rather at selective presentation of evidence, it
must confess vulnerability to criticism and a willingness to
learn from the debate.

For some time I tried to resist including the following
illustration, out of respect and gratitude for the distinguished
contributions Perry Miller has made in the understanding
of the New England mind, particularly in the seventeenth
century, and also for his editing of the so-called "Lost Journal" of Thoreau for the years 1840-41, but Miller has so
strikingly quoted Thoreau out of context as to falsify completely the meaning of a central passage. This error inval-
idates the supposedly withering charge of blasphemy that
he brings with rhetorical flourishes against Thoreau. The
passage is significant because Thoreau is speaking out of
sustained and reflected-upon anguish as he resumes his
Journal after the death by lockjaw of his older brother, John,
whom he adored. Beyond what it shows us about Thoreau's
dialogue with God, it demonstrates how completely even a
very competent scholar may fail to see the contextual problem of his religion. Let us first examine Perry Miller's reading of the entry from which he quotes only from its third
paragraph.

"My life, my life! why will you linger?" he exclaims, even in the selectivity of a *Journal* out of which spontaneity has been squeezed, on March 11, 1842, after he has come through the "sympathetic" lockjaw attendant on John's demise. Reviving to face the ordeal he could not escape, he dares ask God if He can afford that Henry should forget Him! Recognizing what he has, and all that he has, to work with, Thoreau makes his first venture—what was to become unfortunately a somewhat tiresome habit—into blasphemy:

"Why, God, did you include me in your great scheme? Will you not make me a partner at last? Did it need there should be a conscious material?"

The true "mythology" of the *Journal* is that Henry Thoreau, by the royal light of consciousness, identified himself with the Absolute, not even using Emerson's palliating circumlocution, "Over-Soul." So he fought for what remained of "my life" to be partner with the Almighty. Obviously he who strives to play the drama of such arrogance on the solid soil of Massachusetts is heading recklessly as Tamburlane or Faust toward catastrophe.[14]

It is possible that an alert reader confined only to the sentences quoted from Thoreau might question Miller's interpretation. His suspicion would be thoroughly aroused if he opened the *Journal* to the entry and saw the sentences curiously omitted within the third paragraph between "My life" and the resumption of the passage at "Why, God . . . ?" The reader's questioning, however, would be completely confirmed if he read the first two paragraphs of the entry of March 11, 1842. These paragraphs must now be quoted, not simply to establish Miller's misunderstanding but for the positive contribution they make to an understanding of Thoreau's religion.

March 11. Friday. Chaucer's familiar, but innocent, way of speaking of God is of a piece with his character. He comes readily to his thoughts without any false reverence. If Nature is our mother, is not God much more? God should come into our thoughts with no more parade than the zephyr into our ears. Only strangers approach him with ceremony. How rarely in our English tongue do we find expressed any affection for God! No sentiment is so rare as love of God,—universal love. Herbert is almost the only exception. "Ah, my dear God," etc. Chaucer's was a remarkably affectionate genius. There is less love and simple trust in Shakespeare. When he sees a beautiful person or object, he almost takes a pride in the "maistry" of his God. The Protestant Church seems to have nothing to supply the place of the Saints of the Catholic calendar, who were at least channels for the affections. Its God has perhaps too many of the attributes of a Scandinavian deity.

We can only live healthily the life the gods assign us. I must receive my life as passively as the willow leaf that flutters over the brook. I must not be for myself, but God's work, and that is always good. I will wait the breezes patiently, and grow as Nature shall determine. My fate cannot but be grand so. We may live the life of a plant or an animal, without living an animal life. This constant and universal content of the animal comes of resting quietly in God's palm. I feel as if I could at any time resign my life and the responsibility of living into God's hands, and become as innocent, free from care, as a plant or stone.[15]

In the first paragraph Thoreau yearns to express his love for God, recognizing how rarely it has been done in the English tongue and feeling a poverty in the expression of the affections in Protestantism, as against Catholicism with its communion of saints. In the second paragraph he turns even more concretely to his own situation. The "arrogance," identification "with the Absolute," and "blasphemy" detected by Miller is difficult to see in the words, "I must not be for myself, but God's work, and that is always good." They are not evident in the sense of liberation through commitment to God in the sentence immediately preceding Miller's first quotation from the entry. "I feel as if I could at any time resign my life and the responsibility of living into God's hands, and become as innocent, free from care, as a plant or stone."

Before leaving this entry it will be useful to look at the last paragraph. In it Thoreau turns to his friend Emerson, who is also in grief at the recent death of his five-year-old son Waldo. Thoreau would like to share his deepest feelings, but it became a tragedy of their friendship that Thoreau, very much like Kierkegaard, could not really communicate them.

My friend, my friend, I'd speak so frank to thee that thou wouldst pray me to keep back some part, for fear I robbed myself. To address thee delights me, there is such clearness in the delivery. I am delivered of my tale, which, told to strangers, still would linger on my lips as if untold, or doubtful how it ran.[16]

Thoreau was not given to discussing the depths of his religious orientation with others and was very suspicious of voluble revivalists with their religious chatter. When a neighbor who had just completed an expensive house staged a showy illumination, supposedly to celebrate the Atlantic telegraph, with "Glory to God in the highest" blazoned in great letters, Thoreau was critical. "I felt a kind of shame for [it], and was inclined to pass quickly by, the ideas of indecent exposure and cant being suggested. What is religion? That which is never spoken."[17]

This last definition, should it be taken literally as Thoreau's only position on the question, would bring this inquiry to a screeching halt. It should at the very least remind us that the only trustworthy authority on his religion is Thoreau himself, and not his contemporaries. They may have felt they knew, but they were largely drawing conclusions from fragmentary evidence, almost never from exhaustive discussion with Thoreau himself on a topic which he treated with reserve. Accordingly, after this introductory chapter there will be little discussion with other students of Thoreau about their analyses of his religion and only limited quotation from his contemporaries. The solid body of Thoreau's own writings, now being restored to us in accurate texts by a dedicated company of Thoreau scholars drawn together by Professor Harding and the Princeton University Press, must remain the absolutely primary source for the interpretation of his religion. This method also makes it necessary to quote extensively from Thoreau's writings, so that the reader can judge for himself. This decision to concentrate upon Thoreau himself will of necessity bar much consideration of his borrowings from his fellow Transcendentalists, especially Emerson. There are many instances when Thoreau uses phrases that are found in Emerson in a way quite different from Emerson's meaning in context. The important issue is what Thoreau meant by the words he used, regardless of their supposed source elsewhere.

The last commitment of this study to be recorded here is the attempt to understand the developmental aspect of Thoreau's religion, for it was not a static thing. In preparation for writing this book, the *Journal,* his letters, poetry, two published books, and the essays were completely reread in chronological order, or as near to this as it is possible to get with a number of essays that were only published after his death. These articles or lectures were revised many times by him during his lifetime. The two published books, moreover, had gestation periods of ten and eight years respectively. The order of chapters will be approximately chronological. There is a table of events and writings to help the reader chronologically. Amid the dense vegetation of a primitive wood, a winter tote road becomes at times visible, now lost in swamps, now obscured on rocky ground, now merging with a well-worn portage trail. It leads to an appreciation of his religion.

The chapter began with Thoreau's response to the Association for the Advancement of Science and his declaration, "I am a mystic, a transcendentalist, and a natural philosopher to boot." It may fitly end with an illustration of his first two descriptions of himself, not so much as a solemn statement of self-recognition but as the unconscious background for one of his better-known poems. His poetry is seldom distinguished—his versification is often singsong rather than musical—but it contains nuggets of his thought and feelings. One seems to be hearing echoes from Donne and Herbert, for Thoreau had a genuine fondness for the metaphysical poets. Since "Inspiration" is one of his longer poems, it will be necessary to use only limited quotations from it here. It is essentially a description of an experience of illumination that comes to a mystic, of deeper levels of awareness opened up not by the poet's striving but by his response to God's initiative, and of Thoreau's commitment to a divine love that is seen not only as supportive but redemptive in quality.

> Whate'er we leave to God, God does,
>   And blesses us;
> The work we choose should be our own,
>   God lets alone. . . .
>
> But now there comes unsought, unseen,
>   Some clear, divine electuary,
> And I who had but sensual been,
>   Grow sensible, and as God is, am wary.
>
> I hearing get who had but ears,
>   And sight, who had but eyes before,
> I moments live who lived but years,
>   And truth discern who knew but learning's lore.
>
> I hear beyond the range of sound,
>   I see beyond the range of sight,
> New earths and skies and seas around,

And in my day the sun doth pale his light. . . .

I will not doubt forever more,
    Nor falter from a steadfast faith,
For though the system be turned o'er,
    God takes not back the word which once he saith.

I will then trust the love untold
    Which not my worth nor want has bought,
Which wooed me young and woos me old,
    And to this evening hath me brought.

My memory I'll educate
    To know the one historic truth,
Remembering to the latest date
    The only true and sole immortal youth.

Be but thy inspiration given,
    No matter through what danger sought,
I'll fathom hell or climb to heaven,
    And yet esteem that cheap which love has bought.[18]

2

SIGNING OFF FROM ORGANIZED RELIGION

A fascinating discovery among Thoreau documents was made in 1972 from town records deposited in the Concord Free Public Library. In a letter of one sentence, Thoreau signed off from the First Parish, the church in which his family worshiped, in which he had been baptized by the patriarchal Rev. Ezra Ripley, and in which he had been instructed, he later said, to his displeasure in church school.

Concord Jan. 6th 1841

Mr. Clerk

Sir

I do not wish to be considered a member of the First Parish in this town.

Henry D. Thoreau[1]

In his essay on "Civil Disobedience," published in 1849, he explained his earlier brush with the state over the surviving elements of the Puritan religious establishment. It was an act of dissociation that prefigured his refusal to pay his poll tax in 1846 and symbolized his lifelong criticism not merely of state churches but of organized religion in any form.

Some years ago, the State met me in behalf of the Church, and commanded me to pay a certain sum toward the support of a

clergyman whose preaching my father attended, but never I myself. "Pay," it said, "or be locked up in the jail." I declined to pay.
But, unfortunately, another man saw fit to pay it. I did not see
why the schoolmaster should be taxed to support the priest, and
not the priest the schoolmaster; for I was not the State's schoolmaster, but I supported myself by voluntary subscription. . . .
However, at the request of the selectmen, I condescended to make
some such statement as this in writing:—"Know all men by these
presents, that I, Henry Thoreau, do not wish to be regarded as a
member of any incorporated society which I have not joined."
This I gave to the town clerk; and he has it. The State, having thus
learned that I did not wish to be regarded as a member of that
church, has never made a like demand on me since; though it said
that it must adhere to its original presumption that time.[2]

In order to relate the signing off from the First Parish
(Unitarian) of Concord to Thoreau's thoughts at the time, it
is necessary to consult the *"Lost Journal"* for January 1841.
Two days after writing the town clerk he entered a mocking
poem somewhat in imitation of the New England Primer:

The church bell is not a natural sound to the church goer.

> Who hears the parson
> Will not hear the bell,
> But if he deafly pass on
> He will hear of hell.
>
> I' faith the people go to church
> To leave the devil in the lurch,
> But since they've carpeted the pews
> To squat with hymn book he doth use.[3]

Within a week, however, he recorded in the *Journal* a
solemn religious commitment about the significance of
keeping his journal. He may not have looked to the institutional church for guidance, but he embarked upon a spiritual pilgrimage that shaped alike his life and his journal.
He one time advised that when knocking at the gate of
heaven one should ask for the master and not be put off
by the servants.

We should offer up our *perfect* thoughts to the gods daily—our
writing should be hymns and psalms. ·Who keeps a journal is

purveyor for the gods. There are two sides to every sentence; the one is contiguous to me, but the other faces the gods, and no man ever fronted it. When I utter a thought I launch a vessel which never sails in my haven more, but goes sheer off into the deep. Consequently it demands a godlike insight—a fronting view, to read what was greatly written.[4]

Thoreau's family were churchgoers and kept the New England institution of the long sabbath. An amusing anecdote is told of Henry at the age of three or four years. He announced that he did not want to die and go to heaven because his sled was not fine enough for that place, for the boys with whom he had been coasting told him his sled, not being shod with iron, was not worth a cent. Another childhood incident was described by his mother. When she found him still awake in bed she asked, "Why, Henry dear, why don't you go to sleep?" "Mother," said he, "I have been looking through the stars to see if I couldn't see God behind them."[5] In a sense, that search was precisely his task for the rest of his life, as both a pilgrim and a literary craftsman. From age eleven or twelve, there survives a short essay on "The Seasons," suggesting again the theme of so much adult attention and prefaced by four lines of poetry with a sense of the creator's power.

> Why do the seasons change? and why
> Does Winter's stormy brow appear?
> Is it the word of him on high
> Who rules the changing varied year?[6]

Pastor Ezra Ripley ran a tight ship but seemed somehow to carry his people with him in the early disputes that saw Unitarianism emerge out of the Congregational Church. The Concord parish dropped the shorter catechism and then specific Trinitarian references. In 1826, however, the conservatives, largely Calvinist, protested and out of the disruption founded an Orthodox Trinitarian Church with Elizabeth, Jane, and Maria Thoreau, Henry's aunts, as charter members. Cynthia Thoreau, Henry's mother, also seceded in 1827 but for some reason, perhaps because of her independent spirit, was adjudged by the new church ineligible for fellowship. In some embarrassment she returned to the First Parish, where she continued a member until her death, outliving all her children except Sophia. This zealous sectarian strife was not likely to make a favorable impression on a sensitive ten-year-old boy. The popular picture of Thoreau as the hermit of Walden Pond is badly out of focus. He only spent two years, two months, and two days there. Most of his life was spent in the family circle, with maiden aunts and many paying guests around him. There is evidence that various members of this large family fretted about his lack of orthodoxy, but he seemed to take it all in tolerant spirit, recording once in obvious amusement in his *Journal* his Aunt Maria's complaint to Aunt Jane after he had refused her request that he read a biography of Dr. Chalmers: "Think of it! He stood half an hour today to hear the frogs croak, and he wouldn't read the life of Chalmers."[7] They must, however, have been a trial to him. The afternoon walk would be all his own. It was probably Aunt Maria, moreover, who wrecked his protest against slavery and the Mexican War by promptly paying his poll tax when he was put in jail.

The family skimped and sent Henry to Harvard, after preparation at the Concord Academy. Many found it strange that Henry and not his older brother, John, who seemed far more promising than Henry, should have been the one chosen for higher education. In terms of religious development there is very little to report from the Harvard years 1833-37 until his last year there. Henry attended compulsory chapel and took required courses in religion, studying Paley and Butler, the English theologians. Never given to the niceties of metaphysics or the classic arguments for the existence of God, Thoreau does at times in the *Journal* seem to have Paley's and Butler's arguments from design as a working hypothesis behind his exclamations of beauty and order. A pupil of Henry's, when Henry taught for a short time after graduation with his brother at the Concord Academy, recalled his talks following morning prayers "on design in the universe, strikingly illustrated for children's minds."[8] During a break from college he taught school at Canton and stayed in the house of Orestes Brownson, that excited reformer, who passed through Presbyterianism, Unitarianism, and various social experiments to find an anchor afterward in Roman Catholicism. By the evidence of the correspondence he kindled a response in Henry as they studied German together and discussed the rising tide of Transcendentalism.

A number of Thoreau's essays written on topics assigned by Harvard's professor of rhetoric, Edward Channing, have been preserved. For the most part they are conventional in their handling of religious matters, but now and then a gleam of independent questioning appears. One theme, numbered seventeen in Sanborn's editing and dated by him in late spring of 1837, deals with "The Sublime." The following paragraph begins with orthodox Christian presuppositions and then rises toward a perspective all Thoreau's own.

Nay, further,—can anything be conceived more sublime than that second birth, the Resurrection? It is a subject which we approach with a kind of reverential awe. It has inspired the sublimest efforts of the poet and the painter. The trump which shall awake the dead is the creation of poetry; but (to follow out the idea) will its sound excite in us no emotion? or will the Blessed, whom it shall summon to forsake the mouldering relics of mortality, and wing their way to brighter and happier worlds, listen with terror or indifference? Shall he who is acknowledged while on earth to have a *soul* for the sublime and beautiful in nature, hereafter, when he shall be *all* soul, lose this divine privilege? Shall we be indebted to the body for emotions which would adorn Heaven? And yet there are some who will refer you to the casting off of this "mortal coil" as the beginning and, I may add, the consummation of all this.[9]

Farther on in the essay he is struggling to find the root of the religious impulse itself. His description begins to approach "the numinous," as it would be analyzed much later by Rudolph Otto in his classic *The Idea of the Holy*. Thoreau is reaching out toward that precritical, undifferentiated matrix of "religious awe" before it is moralized in subsequent advances. It will be interesting later to see how his growing interest in "the wild" will be related to his primary insight into the religious phenomenon.

The emotion excited by the Sublime is the most unearthly and godlike we mortals experience. It depends for the peculiar strength with which it takes hold on and occupies the mind, upon a principle which lies at the foundation of that worship which we pay to the Creator himself. And is fear the foundation of that worship? Is fear the ruling principle of our religion? Is it not, rather, the mother of superstition?

Yes, that principle which prompts us to pay an involuntary homage to the Infinite, the Incomprehensible, the Sublime, forms the very basis of our religion. It is a principle implanted in us by our Maker,—a part of our very selves. We cannot eradicate it, we cannot resist it; fear may be overcome, death may be despised;

but the Infinite, the Sublime, seize upon the soul and disarm it. We may overlook them, or rather, fall short of them; we may pass them by,—but so sure as we meet them face to face, we yield.[10]

Another essay of his senior year, perhaps reflecting discussions with Brownson that may have led him to withdraw Benjamin Constant's *On Religion* from the Harvard Library on April 27, 1837, shows him boldly advocating Constant's rejection of traditional religion as a necessary step to moral excellence. The way was being prepared for signing off from the First Parish.

None, in fine, but the highest minds, can attain to moral excellence. With by far the greater part of mankind, religion is a habit, or rather, habit is religion, their views of things are illiberal and contracted, for the very reason that they possess not intellectual power sufficient to attain to moral excellence. However paradoxical it may seem, it appears to me that to reject Religion is the first step towards moral excellence; at least, no man ever attained to the highest degree of the latter by any other road.[11]

At his commencement exercises in a "conference" on "The Commercial Spirit of Modern Times, Considered in Its Influence on the Political, Moral, and Literary Character of a Nation," Thoreau, who had been selected as a speaker, condemned materialism and showed how it corrupted patriotism, domestic relations, and (enlarging the topic) religion. He pled for men to lead "manly and independent" lives and attacked the commercial exploitation of the world with a wisdom toward which we are being driven today by our worsening ecological crisis. Many of the chief themes of his future authorship were handled in this address.

This curious world which we inhabit is more wonderful than it is convenient; more beautiful than it is useful; it is more to be admired and enjoyed than used. The order of things should be somewhat reversed; the seventh should be man's day of toil, wherein to earn his living by the sweat of his brow; and the other six his Sabbath of the affections and the soul,—in which to range this widespread garden, and drink in the soft influences and sublime revelations of Nature.[12]

The greatest influence upon Thoreau in the first years out of college was his deepening friendship with Ralph Waldo

Emerson, fourteen years his senior. Emerson was an established figure when in 1834 he settled down in the Concord of his ancestral ties. Some called him a grand old man at age forty. He had already given up the ministry of the Second Church in Boston from misgivings about celebrating the Lord's Supper. His Concord home rapidly became a magnet for reformers from all over the country and abroad. His generous personality and sociability attracted many friends to take up residence in the village. His effect upon the young Thoreau was dynamic. The ultimate recognition of Thoreau's genius was long postponed partly because so many critics insisted on viewing Thoreau as Emerson's disciple. This he was with passionate intensity in his early years, but he soon began to outgrow this apprenticeship with a cooling of their earlier relationship, a development not understood by many of Thoreau's early interpreters. The seminal book of Thoreau's late-college reading and early postgraduate period was Emerson's *Nature,* published in 1836. Thoreau took his platform for action directly from the book and then proceeded to begin its realization with such fidelity and discipline that he soon outdistanced his teacher.

The foregoing generations beheld God and nature face to face; we, through their eyes. Why should not we also enjoy an original relation to the universe? Why should not we have a poetry and philosophy of insight and not of tradition, and a religion by revelation to us, and not the history of theirs?[13]

These words without any alteration could serve as a statement of the purpose and even of the remarkable realization of Thoreau's entire life. Emerson in the next few years followed up this program by delivering his well-received address at Harvard on the "American Scholar" and then by giving at the Divinity School a talk in 1838 that so alienated the conservative faculty that he was not invited back for some twenty years. At the Divinity School he complained that clergy took a backward view of revelation, with the result that they spoke and acted "as if God were dead." Emerson was really the first of the "God is dead" theologians. Thoreau took over many of the terms and phrases of Emerson's analysis, as can be seen from his *Journal,* but he remained quite independent of Emerson's special ways of reasoning.

Partly this original divergence which would increase with the years was stylistic; Emerson tended to make sweeping generalizations in fairly abstract terminology, whereas Thoreau retained concreteness and specificity at all stages. Emerson was perceptive of this difference: "In reading Thoreau, I find the same thoughts, the same spirit that is in me; but he takes a step beyond, and illustrates by excellent images, that which I should have conveyed by a sleepy generalization."[14]

Partly the divergence came from their temperaments and from quite different histories of mental and life struggle. Emerson had pioneered in the movement away from the older Unitarian divines; he had to a great degree borne the heat and battle of the day in giving shape to Transcendentalism. Henry Thoreau was almost a second-generation phenomenon. He went quickly from a conventional college outlook to a wholehearted acceptance of the movement with little of the blood, sweat, and tears of the early Emerson. In great agony of soul and at times depression of spirit, Emerson withdrew from the ordained ministry; with a stroke of the pen Thoreau withdrew from the First Parish. Emerson brought with him during this transition period all the baggage of his professional theological education. Paradoxically, this gave him points of continuity with what went before (which Thoreau lacked), but it also brought him to feel a need to formulate his theological positions with precision in a way that Thoreau never seemed compelled to do.

To illustrate, early in his essay *Nature* Emerson wrote the following sentence, which in one sense is at once a more explicit statement of pantheism and yet a more vapid definition than Thoreau would ever make. No person conversant with Thoreau's writings could ever make the mistake of attributing this sentence of Emerson's to him: "I become a transparent eye-ball; I am nothing; I see all; the currents of Universal Being circulate through me; I am part or parcel of God."[15]

Scholars are accustomed to approach Transcendentalism in fear and trembling because of the many disputes about its origins, influence, and basic tenets. It is best understood as a distinctively American idealist and romantic phenomenon, although its contributors were Greek (Plato, Plotinus), German (Kant, Jacobi, Fichte, Shelling, Schleiermacher, Goethe), English (Wordsworth, Coleridge, Carlyle), and French (Chateaubriand, Constant), together with the native evolution of the Puritan moral theology from the Mathers to Jonathan Edwards and on through the first generation of Unitarians. Into the American melting pot they went, and out of it emerged a New England Renaissance. It was "romanticism in a Puritan setting," to use a phrase quoted by F. O. Matthiessen. From the side of the theory of knowledge, it represented a revolt from the dominance of the empirical movement in British philosophy. Locke had typified this empiricism with his test for truth as conformity to the evidence of the senses. Its very name reflected Kant's conviction that in addition to the empirical basis in knowledge there are a priori categories that are the result of intuition. This complex of experience is then clarified by three "transcendental" ideals of the reason, that of self, of world, and ultimately of God. Kant looked also to the moral law for knowledge of God. The New England Transcendentalists made conscience the infallible guide. Professor Ahlstrom makes a helpful comment:

The term "transcendentalist" is of uncertain origin and ambiguous in meaning. Kant gave currency to the term, but the early Transcendentalists were not rigorously Kantian. The term, whether used in ridicule or as finally accepted, indicated their concern for the higher use of Reason and its objects: the Good, the True, the Beautiful, the Divine.[16]

To the conservatives of that time, many of whom were not so much descendants of the older Calvinists as of the rationalistic Unitarians—"corpse-cold," to use Emerson's epithet—it was a threatening counterculture. It had coteries and the headiness of being "in" or "with it," until the bubble burst after about fifteen years as its gains became culturally acclimatized and its shocking newness began to seem old hat. To a remarkable degree, it was a clerical movement. Margaret Fuller, as a laywoman, had to keep pushing in order to be recognized. Thoreau, also a layman, was not interested in struggling to be recognized by the parsons or ex-clerics. Ironically, Octavius Brooks Frothingham's classic *Transcendentalism in New England* fails to discuss him at all. Published in 1876, the book is indispensable for understanding the movement through which the author and his father lived. It was an Indian Summer manifestation of Transcendentalism itself, as the following quotation so well brings out in style and content.

It possessed the character of indefiniteness and mystery, full of sentiment and suggestion, that fascinates the imagination, and lends itself so easily to acts of contemplation and worship. . . . Religion felt it, literature, laws, institutions. . . . The various reforms owed everything to it. New England character received from it an impetus that never will be spent. It made young men see visions and old men dream dreams. There were mounts of Transfiguration in those days, upon which apostles thought they communed visibly with lawgivers and prophets.[17]

If, however, we wish to see Transcendentalism in its real expression and not a humpty-dumpty collection of scholarly eggshells, we must examine the *Dial,* its early literary organ, edited first by Margaret Fuller and then by Emerson, assisted by Thoreau, who actually put the April 1843 issue together himself. Thoreau contributed thirty-one articles, essays, poems, and translations to the *Dial.* Emerson already looked upon "his Henry" as the writer destined to realize his fondest hopes for the new, self-reliant American. More than that, Henry could garden, graft an orchard, repair broken things, and take the children blueberrying. On April 26, 1841, Emerson induced Henry to move in with them as odd-jobs man for almost two years, with his room at the head of the stairs. He had the run of the library with all those fascinating Oriental books for which he had apparently been acquiring a taste at college but which now became, for a time, almost a passion. Later in May of 1843, as part of Emerson's plan for getting him close to publishing and literary circles in New York, he arranged to have Thoreau live with his brother's family on Staten Island as tutor to the children. Thoreau, however, was not happy and returned to Concord after Thanksgiving, never again to give up permanent residence there.

The July 1842 *Dial* carried his "Natural History of Massachusetts," supposedly a review of a number of books on the flora and fauna of the state but actually more of a mosaic of passages from the *Journal.* In it he criticizes "some creeds in vestries and churches" and the dreariness of "sedentary sects," affirming joy as "the condition of life." Thoreau reports that seventy-five genera and one hundred and seven species of fish are covered in the report, but adds that he is wiser "for knowing that there is a minnow in the brook." Then he introduces us to the idea of the brotherhood of creation, which will become a central ecological theme as the years develop. "Methinks I have need even of his sympathy, and to be his fellow in a degree."[18]

The October 1843 *Dial* printed his "Winter Walk," after severe revisions by Emerson. Near the close of the essay there is some imaginative assessment of the need for religious revelation to be ecologically appropriate to its natural and seasonal setting.

The good Hebrew Revelation takes no cognizance of all this cheerful snow. Is there no religion for the temperate and frigid zones? We know of no scripture which records the pure benignity of the gods on a New England winter night. Their praises have never been sung, only their wrath deprecated. The best scripture, after all, records but a meager faith. Its saints live reserved and austere. Let a brave devout man spend the year in the woods of Maine or Labrador, and see if the Hebrew Scriptures speak adequately to his condition and experience, from the setting in of winter to the breaking up of the ice.[19]

There is a poem of Thoreau's from the *Dial* which is a remarkable testament of faith. The view of God presupposed is hardly that of Emerson's "I am part or parcel of God." God for Thoreau, even at the time of maximum Emersonian influence, is still one who is believed capable of answering petitions for concrete requests. In a survival from the Puritan belief in special providence, the poet believes that God has secretly made a covenant with his worshiper, who prays to know and realize his "purpose" and "designs" as "an elect individual." Suspicion about one's friends, a problematic but common theme in Thoreau, is not grounded here in the misanthropy with which his critics charge him, but is seen as a by-product of the poet's intimacy with God and of dedication to his purposes. The editor of Thoreau's poetry comments that "this prayer is peculiarly characteristic of Thoreau."

> Great God, I ask thee for no meaner pelf
> Than that I may not disappoint myself,
> That in my action I may soar as high,
> As I can now discern with this clear eye.
>
> And next in value, which thy kindness lends,
> That I may greatly disappoint my friends,
> Howe'er they think or hope that it may be,
> They may not dream how thou'st distinguished me.

That my weak hand may equal my firm faith,
And my life practice more than my tongue saith;
That my low conduct may not show,
Nor my relenting lines,
That I thy purpose did not know,
Or overrated thy designs.[20]

There is one element in Thoreau's religion which, according to the evidence of a quarter of a century of journal keeping, did not change. It was his continuous criticism of the churches and, even more, of their professional leaders, the clergy. There were solid grounds for the criticism, values often deeply central in the churches themselves but sacrificed readily by them in institutional conformance to the militant materialism of America. There was also, however, in Thoreau a carping bitterness and a loveless contempt that becomes, for anyone who reads the *Journal* to list his references to organized religion, a weariness to the flesh. One can enjoy the irony, humor, and satire when it is present, but the fatiguing sameness of the denunciation resembles nothing so much as a phonograph needle catching in the same groove or the irksome habit of the sectarians in early seventeenth-century England of "railing against meeting house steeples." Thoreau, particularly sensitive to sound, often reacted in a Pavlovian way when he heard the church bell ring.

One might speculate about causative factors in this compulsive criticism. He had grounds for bitterness. His teaching in the Concord public school came to an end when he refused to keep order by whipping at the demand of a school board member, a deacon of the church. Behind Ellen Sewall's rejection first of John's offer of marriage (for the younger brother stood aside to give the elder first chance) and then of his own perhaps too feebly pressed and cryptic request for her hand, there loomed constantly the disapproval of Ellen's father, a conservative Unitarian clergyman at Scituate who considered the Thoreaus dangerous examples of the newest form of infidelity, Transcendentalism. Of course Ellen herself made the decision. Thoreau had refused to go to church with Ellen when she visited Concord. His letter signing off from the First Church was written within two months of Ellen's rejection of him. His nonconforming views about religious matters, moreover, brought him trouble in the reviews of his books and battles with editors, who, to his mounting anger, took it upon themselves to censor his articles. He might have hoped for a favorable review for *A Week* from the New York *Tribune*, with its editor Horace Greeley a friend, but Greeley's review, while favorable to elements in the book, criticized his "Pantheistic egotism" and read him a long lecture on biblical inspiration. The review undoubtedly kept readers from the book. He had trouble with editors sensitive to his criticism of the Roman Catholic Church in *A Yankee in Canada* and to the Protestant establishment in *Cape Cod*. The most famous incident, of course, was his clash with James Russell Lowell, then editor of the *Atlantic*, who without his permission simply deleted the following line from "Chesuncook," the essay that would appear after his death as the second in the trilogy, *The Maine Woods*: "It [the pine tree cut down] is as immortal as I am, and perchance will go to as high a heaven, there to tower above me still."[21] Lowell, wounded by Thoreau's angry letter, as Emerson has testified, criticized Thoreau's writing after his death in a way that did much to hold back the recognition of his stature. In spite of these tribulations it is difficult to make a case that Thoreau felt personally persecuted by orthodox religious forces or that his attitude toward the churches and their clergy was conditioned by a "sour grapes" syndrome. The sorry performance of these nineteenth-century churches, all too obvious today, is explanation enough. His criticism of them had all the rough honesty and harshness of a biblical prophet.

Thoreau's basic charge was that they were taking their ease in Zion, having lost their revolutionary thrust and having been paid off by the exploiters of the people and the comfortable advocates of materialism. He sensed that "respectable Christianity" was no Christianity at all. Even Jesus was redrawn as a gentleman, the prototype of a successful businessman.

Neither England nor America have any right to laugh at that sentence in the rare book called *The Blazon of Gentry*, written by a zealous student of heraldry, which says after due investigation that "Christ was a gentleman, as to the flesh, by the part of his mother, . . . and might have borne coat-armor." . . . Whatever texts we may quote or commentaries we may write, when we consider the laws and customs of these two countries we cannot fail to perceive that the above sentence is perfectly of a piece with our practical commentary on the New Testament. The above is really a pertinent reason offered why Christianity should be embraced in England and America. Indeed, it is, accordingly, only what may be called "respectable Christianity" that is at all generally embraced in the two countries.[22]

More particularly, Thoreau correctly charged the churches as being accomplices with the state in defending and perpetuating slavery. He acknowledged that there was a ministry of church people and clergy dedicated to the eradication of the evil, like Daniel Foster, the Universalist pastor of Concord, who, he was glad to hear, had been at the demonstration on the Boston waterfront against the forced return of Sims to slavery by federal officials acting under the Fugitive Slave Law. He rejoiced that it was a Concord citizen who had offered prayer there for the victim and for the abolition of slavery. He recorded on another occasion that Foster had said in a sermon, "Thank God, there is no doctrine of election with regard to Nature! We are all admitted to her."[23] Thoreau gave Foster an autographed copy of A Week, but he did not go to his church.

The churches, however, were not only outraging the common feelings of humanity, in their cowardly acquiescence in state-protected slavery, but were contradicting the solemn law of Christ. Thoreau took very seriously Jesus' parable in Matthew 25 about the help to the poor, the sick, the hungry, the naked, and the imprisoned as being a service to Christ himself and the denial of such help a persecution of Christ himself.

A government that pretends to be Christian and crucifies a million Christs every day! . . . a church that can never have done with excommunicating Christ while it exists. . . . The United States exclaims: "Here are four millions of human creatures which we have stolen. We have abolished among them the relations of father, mother, children, wife, and we mean to keep them in this condition. Will you, O Massachusetts, help us to do so?" And Massachusetts promptly answers, Aye![24]

When the chips were down and the American people were confronted by John Brown's raid, the churches either remained silent or criticized any resort to violence. Even the abolitionists in their professional organizations and papers went by on the other side of the road. They had institutionalized reform into an establishment that ministered as much to the neurotic needs of the reformers, Thoreau thought, as showed compassion for the victims of injustice. Thoreau recorded in his *Journal* the *Liberator*'s verdict that Brown's raid was "a misguided, wild, and apparently insane . . . effort" and Thoreau shot back, "If Christ should appear on earth he would on all hands be denounced as a mistaken, misguided man, insane and crazed."[25] Earlier he had written, unconsciously prophetic of just that element in Islam which in our day would seem a liberating gospel from white Christianity to many blacks:

I perceive no triumphant superiority in the so-called Christian over the so-called Mahometan. That nation is not Christian where the principles of humanity do not prevail, but the prejudices of race. I expect the Christian not to be superstitious, but to be distinguished by the clearness of his knowledge, the strength of his faith, the breadth of his humanity.[26]

Another of Thoreau's charges against the churches of his day was their timidity of spirit, their lack of adventurousness in the life of the spirit, their backward look to the authority of past revelation rather than receptivity to new revelation. "The church is the hospital for men's souls, but the reflection that he may one day occupy a ward in it should not discourage the cheerful labors of the able-bodied man."[27] Much in this vein is to be compared with Dietrich Bonhoeffer's criticism of a presentation of the Christian faith that exploits the weakness of man rather than builds upon his strength, that tries to insert religion into the crisis areas of life rather than witness to God at the very center of existence. Thoreau scoffed at the church as "a baby house made of blocks." It denied freedom of speech in a nervous pressure for conformity. There was no policeman like the parson. It was "like stale gingerbread." One must not take a deep breath lest the edifice come tumbling down. "It is eminently the timid institution, and the heads and pillars of it are constitutionally and by principle the greatest cowards in the community. . . . The best 'preachers,' so called, are an effeminate class; their bravest thoughts wear petticoats." He added that on his trips to lecture he tried to stimulate the audience by reporting the best of his experience, but "I see the craven priest looking round for a hole to escape at, alarmed because it was he that invited me thither, and an awful silence pervades the audience. They think they will never get me there again. But the seed has not fallen in stony and shallow ground."[28] This last sentence illustrates Thoreau's detailed knowledge of the Bible and his ability to give authority to his own words by a clever twist or turn of the original passage. Often Thoreau's seeming heterodox point or impious act is established by a delicious irony as true on the basis of Christ's teaching.

One of the worst flaws of church life was the suppression of the child's questions rather than a welcoming of his new insights. Did Thoreau speak from his experience of being indoctrinated in Sunday school?

It is remarkable that the highest intellectual mood which the world tolerates is the perception of the truth of the most ancient revelations, now in some respects out of date; but any direct revelation, any original thoughts, it hates like virtue. The fathers and the mothers of the town would rather hear the young man or young woman at their tables express reverence for some old statement of the truth than utter a direct revelation themselves. They don't want to have any prophets born into their families,—damn them! . . . We check and repress the divinity that stirs within us, to fall down and worship the divinity that is dead without us. . . . They think they love God! It is only his old clothes, of which they make scarecrows for the children. Where will they come nearer to God than in those very children?[29]

At times Thoreau's criticism has some resemblance to Soren Kierkegaard's *Attack on Christendom,* in which truly prophetic criticism tends to lose its effectiveness and be overwhelmed by querulousness and blather.

If it were not for death and funerals, I think the institution of the church would not stand longer. The necessity that men be decently buried—our fathers and mothers, brothers and sisters and children (notwithstanding the danger that they be buried alive)—will long, if not forever, prevent our laying violent hands on it. . . . What is the churchyard but a graveyard? . . . The cry that comes up from the churches in all the great cities in the world is, "How they stink!"[30]

Again and again, however, the situation is rescued by some keen flash of insight that recognizes that behind the corruptions of the organization there is the foundation of truth, a truth revolutionary in its potential. Within a few months of the foregoing diatribe Thoreau wrote, on March 5, 1852:

It is encouraging to know that, though every kernel of truth has been carefully swept out of our churches, there yet remains the dust of truth on their walls, so that if you should carry a light into them they would still, like some powder-mills, blow up at once.[31]

When we shift our attention from the church as such to the people who compose it we discover another source of Thoreau's hostility to organized religion. He is a mystic of such developed individualism, both in practice and theory, that he just cannot see a group of people meaningfully relating to each other and to a wider compass beyond them and mediating what for him must remain an essentially incommunicable experience. He regards the word church as belonging to a class of words "which are spurious and artificial. . . . It is in vain to try to preserve them by attaching other words to them as the *true* church, etc. It is like towing a sinking ship with a canoe."[32] For Thoreau the deepest religious experience has about it all the marks of the particularity and individual creativeness of the poet.

A great cheerfulness have all great wits possessed, almost a prophane levity to such as understood them not, but their religion had the broader basis in proportion as it was less prominent. The religion I love is very laic. The clergy are as diseased, and as much possessed with a devil, as the reformers. They make their topic as offensive as the politician, for our religion is as unpublic and incommunicable as our poetical vein, and to be approached with as much love and tenderness.[33]

Although Thoreau heaped most of his censure upon the clergy, he found little to reassure him in the laity. All their prayers, he said, began with "Now I lay me down to sleep." They wanted nothing to change; surprises were anathema. The modern Christian made his historic liturgies into an opiate as he showed "the whites of his eyes on the Sabbath and the blacks all the rest of the week."[34]

No one has reported Thoreau as saying, "Some of my best friends are clergy, but—." He was a dedicated anticlerical, carrying his feeling like a chip on his shoulder. When he met the Rev. John Weiss, an old Harvard classmate, he baited a trap. "Have you ever yet in preaching been so fortunate as to say anything?" Weiss allowed he had. "Then your preaching days are over. Can you bear to say it again? You can never open your mouth again for love or money."[35] It took an extraordinary event for him to attend church. He went, however, in Concord to hear his old teacher from Harvard, Henry Ware, Jr., and Father Taylor of the Boston waterfront, the colorful original of Father Mapple in *Moby Dick;* both men were regarded as saints. Emerson recorded in his diary that it was "droll" to see Thoreau in church. With Bronson Alcott he went to hear Henry Ward Beecher at the Plymouth Church in Brooklyn, but found it "pagan," an interesting pejorative use of the adjective for Thoreau. It was probably the emotionalism and confident air of Beecher that put him off, for he later wrote snappishly in his *Journal,* "If Henry Ward Beecher knows so much more about God than another, if he has made some discovery of truth in this direction, I would thank him to publish it in *Silliman's Journal,* with as few flourishes as possible."[36]

With the poet Ellery Channing, his most intimate friend, he took a special excursion by train to Canada in 1850. He was impressed with the opportunities for individual silent worship in Notre Dame in Montreal and in the simple village churches. He contrasted the piety of the French Canadians with the Yankee failure to use the church save for corporate worship, and often participation in that only in the local building in town. "As if you were to catch some farmer's sons from Marlboro, come to cattle-show, silently kneeling in Concord meeting-house some Wednesday! Would there not soon be a mob peeping in at the windows?"[37] One must not conclude, however, that Thoreau was ripe for conversion to Catholicism, although an acquaintance of his at their boarding table in Concord, who later became a priest and founded the Paulist Order, Isaac Hecker, unrealistically hoped for this from the evidence of some interesting letters that passed between them.[38] Thoreau qualified his admiration for Quebec Catholicism by saying that it seemed to him that priests and people had "fallen behind the significance of their symbols" and then by concluding that "this Catholic religion would be an admirable one if the priest were quite omitted."[39] It is now clear why Emerson in his funeral oration called him "a born protestant . . . a protestant à *outrance.*"[40] As they camped beside Moosehead Lake, his Indian guide, Joe Polis, criticized Thoreau's way of spending the sabbath. "He stated that he was a Protestant, and asked me if I was. I did not at first know what to say, but I thought that I could answer with truth that I was."[41]

There was one exception to his anticlericalism. He greatly admired the labors of the Jesuits among the Indians, quoting some more than three hundred pages from the *Jesuit Relations* in the eleven manuscript volumes of his Indian Notebooks.[42] He also was delighted by many of the early Puritan ministers who wrote their charming local histories of New England towns. For him, it would not be an exaggeration to say, the only good clergyman was a dead clergyman.

Even the liberal clergyman fared ill at his hands. There was always the suspicion of a "system," even as a presupposition when the more obvious external institutions had been removed. One journal passage must serve as the representative for many of similar emphasis.

But in the clergyman of the most liberal sort I see no perfectly independent human nucleus, but I seem to see some indistinct scheme hovering about, to which he has lent himself, to which he belongs. It is a very fine cobweb in the lower stratum of the air, which stronger wings do not even discover. . . . Whatever he may say, he does not know that a man's creed can never be written, that there are no particular expressions of belief that deserve to be prominent. He dreams of a certain sphere to be filled by him, something less in diameter than a great circle, maybe not greater than a hogshead. All the staves are got out, and his sphere is already hooped. What's the use of talking to him? When you spoke of sphere-music he thought only of a thumping on his cask. . . . What great interval is there between him who is caught in Africa and made a plantation slave of in the South, and him who is caught in New England and made a Unitarian minister of? In course of time they will abolish the one form of servitude, and, not long after, the other. . . . Here's a man who can't butter his own bread, and he has just combined with a thousand like him to make a dipped toast for all eternity![43]

The Quakers, with their simplicity and plainness and lack of an ordained clergy, fared better than the others, but Thoreau would be suspicious even of silence when it became a corporate "method," not to speak of that inevitable substitute for a cleric, "the weighty Friend." To his sister Helen he wrote about attending the Friends Meeting in Hester Street, New York, and how the Quaker bonnets and handkerchiefs made the women look like chickadees.

At length, after a long silence, waiting for the spirit, Mrs. [Lucretia] Mott rose, took off her bonnet, and began to utter very deliberately what the spirit suggested. Her self-possession was something to say, if all else failed—but it did not. Her subject was the abuse

of the Bible—and thence she straightway digressed to slavery and
the degradation of woman. It was a good speech—transcendentalism in its mildest form. . . . On the whole I liked their ways, and
the plainness of their meeting house. It looked as if it was indeed
made for service.[44]

But he was always quick to spot hypocrisy under any piety.
On a visit to his friend Daniel Ricketson in New Bedford
he sought out the only pure-blooded Indian left in those
parts. "A conceited old Quaker minister, her neighbor, told
me with a sanctified air, 'I think that the Indians were human
beings; dost thee not think so?' He only convinced me of
his doubt and narrowness."[45]

Eight Worcester ministers received better treatment than
the rest. They wrote asking his advice for a camping trip in
the White Mountains. He replied at great length about
clothing, food, bough beds, and shelter. Now there were
ministers for you! Perhaps he felt something like he did
when he recorded in his *Journal* a visit to Amherst, New
Hampshire: "Lectured in basement of the orthodox church,
and I trust helped to *undermine* it."[46] It is amusing that with
his solemn manner he was mistaken more than once for a
clergyman. Mrs. Minot Pratt remembered that "he was more
like the ministers than others; that is, like they would wish
and try to be."[47] Thoreau would not have regarded it as a
compliment. Most amusing of all, however, is to find him
writing the president of Harvard and virtually claiming
"benefit of clergy" for himself by an interpretation which
would allow him to take books from the library under the
provision that neighboring clergymen might borrow books.

Both Thoreau and Abraham Lincoln are reported to have
enjoyed telling the story of the boy making a church out of
mud. They shared a common dislike for the petty sectarian-
ism of their day. The Thoreau version of the story runs as
follows: "Why, making a meeting house out of that stuff?"
asked the minister. "I am," replied the boy, "and I expect to
have enough left over to make a Methodist minister
besides."[48]

When Frank Sanborn settled in Concord, he was told that
there were three churches there—the Unitarian, the Orthodox, and the Walden Pond Society. Needless to say, Thoreau
was the unofficial priest of the third. He had written after
the visit to Notre Dame in Montreal, "In Concord, to be

sure, we do not need such. Our forests are such a church, far grander and more sacred."[49]

We have seen that the greater part of Thoreau's criticism of organized religion arises from values central to the biblical revelation itself. He often quotes from the Gospels to make his point. While there are tiresome tirades, most of the criticism springs from a feeling of perfectionism that he was prepared to apply to any religious institution as well as to his friends and to himself. He detested hypocrisy. Part of the liberation that he would find in the Oriental books was that he could pick and choose without regard to the expression of these literary sources in the actual living religious institutional expression of these faiths. He did, however, meet some of this organizational context of the Oriental faiths in his omnivorous reading of travel books, and it is clear that he did not always like what he found.[50] The point to be made is that his individualism and mysticism made him incapable of sympathy for any communal expression of the religious impulse, with very few exceptions. Creeds, methods, systems were all alike suspect wherever found, not just in the Judeo-Christian tradition.

A fitting conclusion to this chapter is one of his most beautiful poems, recalling Simonides but better than any of his, according to Emerson. The poem describes the ascent of smoke from his hearth, presumably at Walden. The poet knows where he stands ("this clear flame") and offers his life and activity as incense on the altar, but he recognizes the danger of pride (the Greek *hybris*) and therefore asks pardon of the gods.

> Light-winged Smoke, Icarian bird,
> Melting thy pinions in thy upward flight,
> Lark without song, and messenger of dawn,
> Circling above the hamlets as thy nest;
> Or else, departing dream, and shadowy form
> Of midnight vision, gathering up thy skirts;
> By night star-veiling, and by day
> Darkening the light and blotting out the sun;
> Go thou my incense upward from this hearth,
> And ask the gods to pardon this clear flame.[51]

3

THE RELIGIONS
OF *A WEEK*
ON *THE CONCORD*
AND MERRIMACK RIVERS

Three events in Thoreau's life led up to his writing *A Week on the Concord and Merrimack Rivers* over a period of ten years, with its publication finally in 1849 at his own expense. First, there was the vacation trip itself. In August 1839 Thoreau and John, both teachers at the Concord Academy, rowed northward down the Concord River and then, by the linkage of the old Middlesex Canal, up the Merrimack to just below Concord, New Hampshire. Leaving their home-made boat there, they hiked through the White Mountains and returned home, a trip of about two weeks' duration. The *Journal* for 1839 gives only the briefest outline, but an entry about nine months after that begins the process of recollection and shows the basic pattern that the book would take, an exploration by river into the stream of thought. "So with a vigorous shove we launch our boat from the bank, while the flags and bulrushes curtsy a God-speed, and drop silently down the stream. As if we had launched our bark in the sluggish current of our thoughts and were bound nowhither."[1]

The second event, the sudden and shattering death of John in January 1842, led Thoreau to conceive of his writing project as a memorial to his brother. Many of the things said about friendship in *A Week* and in the *Journal,* which are automatically referred by most commentators to Emerson, probably have John as their primary reference.

The third event was Thoreau's decision to leave his noisy

family house for a time and go live at Walden Pond. After he had built his small house near the shore on Emerson's newly acquired woodlot, he moved in with his simple belongings on Independence Day 1845. There were many reasons for the Walden experiment, but one of the most obvious was to find a block of time to write the *Week*.

The previous chapter discussed some of Thoreau's contributions to the *Dial,* but it remains here to examine one of his chief features for that magazine as a prelude to his writing of the *Week*. Urged on by Emerson, Thoreau excerpted from the Oriental books passages which he liked from Hinduism, Confucianism, Sufi Islam, Buddhism, and others and published them in four installments in the *Dial* for the years 1843 and 1844. Emerson had begun this serial feature in the July 1842 issue with a preface that both set the ground rules for the project and undoubtedly influenced Thoreau's handling and evaluation of materials.

We commence in the present number the printing of a series of selections from the oldest ethical and religious writings of men, exclusive of the Hebrew and Greek Scriptures. Each nation has its Bible more or less pure; none has yet been willing or able in a wise and devout spirit to collate its own with those of other nations, and sinking the civil-historical and ritual portions to bring together the grand expressions of the moral sentiment in different ages and races, the rules for the guidance of life, the bursts of piety and of abandonment to the Invisible and Eternal,—a work inevitable sooner or later, and which we hope is to be done by religion and not by literature.[2]

The important thing to be grasped at this point is the highly eclectic and subjective use which Thoreau made of these documents. Quotations were torn from their context in such a way that it almost becomes more significant for our understanding of Thoreau's attitudes to the Eastern religions to see what was deliberately cast aside than what was admitted to the new Transcendentalist canon of world scriptures.[3] There is one later example of this practice from the *Week* which is particularly illuminating. It shows that Thoreau chose what interested him in terms of imaginative insight and metaphor even at the expense of suppressing part of the context and in this case the very quotation itself, when it became too metaphysical or dogmatic for his tastes. "It is the attitude of these men," he writes, "more than any communication which they make, that attracts us." Then he praises the Brahmans for a "conception of creation [as] peaceful as a dream. 'When that power awakes, then has this world its full expansion; but when he slumbers with a tranquil spirit, then the whole system fades away.' "[4] This quotation is from his favorite *Laws of Menu,* but it will now be given in full as it occurs in the Jones translation which Thoreau used, with the section omitted by Thoreau placed in italics.

When that power awakes, *for, though slumber be not predicable of the sole eternal mind, infinitely wise and infinitely benevolent, yet it is predicated of Brahma, figuratively, as a general property of life,* then has this world its full expansion; but, when he slumbers with a tranquil spirit, then the whole system fades away.[5]

Thoreau's conclusion drawn from this quotation, after he has licked it into shape, is fascinating. His mysticism leads him to praise the "very indistinctness" of the conception, his inheritance through Puritanism produces the biblical stress on the transcendence of God, and his poetic instinct seizes upon the picture of divinity awakening and slumbering. Thoreau was delighted when any "system fades away" even if, as here, he had to give it a shove. "In the very indistinctness of their theogony a sublime truth is implied. It hardly allows the reader to rest in any supreme first cause, but directly it hints at a supremer still which created the last, and the Creator is still behind increate."[6] This passage from *A Week* derives from the *Journal,* in which the section concludes with this addition, "The divinity is so fleeting that its attributes are never expressed."[7]

The idea that the *Week* is an attack upon Christianity in favor of the Eastern religions, a view taken by early reviewers of the book and still surprisingly accepted by too many modern commentators, is far too simplistic an analysis. Thoreau's intense individualism and mysticism make him critical of any social, institutional expression of religion in any form, whether Western or Eastern. At times he is prepared to favor Eastern mysticism over the Judeo-Christian tradition in which mysticism has been historically mediated, but at other times it will often be values from the biblical heritage of Puritanism and Transcendentalism that lead him to criticize elements in the Eastern religions. Although the *Week* is a far more theoretical book than *Walden,* it would be a mistake to read it as a carefully reasoned essay in the philosophy of religion, with clear judgments on the various forms of the human religious enterprise. Thoreau's evaluations are often cryptically expressed in one sentence, seldom developed into a sustained paragraph. Like a guest confronted with a smorgasbord, he chooses here and there at will and in peril of indigestion. In later years he would stress simpler eating habits. The hunger, however, is genuine; Thoreau hungers and thirsts for vision. The following passage should be accorded a far more central position in Thoreau criticism than it has had:

The most glorious fact in my experience is not anything that I have done or may hope to do, but a transient thought, or vision, or dream, which I have had. *I would give all the wealth of the world, and all the deeds of all the heroes, for one true vision.* But how can I communicate with the gods, who am a pencil-maker on the earth, and not be insane?[8]

The *Week* is a highly poetic, tentative grappling with the religious dimension of human existence. It is expressed historically in the analysis of religions in the essays of "Sunday" and "Monday," but it is chiefly described in terms of personal experience in "Tuesday" on the heights of Greylock, the mountain of theophany, the symbolical Sinai of Thoreau's Transcendentalism.

There were still other elements of delight to be discovered in these Eastern books. Perhaps the single most exciting find was the realization by Emerson and Thoreau that their own New England Transcendentalism had been underwritten thousands of years before them by these great cultures of high morality and enthusiastic piety. To these pioneer Americans, almost the first to take the explosion of translations of the sacred books of the East seriously, new planets were appearing. Arthur Christy's *The Orient in American Transcendentalism*, an early study in this field which needs some correction, saw the point very clearly in its discussion of the idealistic philosophy of the Hindus, the down-to-earth wisdom of Confucius, and the artistic poetry of the Mohammedan Sufis.

These three Oriental cultures were eclectically blended, despite their inherent contradictions, into a composite which in miniature is an excellent representation of that larger Transcendentalism composed of borrowings from Greek, English, French, German, and native thought. . . . The common denominator of all that Thoreau took from the Hindus, Chinese, and Persians was a mystical love for Nature.[9]

Emerson and Thoreau found different jewels and gems in this Eastern treasure chest. Both could approve the practical wisdom of Confucius, but Thoreau would reject strongly the emphasis upon conformity and deference to authority. Indeed, one of the points that would come to irritate Thoreau more and more would be Emerson's mandarin quality in the village, his emphasis upon fine manners and the social amenities. Emerson would deal much more metaphysically with the Hindu documents than Thoreau, seeing in Brahma his own "Over-Soul" and reading Karma as his own "Compensation." Thoreau valued them especially for their ascetic disciplines, a topic to be discussed later in the chapter on mysticism. He did not like the caste structure ("Hindu tyranny"), the mendicant way of life, the element of historical stagnation, or the generally pessimistic outlook of the *Upanishads*. Even in his beloved *Bhagavad-Gita* he was uneasy with Arjuna's hesitancy to act with a decisiveness that would be expected of any New Englander of heroic Transcendentalist morality.[10]

Thoreau was particularly drawn to early books. Many of the quotations in the *Week* are from the journals of the early explorers of America or from the chronicles of New England towns. This quest for the ancient documents naturally led him to Homer and to the Eastern books. The first outburst of enthusiasm in the *Journal* comes from August 22, 1838. "How thrilling a noble sentiment in the oldest books—in Homer, the *Zendavesta*, or Confucius! It is a strain of music wafted down to us on the breeze of time, through the aisles of innumerable ages. By its very nobleness it is made clear and audible to us."[11]

This ancient wisdom is really poetry. "If I were to complete a volume to contain the condensed wisdom of mankind, I should quote no rhythmless line."[12] From the enthusiastic entries in the *Journal,* in the months immediately following his going to live with the Emersons in 1841, we find this question: "Who is writing better Vedas?"[13]

"In the Hindoo scripture the idea of man is quite illimitable and sublime. There is nowhere a loftier conception of his destiny."[14] At times he probed behind his enthusiasm, looking for principles of criticism.

It is now easy to apply to this ancient scripture such a catholic criticism as it will become the part of some future age to apply to the Christian,—wherein the design and idea which underlies it is considered, and not the narrow and partial fulfillment.

These verses are so eminently textual, that it seems as if those old sages had concentrated all their wisdom in little fascicles, of which future times were to be the commentary; as the light of this lower world is only the dissipated rays of the sun and stars. They seem to have been uttered with a sober morning prescience, in the dawn of time. There is a sort of holding back, or withdrawal of the full meaning, that the ages may follow after and explore the whole.[15]

In a sense, Thoreau had anticipated these principles of evaluation when he first began to keep his *Journal* back in 1837, in a comment on the Druids, before his anticlericalism became a settled landmark.

In all ages and nations we observe a leaning towards a right state of things. This may especially be seen in the history of the priest, whose life approaches most nearly to that of the ideal man. . . . In the last stage of civilization Poetry, Religion, and Philosophy will be one; and this truth is glimpsed in the first.[16]

A common criticism of *A Week on the Concord and Merrimack Rivers* is that the narrative, telescoped for dramatic presentation from a fortnight into one week, is fragmented by long insertions of extraneous material. James Russell Lowell complained in his review that "choiceness of material has been of less import than suitableness to fill up . . . plastic and broken bricks from old buildings, oyster-shells, and dock mud have been shot pell-mell together."[17] The *Week*, however, does possess a large measure of organic unity that grows on one after a number of readings. It may not be as obvious as in *Walden*, in which the craftsmanship is superior, but it could be argued that the *Week* is more typical of its author's Transcendentalism. Its unity is in part that of a fresh scripture of the movement or, perhaps more accurately, that of a catalyst inviting the reader to experience Transcendentalism for himself. One of Thoreau's earliest entries in the *Journal* stated an aim which he cultivated throughout his life and of which the Week is the first extended public demonstration. "How indispensable to a correct study of Nature is a perception of her true meaning. The fact will one day flower out into a truth. The season will mature and fructify what the understanding had cultivated."[18]

After a brief introductory essay entitled "Concord River," Thoreau and his brother launch their rowboat, "painted green below, with a border of blue, with reference to the two elements in which it was to spend its existence."[19] Under "Saturday" he presents a study of the river fishes, with an ecological feeling for "the fish principle" in nature. "I have thus stood over them [the breams] half an hour at a time, and stroked them familiarly without frightening them . . . and have even taken them gently out of the water with my hand."[20] One of Thoreau's amazing qualities was his intimacy with all forms of life. He feels himself a fellow creature with the shad, frustrated as its instincts lead it to seek its ancestral spawning grounds only to be met by barrier dams. The dams in the Week symbolize the triumph of commercial, exploitative interests over the wild and over the potentialities of natural and spiritual life.

Poor shad! where is thy redress? When Nature gave thee instinct, gave she thee the heart to bear thy fate? . . . I for one am with thee, and who knows what may avail a crowbar against that Billerica dam? . . . Who hears the fishes when they cry? It will not be forgotten by some memory that we were contemporaries.[21]

"Sunday" brings a "natural Sabbath" to the voyagers, "as if it dated from earlier than the fall of man, and still preserved a heathenish integrity."[22] After a description of the founding of churches in the towns they are passing on the riverbank, Thoreau discusses with considerable realism the encounter between the whites and the Indians. Again, there is a feeling for the ecological at-homeness of the latter in their environment.

We talk of civilizing the Indian, but that is not the name for his improvement. By the wary independence and aloofness of his dim forest life he preserves his intercourse with his native gods, and is admitted from time to time to a rare and peculiar society with Nature. He has glances of starry recognition to which our saloons are strangers. . . . The Indian's intercourse with Nature is at least such as admits of the greatest independence of each.[23]

There follows a short essay on mythology, suggestive of more recent studies by Ernst Cassirer and Mircea Eliade, which is absolutely central to what Thoreau will try to convey to his readers. The "fable" is mankind's approach to a common language; it is proof of a common humanity; it binds early human beings to our contemporaries. Mythology, he claims, is a form of general revelation through which God discloses himself, in accordance with a cryptic remark made earlier in his *Journal* to the effect that "the unconsciousness of man is the consciousness of God."[24]

But what signifies it? In the mythus a superhuman intelligence uses the unconscious thoughts and dreams of men as its hieroglyphics to address men unborn. In the history of the human mind, these glowing and ruddy fables precede the noonday thoughts of men, as Aurora the sun's rays. The matutine intellect of the poet, keeping in advance of the glare of philosophy, always dwells in this auroral atmosphere.[25]

Disapproving looks from churchgoers as the brothers pass under the last bridge over the Middlesex Canal precipitate Thoreau's criticism of his "country's God." He feels that Jehovah, despite his unapproachableness, is far less apotheosized than the Greek gods because "so wholly masculine," and thus Thoreau anticipates the widespread discussion today about the almost exclusively masculine language of "God-talk" in the Judeo-Christian tradition.[26] Then he playfully shocks the orthodox of his day by invoking Pan. Although his friends called Thoreau "young Pan," to most modern readers he looks like a thoroughgoing Puritan Pan.

In my Pantheon, Pan still reigns in his pristine glory, with his ruddy face, his flowing beard, and his shaggy body, his pipe and his crook, his nymph Echo, and his chosen daughter Iambe; for the great god Pan is not dead, as was rumored. No god ever dies. Perhaps of all the gods of New England and of ancient Greece, I am most constant at his shrine.[27]

Then, with the insight of a biblical prophet condemning idolatry and with some feeling for the relativities of culture, Thoreau argues that the God worshiped in civilized countries is not at all divine but an imperfect deification of the "authority and respectability of mankind combined. . . . The Christian fable" is a memorable addition to the mythology of mankind, Christ being "the new Prometheus. . . . It would seem as if it were in the progress of our mythology to dethrone Jehovah, and crown Christ in his stead." Considering the "snappish tenacity" with which Christianity is still preached, Thoreau wonders that "the humble life of a Jewish peasant should have force to make a New York bishop so bigoted."[28] Then, in a memorable paragraph that sums up all his distrust of the deforming nature of tradition, revealing again his intense mysticism and individualism, he pleads for tolerance because the basic reality behind all religious manifestations is God and the appropriate human response should be love.

I trust that some may be as near and dear to Buddha, or Christ, or Swedenborg, who are without the pale of their churches. It is necessary not to be Christian to appreciate the beauty and significance of the life of Christ. I know that some will have hard thoughts of me, when they hear their Christ named beside my Buddha, yet I am sure that I am willing they should love their Christ more than my Buddha, for the love is the main thing, and I like him too. "God is the letter Ku, as well as Khu." Why need Christians be still intolerant and superstitious?[29]

Thoreau asserts that he has never found any authority for Trinitarianism. He says, "The wisest man preaches no doctrines; he has no scheme; he sees no rafter, not even a cobweb, against the heavens."[30] The problem, of course, with this assertion is that it is itself a "doctrine" and a "scheme," but Thoreau chooses to ignore this flaw in his presentation. "Even Christ, we fear, had his scheme, his conformity to tradition, which slightly vitiates his teaching."[31] The contemporary Christian whose historical methods have freed him from the bondage to propositional religious truth, which was nearly universal in Thoreau's day, should have few of the problems here that Thoreau's contemporaries found.

Your scheme must be the framework of the universe; all other schemes will soon be ruins. The perfect God in his revelations of himself has never got to the length of one such proposition as you, his prophets, state. Have you learned the alphabet of heaven and can count three? . . . Do you presume to fable of the ineffable?[32]

Thoreau confesses to having been slightly prejudiced

against the New Testament "in my very early days by the church and the Sabbath-school." *Pilgrim's Progress,* Thoreau believes, is the best sermon ever preached on it. This judgment reveals clearly his predisposition toward elements of his Puritan heritage. He never reads novels, but "the reading which I love best is the scriptures of the several nations, though it happens that I am better acquainted with those of the Hindoos, the Chinese, and the Persians, than of the Hebrews, which I have come to last."[33] In his review of *A Week,* Horace Greeley took this last playfully shocking line literally and belabored Thoreau for daring to criticize what he had not thoroughly studied. But Thoreau had indeed studied the Bible thoroughly; the text of *A Week* reveals this to a discerning reader. What he may have been trying to convey in his tongue-in-cheek remark was that he had only come to appreciate it of late since his liberation from Christian editing of the book or, possibly, that he did not know the Old Testament as well as the New. What is remarkable by way of development from the *Week* to *Walden* is that the biblical references become so numerous in the latter that no discerning critic could possibly bring the charge of ignorance against him as Greeley had. Whether this intensification of biblical style and references was a conscious or unconscious response to criticism is debatable. What is more probable is that *Walden* represents a more mature religious orientation than the *Week,* however we account for the intervening development.

Thoreau in delicious irony would like to get his friends to read the New Testament, because "it fits their case exactly." Then, in a burst of rhetoric that reveals his own attachment to that part of Christ's teaching which supports his Transcendentalism and his vocation of simplification of life, he preaches a powerful sermon:

It is remarkable that, notwithstanding the universal favor with which the New Testament is outwardly received, and even the bigotry with which it is defended, there is no hospitality shown to, there is no appreciation of, the order of truth with which it deals. I know of no book that has so few readers. There is none so truly strange, and heretical, and unpopular. To Christians, no less than Greeks and Jews, it is foolishness and a stumbling-block. There are, indeed, severe things in it which no man should read aloud more than once. "Seek first the kingdom of heaven." "Lay not up for yourselves treasures on earth." "If thou wilt be perfect, go and sell that thou hast, and give to the poor, and thou shalt have treasure in heaven." "For what is a man profited, if he shall gain the whole world, and lose his own soul? Or what shall a man give in exchange for his soul?" Think of this, Yankees! . . . Think of repeating these things to a New England audience! thirdly, fourthly, fifteenthly, till there are three barrels of sermons! Who, without cant, can read them aloud? Who, without cant, can hear them, and not go out of the meeting-house? They never *were* read, they never *were* heard. Let but one of these sentences be rightly read, from any pulpit in the land, and there would not be left one stone of that meeting-house upon another.[34]

Then, as though he would seem to be making too much of a commitment to the New Testament or to Christ, he draws back and makes his criticisms. "Yet the New Testament treats of man and man's so-called spiritual affairs too exclusively, and is too constantly moral and personal, to alone content me, who am not interested solely in man's religious or moral nature, or in man even."[35] Modern biblical criticism, which of course was unavailable to him, would have helped Thoreau to liberate himself from the caricature of the New Testament for which he criticized his contemporaries, but which he unfortunately then projected backwards and read into the text himself. Not understanding the eschatological nature of Christ's teaching, that it is a description of life in the kingdom of God meant to be realized within this world, Thoreau hears it just as those he criticized heard it as "an other-worldly ethic." "Yet he [Christ] taught mankind but imperfectly how to live; his thoughts were all directed toward another world."[36] What is actually remarkable about Christ's life and teaching about God is the relatively meager interest in religious things and the overwhelming concentration upon finding God in the center of one's daily life. This feature of Christ's life-style is one of the solid foundations of the contemporary "theology of the secular," a movement still regarded with suspicion within the churches. Because Thoreau shared some of the misconception of most of his contemporaries that Christianity was about an afterlife or the next world in a sort of Platonic dualism, his own counsel of adjustment to reality misses his usual prophetic fire. "Even here we have a sort of living to get, and must buffet it somewhat longer. There are various tough problems yet to solve, and we must make shift to live, betwixt spirit and matter, such a human life as we can."[37]

The charge that the New Testament is "too constantly moral and personal" will have to be dealt with later, as Thoreau's own intense devotion to the moral (as against an inferior acceptance of the moral imperative that leads to self-regarding and self-righteous "moralism") is analyzed. One limitation of his genius may very well be an overdevelopment of the moral side of reality, probably also an inheritance from the Puritan ethos, that makes him read nature with glasses that look to most of our contemporaries as having lenses that magnify the moral. Some of Thoreau's criticism here may be of the nature of a lecture to himself, just as we all project our weaknesses outward upon others. It is a difficult subject in Thoreau criticism, but is related to his dislike of repentance. He sees the problem clearly when he writes, "The conscience really does not, and ought not to monopolize the whole of our lives, any more than the heart or the head."[38]

Thoreau's charge that the New Testament has too exclusive a concern for man alone rests on solid ground, although the churches even today may be defensively resistant to the charge. Perhaps the very fact that they are Johnny-come-latelies to the ecological movement, if indeed they have "come" at all, sufficiently demonstrates the truth of Thoreau's criticism. The New Testament here needs the perspective of the Old Testament to give it greater rootage in ecology, just as Christianity needs the supplementation of other religions, philosophies, and science on this issue. It is paradoxical that early Puritanism, before it was corrupted by man's self-concern, with its pristine emphasis upon God's glory and the world as a theater of his majesty, offered just that refocusing of the revelation that in another context is needed today to reduce an excessive anthropocentricism. In this area Thoreau remains a prophet.

Another criticism Thoreau makes against Christianity is a corollary of his misplaced charge of otherworldliness against Christ's teaching. "Resignation" at one's sad lot in this world, which was the burden of the Christianity of his day and particularly noticeable in the hymnody of the time, he castigates wherever he finds it, but he unfortunately lets its contemporary prevalence blind him to the fact that it is a caricature. He too reads it back into its origins. "Christianity only hopes. It has hung its harp on the willows, and cannot sing a song in a strange land. It has dreamed a sad dream, and does not yet welcome the morning with joy."[39] The dynamic of the resurrection of Christ, on the other hand, gives to the New Testament a joyousness which Western tradition has never adequately reflected. The excitement of "the Word made flesh" reverberates in the New Testament writers as it did so strongly in Donne, Herbert, Quarles, Fletcher, and other of the English metaphysical poets whom Thoreau especially liked. When he quotes their poetry, however, in the *Week* he curiously expurgates it to remove the joyous references to Christ, the Incarnate Redeemer. An illustration occurs in a four-line quotation from Giles Fletcher's "Christ's Victory in Heaven," which he quotes for "Friday."

> There is a place beyond that flaming hill,
> From whence the stars their thin appearance shed,
> A place beyond all place, where never ill,
> Nor impure thought was ever harbored.[40]

Thoreau does not let his readers know that the next four lines exist, but they supply just that emphasis upon joy for the supposed lack of which he has here faulted Christianity.

> But saintly heroes are for ever su'd
> To keep an everlasting Sabbath's rest;
> Still wishing that, of what th'are still possest;
> Enjoying but one joy, but one of all joys best.[41]

The lockman lowers them into the Merrimack at Middlesex, and the upstream part of the voyage begins in earnest. There is much more included in this day from the classics, from the early history of Dunstable, and from Puritan missions to the Indians, as well as a profile of the Merrimack River, tying it to its environment. Thoreau offers two further comments that throw light upon his own religious perspective, from which he has criticized his "country's God."

A man's real faith is never contained in his creed, nor is his creed an article of his faith. The last is never adopted. This it is that permits him to smile ever, and to live even as bravely as he does. And yet he clings anxiously to his creed, as to a straw, thinking that that does him good service because his sheet anchor does not drag.[42]

This conviction of Thoreau's, which he shared with Transcendentalism in general, remained so strongly a feature of his outlook throughout life that it may, paradoxically, be described as an article of his faith. The second point arose from the mystic's thirst for authenticity in experience. Here he is at one with Martin Luther, who said that everyone has got to do his own believing just as he must do his own dying.

There is a chasm between knowledge and ignorance which the arches of science can never span. A book should contain pure discoveries, glimpses of *terra firma*, though by shipwrecked mariners, and not the art of navigation by those who have never been out of sight of land.[43]

The voyagers embark early on Monday morning and soon come upon a ferry carrying many people back and forth across the Merrimack. Thoreau speculates that some must be ministers traveling home "with sermons in their valises all read and gutted" with the prospect before them of "vacation now for six days."[44] The brothers stop for their nooning, for "at this season of the day, we are all, more or less, Asiatics, and give over all work and reform."[45] The stage has been set for his discussion of the Eastern religions. The whole book contains only one clear expression of social concern. "I do not wish, it happens, to be associated with Massachusetts, either in holding slaves or in conquering Mexico. I am a little better than herself in these respects."[46] The reason for this is apparently his desire not to break open its mood of contemplation. He was actually preparing "Civil Disobedience" for publication as he dealt with the proofs of the *Week*.

There is a discussion of true conservatism initiated by a brief analysis of the *Bhagavad-Gita*. "It is unquestionably one of the noblest and most sacred scriptures which have come down to us. . . . Western philosophers have not conceived of the significance of Contemplation in their sense."[47] Thoreau seeks to bring the Bible and the *Bhagavad-Gita* together as mutually needing each other. This principle of ecumenism may seem somewhat surprising at this point, for the spirited criticism of yesterday of the Judeo-Christian tradition might seem to suggest the displacement of it by the Eastern faiths, but that is not Thoreau's purpose at all. The high evaluation of New Testament morality that emerges in the discussion of "Monday" is the clue to Thoreau as a biblical prophet, to the reconciliation of the essay on "Civil Disobedience" with *Walden*. Radical reformer and nature mystic, the two sides of Thoreau that polarized many of his followers into opposite camps, are really united in his religious dialectic, which is complex and which is passing through an interesting development in the *Week*. (He would later bring the two sides together in his splendid essay "Life Without Principle.") "The New Testament is remarkable for its pure morality; the best of the Hindoo Scripture, for its pure intellectuality."[48]

The following paragraph, although long, must be quoted in its entirety, for it provides clues to many questions about Thoreau's personal religious orientation. It shows, for that time, a daring attempt to understand the incarnation of Christ in terms of what Thoreau elsewhere calls "the vast and cosmogonal philosophy of the Bhagvat-Geeta"[49] in much the same way that the writer of the Gospel of John employed the Logos philosophy of the Greco-Roman world to explicate "the Word made flesh."

Christianity, on the other hand, is humane, practical, and, in a large sense, radical. So many years and ages of the gods those Eastern sages sat contemplating Brahm, uttering in silence the mystic "Om," being absorbed into the essence of the Supreme Being, never going out of themselves, but subsiding farther and deeper within; so infinitely wise, yet infinitely stagnant; until, at last, in that same Asia, but in the western part of it, appeared a youth, wholly unforetold by them,—not being absorbed into Brahm, but bringing Brahm down to earth and to mankind; in whom Brahm had awaked from his long sleep, and exerted himself, and the day began,—a new avatar. The Brahman had never thought to be a brother of mankind as well as a child of God. Christ is the prince of Reformers and Radicals. Many expressions in the New Testament come naturally to the lips of all Protestants, and it furnishes the most pregnant and practical texts. There is no harmless dreaming, no wise speculation in it, but everywhere a substratum of good sense. It never *reflects*, but it *repents*. There is no poetry in it, we may say, nothing regarded in the light of beauty merely, but moral truth is its object. All mortals are convicted by its conscience.[50]

Plainly Thoreau seeks to relate these two traditions by the way of mutual enrichment once the weak points of each have been recognized. It may have seemed to the reader up to this point that a strongly criticized Christianity was being asked to stop being intolerant to a Hinduism that has been extravagantly and enthusiastically praised, but Thoreau's dialectic is more evenhanded than that. Now he begins a trenchant criticism of the Hindu books, in particular of the

Bhagavad-Gita. One can sense why the crucifixion, so central to Christianity, becomes a stumbling block in the Hindu milieu. Thoreau's interpretation here will become significant for his own handling of the problem of evil. He drives home his point concretely.

This teaching is not practical in the sense in which the New Testament is. It is not always sound sense in practice. The Brahman never proposes courageously to assault evil, but patiently to starve it out. His active faculties are paralyzed by the idea of caste, of impassable limits of destiny and the tyranny of time. Kreeshna's argument, it must be allowed, is defective. No sufficient reason is given why Arjoon should fight. . . . The Brahman's virtue consists in doing, not right, but arbitrary things.[51]

Thoreau is not playing an intellectual game with the religions of humanity, now neatly catalogued according to his own dialectic. He suggests no armchair synthesis. He is driven on by a deep piety, even a missionary zeal for his project of the "ethnical scriptures" of humankind. At this point the mystic surprisingly enlists the aid of religious institutions, for sacred books are certainly institutions. His unwillingness to treat the New Testament on a par with the others is most significant, not just as a concession to the feelings of his immediate contemporaries but as suggesting, when combined with what he has said before of its ability "to convict all mortals by its conscience," that he regards it in some sense as more authoritative than others for "pure morality." There is a New Testament prophet here, behind the eclectic compiler of ethnical scriptures, that the history of his times will draw out. The view of its authority, however, unlike the traditional one with its dogma of verbal infallibilism, would have to be a liberal one to suit him.

It would be worthy of the age to print together the collected Scriptures or Sacred Writings of the several nations, the Chinese, the Hindoos, the Persians, the Hebrews, and others, as the Scripture of mankind. The New Testament is still, perhaps, too much on the lips and in the hearts of men to be called a Scripture in this sense. Such a juxtaposition and comparison might help to liberalize the faith of men. This is a work which Time will surely edit, reserved to crown the labors of the printing-press. This would be the

Bible, or Book of Books, which let the missionaries carry to the uttermost parts of the earth.[52]

This is an appropriate place to examine the overall impact of the Oriental religious books on Thoreau, although we have still in later chapters to analyze their influence on *Walden* and their contribution to his mysticism. In the early 1840s when he ransacked Emerson's library and made anthologies for the *Dial* they are greeted with overwhelming enthusiasm, an "extravagant outpouring of praise," according to Christy.[53] *Journal* entries catch what could be called the zeal of a convert. In the years at Walden Pond their atmosphere influences his periods of contemplation, furnishes a dynamic for his ascetic exercises, and provides him with material for living and discussing the good life. In the later 1840s he gains access in the Harvard Library to still new titles in this field and, for example, translates from a French version of the Hindu *Harivansa, The Transmigration of the Seven Brahmans.* The necessity of trying at least to communicate to his readers in the *Week* some principles of interpretation in this vast and complex area led him to revise his *Journal* entries for inclusion into the *Week,* moderating somewhat his criticism of the Old Testament and expressing his enthusiasm for the Eastern books in much more measured terms. Some of this editing resulted from stylistic needs, but much indicates a development in his own attitudes.

The next test of change, and a decisive one, comes with the gift from Thomas Cholmondeley sent to him from England in 1855 of a collection of forty-four Oriental books. Cholmondeley had visited Emerson the year before but then stayed on to come to know Thoreau and to take an excursion with him to Wachusett.[54] Some have claimed that these books made Thoreau the owner of the most extensive Oriental library in the hands of an individual at that time in America. Thoreau wrote excitedly to his New Bedford friend, Daniel Ricketson, "I am familiar with many of them & know how to prize them. I send you information of this as I might of the birth of a child."[55] From driftwood collected on the river he built a cradling bookcase for the new addition. His comment to his friend H. G. O. Blake in Worcester was more prophetic than he could know at the time: "I have not made out the significance of this godsend yet."[56] It is doubtful whether he ever did. Not only did he not learn Sanskrit, but there is little evidence in his *Journal* or *Correspondence* that he ever read at all widely in them.

One of his entries some time after the gift deals with Wilson's translation of the *Rig Veda*, showing that he chiefly prized their atmosphere.

While the commentators and translators are disputing about the meaning of this word or that, I hear only the resounding of the ancient sea and put into it all the meaning I am possessed of, the deepest murmurs I can recall, for I do not the least care where I get my ideas, or what suggests them.[57]

The truth of the matter is that his interest in the Oriental books had peaked. They had helped him at one stage of his development, and the memory of their liberating influence would be precious, but he had himself long since become his own man, capable of expounding his thought and experience completely in his own terms. Cholmondeley really missed the boat when he wrote Thoreau, "I had indeed studied your character closely, and knew what you would like."[58]

A more appropriate gift to Thoreau at this stage would have been early French and English narratives of exploration and encounter with the Indians. Thoreau was reading avidly all that he could find on Indian life, a dominating interest that would lead him to compile his Indian Notebooks, a collection of eleven manuscript volumes, now in the Morgan Library, of notes and extracts about the American Indians and other primitive peoples.[59] Had his health been spared, Thoreau's greatest contribution might have been an interpretation of the Indian. His sensitivity might have enriched white culture and led to greater justice for the Indian, for Thoreau, unlike Rousseau, had a realistic understanding of the limitations of wildness as well as a respect for Indian culture, religion, and ecological sanity. A central purpose behind the trips into the Maine woods was to come to know the Indian guides and their Algonquin language, which he also studied from the few dictionaries and grammars available. Soon after his trip on the East Branch of the Penobscot with Joe Polis as guide, he wrote Blake:

I have made a short excursion into the new world which the Indian dwells in, or is. He begins where we leave off. It is worth the while to detect new faculties in man,—he is so much the more divine; and anything that fairly excites our admiration expands us. The Indian, who can find his way so wonderfully in the woods, possesses so much intelligence which the white man does not,— and it increases my own capacity, as well as faith, to observe it. I rejoice to find that intelligence flows in other channels than I knew. It redeems for me portions of what seemed brutish before.[60]

On his last major trip in search of health, when tuberculosis was wracking him, he journeyed to Minnesota and attended the yearly conclave of the Sioux near Redwood. He listened with admiration to the oratory of Chief Little Crow, sympathizing with his protests against white injustice, little realizing that in the very next year Little Crow would lead a Sioux uprising that would bring death to eight hundred Minnesotan settlers. It was a shame that his friend Cholmondeley had not seen Thoreau's statement filed in 1853 with the Association for the Advancement of Science to the effect that his chief interest was "The Manners & Customs of the Indians of the Algonquin Group previous to contact with the civilized man."[61] By a sort of cultural lag in his interpretation of Thoreau, Cholmondeley picked the wrong Indians! Walter Harding, his most comprehensive biographer, sums up the situation: "It is significant that by the time the Cholmondeley collection of Oriental books arrived in Concord he was no longer vitally interested in reading them."[62]

Thoreau follows the section on religious books with an essay on history, glimpses of river scenery, local incidents in King Phillip's War, and finally camp near Penichook Brook. The detailed discussion about the religions of the human family is concluded and, as though to prepare his readers for his own experience of the divine on the morrow on Mount Greylock, he introduces part of his long poem "Inspiration." To gain time and effect, apparently, he collapses many of the stanzas into prose with a beat as steady as the distant drummer's that he has been listening to from their camp.

Heal yourselves, doctors; by God I live.
> Then idle Time ran gadding by
> And left me with Eternity alone;
> I hear beyond the range of sound,
> I see beyond the verge of sight,—
I see, smell, taste, hear, feel, that everlasting Something to which we are allied, at once our maker, our abode, our destiny, our very

Selves; the one historic truth, the most remarkable fact which can become the distinct and uninvited subject of our thought, the actual glory of the universe; the only fact which a human being cannot avoid recognizing, or in some way forget or dispense with.

> It doth expand my privacies
> To all, and leave me single in the crowd.

I have seen how the foundations of the world are laid, and I have not the least doubt that it will stand a good while.

> Now chiefly is my natal hour,
> And only now my prime of life.
> I will not doubt the love untold,
> Which not my worth nor want hath bought,
> Which wooed me young and wooes me old,
> And to this evening hath me brought.[63]

Early on Tuesday morning the voyagers embark on a river covered with fog. Thoreau takes the opportunity to tell the story of how he "once saw the day break from the top of Saddleback Mountain [Greylock] in Massachusetts, above the clouds."[64] He skillfully prepares his readers for a revelation on the mountain, building up their expectation with images suggesting supernatural scenes and struggle.

My route lay up a long and spacious valley called the Bellows, because the winds rush up or down it with violence in storms, sloping up to the very clouds between the principal range and a lower mountain. . . . It seemed a road for the pilgrim to enter upon who would climb to the gates of heaven . . . still gradually ascending all the while with a sort of awe, and filled with indefinite expectations as to what kind of inhabitants and what kind of nature I should come to at last. . . . The thunder had rumbled at my heels all the way. . . . I half believed that I should get above it. . . .

I made my way steadily upward in a straight line, through a dense undergrowth of mountain laurel, until the trees began to have a scraggy and infernal look, as if contending with frost goblins, and at length I reached the summit, just as the sun was setting.[65]

Thoreau makes a shallow well to catch drinking water, cooks rice for supper, and, having no blanket, covers himself with boards from the rude observatory built by Williams College. Early the next morning, before it is yet day, he climbs up the tower. Speculating that colleges should be placed at the base of a mountain, a situation equal at least to one endowed chair, he adds, "Some will remember, no doubt, not only that they went to the college, but that they went to the mountain. Every visit to its summit would, as it were, generalize the particular information gained below, and subject it to more catholic tests."[66] The reader has now been subtly conditioned for the theophany to follow. In it light and water, two of Thoreau's favorite symbols of the higher life, meet together. The valley stream has been tracked to the summit, where it is dissolved into mist. The unusual and the common in nature become transparent to the divine. Political subdivisions fade into unreality. To the Transcendentalist climber, the mountain is one of revelation and transfiguration. Skillfully, Thoreau has prepared us to experience with him the actuality of revelation as we recall similar experiences of the grandeur of God. These experiences of ours may have lain fallow without conscious reference to the divine. Now they are renewed for us and made articulate by Thoreau's vision.

As the light increased, I discovered around me an ocean of mist, which by chance reached up exactly to the base of the tower, and shut out every vestige of the earth, while I was left floating on this fragment of the wreck of a world, on my carved plank, in cloud-land; a situation which required no aid from the imagination to render it impressive. As the light in the east steadily increased, it revealed to me more clearly the new world into which I had risen in the night, the new *terra firma* perchance of my future life. There was not a crevice left through which the trivial places we name Massachusetts or Vermont or New York could be seen, while I still inhaled the clear atmosphere of a July morning,—if it were July there. All around beneath me was spread for a hundred miles on every side, as far as the eye could reach, an undulating country of clouds, answering in the varied swell of its surface to the terrestial world it veiled. It was such a country as we might see in dreams, with all the delights of paradise. . . . It was a favor for which to be forever silent to be shown this vision. . . . But when its own sun began to rise on this pure world, I found myself a dweller in the dazzling halls of Aurora . . . and near at hand the far-darting glances of the god. . . . But my muse would fail to convey an impression of the gorgeous tapestry by which I was surrounded, such as men see faintly reflected afar off in the chambers of the east. *Here, as on earth, I saw the gracious god*

"Flatter the mountain-tops with sovereign eye,
Gilding pale streams with heavenly alchemy."
But never here did "Heaven's sun" stain himself.

But, alas, owing, as I think, to some unworthiness in myself, my private sun did stain himself, and

"Anon permit the basest clouds to ride
With ugly wrack on his celestial face,"—

for before the god had reached the zenith the heavenly pavement rose and embraced my wavering virtue, or rather I sank down again into that "forlorn world," from which the celestial sun had hid his visage . . . [and] descending the mountain by my own route . . . I . . . found myself in the region of cloud and drizzling rain, and the inhabitants affirmed that it had been a cloudy and drizzling day wholly.[67]

The structure of this mystical experience is parallel to that of the prophet Isaiah who, beholding the majesty of God and the whole earth full of his glory, cried out, "Woe is me! I am lost, for I am a man of unclean lips (Isa. 6:5, NEB)."[68] This experience, a central focus for the *Week* and an invitation from Thoreau to his reader to submit himself to similar awakening experience, is followed, to break the intensity, by continuing details of the river trip, more local history, Thoreau's meeting Rice high in the mountain intervales of the Deerfield River on his transit to Greylock, the romance of canalboating, more Indian lore, catching a passenger pigeon to eat, translations by Thoreau of Anacreon's odes, and, finally, camp on the west bank in the town of Bedford.

"Wednesday" begins with thoughts of the smaller bittern, standing in the stream of time, a symbol of nature's mystery.

One wonders if, by its patient study by rocks and sandy capes, it has wrested the whole of her secret from Nature yet. What a rich experience it must have gained, standing on one leg and looking out from its dull eye so long on sunshine and rain, moon and stars![69]

The campers pass the falls of Amoskeag and study the potholes in the stream. There is a satirical description of the physician and the priest, much modified from the first version in the surviving manuscripts. The reader begins to wonder what the chief essay of the day will be. He is not kept waiting long, for around the next river bend he meets a thirty-page discussion of friendship, so often printed in anthologies with the nearly unanimous comment that it was inserted almost at the last moment into the *Week*, where it does not really belong. Then the commentators point out elements of unrealism in its demand for a perfection in friendship that transcends any possible human relations between flesh and blood. "Perhaps there are none charitable, none disinterested, none wise, noble and heroic enough, for a true and lasting Friendship."[70] The reader of the anthology concludes that Transcendentalism is a ridiculous thing and ends up with an amateur Freudian analysis of Thoreau in terms of blocked affection, mother dominance, sibling rivalry, homoerotic tendencies, and repressed aggression. All of this has some justification, including Perry Miller's amusing theory that it was a Transcendentalist game to put your friend in the wrong so that you could feel one up on him and take it out on the cropper usually in lengthy entries in your diary.

But suppose, for a moment, that Thoreau knew what he was about when he introduced the essay, which is really on love rather than friendship, at just this point in his narrative and that he has supplied clues to his reader. We have seen that one of the strongest bonds of unity in the *Week* is a continuous exposure to experiencing the divine: in the ecological integrity of Indian life, in the developed religious consciousness of the great historical religions, and in the mystical experience on Mount Greylock. The next "place" of revelation is in human relationships, particularly friendship, which Thoreau tells us "is the secret of the universe"[71] and which he signals to his reader in his introductory stanza to the whole essay.

> True kindness is a pure divine affinity,
> Not founded upon human consanguinity.
> It is a spirit, not a blood relation,
> Superior to family and station.[72]

With its single word for "love," the English language, often so rich in vocabulary, is poverty-stricken beside classical and New Testament Greek. Plato describes the *eros* that binds lovers together, reaching from sexual desire or simply liking to various forms of sublimation. *Eros* is behind the mystic's love for God. Thoreau's longing for the ideal friend is part of this quest.

The sexes are naturally most strongly attracted to one another by constant constitutional differences, and are most commonly and surely the complements of each other. . . . Yet Friendship is no respecter of sex; and perhaps it is more rare between the sexes than between two of the same sex.[73]

Agape is God's love for people, a love that is primarily self-giving and has Christ as exemplar and agent. By grace this love may be reflected to other people, bringing unselfish service as its distinguishing mark. Thoreau conflates these two types of love as follows: "But sometimes we are said to *love* another, that is, to stand in a true relation to him, so that we give the best to, and receive the best from, him."[74] *Philia* in Greek also describes the mutual love of friends as in this definition of Thoreau's: "Friendship takes place between those who have an affinity for one another."[75] In addition, *storge* stands for love within family relationships. Thoreau lets his capitalized word "Friendship" carry many of these particularized meanings, especially the first three in various combinations. There is a strong element of Platonic *eros* in his mix, and he strongly suspects that Christianity may violate the givenness of the relation.

Friendship is not so kind as is imagined; it has not much human blood in it, but consists with a certain disregard for men and their erections, the Christian duties and humanities, while it purifies the air like electricity. . . . We may call it an essentially heathenish intercourse, free and irresponsible in its nature, and practicing all the virtues gratuitously.[76]

Dietrich Bonhoeffer in a prison letter to his friend Bethge laments that there is no biblical institution of friendship as a state of life. Thoreau, interestingly enough, expands this perception by saying that it is not taught by any religion nor its maxims given in any scripture. Yet he points out that "no word is oftener on the lips of men than Friendship, and indeed no thought is more familiar to their aspirations. All men are dreaming of it, and its drama, which is always a tragedy, is enacted daily."[77] The motivating dynamic for Thoreau is the Transcendentalist search for perfection in human relationships. Thoreau feels he is describing an experience in which the divine may be disclosed. A person, created in the image of God, is most divine when his love is supported and transfigured by the Divine itself.

Between whom there is hearty truth, there is love; and in proportion to our truthfulness and confidence in one another, *our lives
are divine and miraculous, and answer to our ideal.* There are passages of affection in our intercourse with mortal men and women,
such as no prophecy had taught us to expect, *which transcend our
earthly life, and anticipate Heaven for us.* What is this Love that
may come right into the middle of a prosaic Goffstown day, *equal
to any of the gods?*[78]

It is often asserted that the figure behind Thoreau's
"friend" is Emerson or some idealization of him. While not
excluding this as a background, it would seem that the primary reference here is to his much-loved brother John, who
shared that "prosaic Goffstown day" with him, now in death
transfigured and hallowed in memory. There is a double
meaning, it would seem, intended in Thoreau's statement,
"My Friend is not of some other race or family of men, but
flesh of my flesh, bone of my bone. He is my real brother."[79]
There are many other aspects of Thoreau's essay that
deserve comment, one being the place he gives to "pure
hate" in the relationship of friendship. This may have more
honest-to-goodness realism in it than some puzzled commentators allow, but the purpose of this discussion is not an
analysis of the whole essay but only its religious dimension.
Surely, the following paragraph, near the end, both reflects
the author's reason for placing it where he has, following his
example of nature mysticism, and at the same time translates
the theoretical analysis into a warm, loving confession of
faith.

As surely as the sunset in my latest November shall translate me to
the ethereal world, and remind me of the ruddy morning of youth;
as surely as the last strain of music which falls on my decaying ear
shall make age to be forgotten, or, in short, the manifold influences of nature survive during the term of our natural life, so
surely my Friend shall forever be my Friend, *and reflect a ray of
God to me,* and time shall foster and adorn and consecrate our
Friendship, no less than the ruins of temples. As I love nature, as I
love singing birds, and gleaming stubble, and flowing rivers, and
morning and evening, and summer and winter, I love thee, my
Friend.[80]

"Thursday" brings the brothers to the head of navigation
just below Concord. Here they beach their boat and con-

tinue the trip on foot, reaching the summit of Agiocochook before turning homeward. Thoreau, strangely, does not bother to tell the reader that Agiocochook is Mount Washington, nor does he describe the hiking part of the expedition. With their boat launched for home, Thoreau returns to local history, but not as an antiquarian. He was skeptical of historical reconstruction; what concerned him was the contemporary meaning of a historical event. Much of this material he uses to recollect and make present to readers the heroic quality of the settlers and the wilderness character of the Indians. Through these documents Thoreau experiences his immediate environment in the dimension of history, an intensification of the revelatory experience, ecology in a vertical dimension. One of these tales was ideally suited to him because there is virtually an exchange of roles within it, a new identification forged out of struggle, death, and adventure. He tells the story of Hannah Dustan, who, with another white woman and an English boy at night, steal the weapons of their Indian captors and tormentors. They scalp the sleeping Indians, flee downriver in a canoe, eluding pursuit, and arrive at the settlements, presenting the ten bloody scalps for bounty. Thoreau is not telling this tale simply to amuse, he is leading his reader into an experience of dread, of the numinous aspect of reality that in its strange way can also become revelatory of the divine.

They are thinking of the dead whom they have left behind on that solitary isle far up the stream, and of the relentless living warriors who are in pursuit. Every withered leaf which the winter has left seems to know their story, and in its rustling to repeat it and betray them.[81]

He describes the family finally assembled together "except the infant whose brains were dashed out against the apple tree, and there have been many who in later time have lived to say that they have eaten of the fruit of that apple tree."[82] Thoreau was one who ate. His eyes were opened; he knew that there was an ineradicable streak of the wild in him. It would lead him in *Walden* to want to seize and devour a woodchuck raw. He would have to come to terms with this dimension of wildness, both existentially in his life and intellectually in his thought.

Thursday's essays on Goethe and Aulus Persius Flaccus are followed by Friday's on Ossian, Chaucer, and Homer. Thoreau wants us to recognize the divine in the poet who draws upon the work of the scientist and the philosopher.

The poet is no tender slip of fairy stock, who requires peculiar institutions and edicts for his defense, but the toughest son of earth and of Heaven, and by his greater strength and endurance his fainting companions will recognize the God in him. It is the worshipers of beauty, after all, who have done the real pioneer work of the world.[83]

Thoreau wants to cultivate the senses by liberating them from our misapplications. Nature directly expresses God if we can only *see* this with unclouded eyes. Purity is the key.

We need pray for no higher heaven than the pure senses can furnish, a *purely* sensuous life. Our present senses are but the rudiments of what they are destined to become. . . . The ears were made, not for such trivial uses as men are wont to suppose, but to hear celestial sounds. The eyes were not made for such groveling uses as they are now put to and worn out by, but to behold beauty now invisible. May we not *see* God? Are we to be put off and amused in this life, as it were with a mere allegory? Is not Nature, rightly read, that of which she is commonly taken to be the symbol merely?[84]

It is easier by far, Thoreau knows, to discover a new world as Columbus did or new planets like Copernicus and Galileo than to undertake the voyage of inward exploration, to re-affirm the metaphor that binds the book together. With Transcendentalist confidence he wants to get on with the task.

Surely, we are provided with senses as well fitted to penetrate the spaces of the real, the substantial, the eternal, as these out-ward are to penetrate the material universe. Veias, Menu, Zoro-aster, Socrates, Christ, Shakespeare, Swedenborg—these are some of our astronomers.[85]

Before bringing the *Week* to a close, the mystic in Thoreau invokes Silence, with a capital letter. It is an honest appeal, but it also conveniently silences much confusion about who "our astronomers" really are amid these many heavenly bodies, the religions of *A Week on the Concord and Merri-mack Rivers*. "If he make his volume a mole whereon the waves of Silence may break, it is well."[86]

4

A PROPHET EMERGES: "CIVIL DISOBEDIENCE"

The facts about the night Thoreau spent in jail are soon told. Like that earlier shot of the embattled farmers at Concord bridge heard round the world, the repercussions of what happened to Thoreau and, more accurately, of what he made out of the incident continue in our own day as a world revolutionary force for freedom.

A strange thing happened to him on the way to the cobbler's to pick up a mended shoe on a day late in July in 1846, his second year of living at Walden Pond. He had not paid his poll tax for about four years because of his opposition to the federal government on slavery and, more recently, because of his special resistance to the Mexican War, which he saw essentially as a slaveholders' plot to enlarge their influence. Sam Staples, the sheriff and well known to Thoreau, demanded the tax, threatening jail for nonpayment. Thoreau suggested that there was no time like the present. Staples locked him up for the night.

As I stood considering the walls of solid stone, two or three feet thick, the door of wood and iron, a foot thick, and the iron grating which strained the light, I could not help being struck with the foolishness of that institution which treated me as if I were mere flesh and blood and bones, to be locked up.[1]

His cell mate, awaiting trial on a barn-burning charge, "occupied one window, and I the other; and I saw, that, if one stayed there long, his principal business would be to look out the window."[2] In the morning, his tax having been paid without his knowledge by someone, probably his Aunt Maria, Thoreau, furious at having his act of social protest cut short, left jail unwillingly. Picking up his shoe, he was soon leading a huckleberry party on one of Concord's highest hills, where "the State was nowhere to be seen."

The act was not in itself new. Bronson Alcott had been arrested for not paying his poll tax, but again someone intervened and paid it before he could be jailed. Emerson told Alcott that Thoreau's act was "mean and skulking." What was new was Thoreau's reaction to the event, crystallizing in a lecture he gave twice at the Concord Lyceum in the winter of 1848 entitled "The Rights and Duties of the Individual in Relation to Government." At the request of Elizabeth Peabody of Salem, he revised this into an essay called "Resistance to Civil Government" for her one-issue "periodical," *Aesthetic Papers,* at the very time that he was correcting proof for the nearly nonpolitical *Week on the Concord and Merrimack Rivers.* The essay created no stir in its day, was published posthumously with the altered title "Civil Disobedience," and owed its later influence to its having been included by the English biographer of Thoreau, Henry Salt, in an 1890 selection of Thoreau's writings. It was read by Gandhi as a young man and used in his struggle for justice for his people in South Africa. Later, of course, it provided the English equivalent for his Indian word *satyagraha* and inspired the mass movement that led to Indian freedom from British rule. "Civil Disobedience" also influenced Tolstoy and Martin Buber, and its most recent distinguished disciple was Dr. Martin Luther King, Jr., who made it an effective weapon for social change.

During my early college days I read Thoreau's essay on civil disobedience for the first time. Fascinated by the idea of refusing to cooperate with an evil system, I was so deeply moved that I re-read the work several times. I became convinced then that non-cooperation with evil is as much a moral obligation as is cooperation with good. No other person has been more eloquent and passionate in getting this idea across than Henry David Thoreau. As a result of his writings and personal witness we are the heirs of a legacy of creative protest. It goes without saying that the teachings of Thoreau are alive today, indeed, they are more alive today than ever before. Whether expressed in a sit-in .

at lunch counters, a freedom ride into Mississippi, a peaceful protest in Albany, Georgia, a bus boycott in Montgomery, Alabama, it is an outgrowth of Thoreau's insistence that evil must be resisted and no moral man can patiently adjust to injustice.[3]

One of the reasons for quoting this long paragraph from one of the martyred prophets of America is to help establish the type of essay it represents. In "Civil Disobedience" Thoreau speaks through his Transcendentalism as a biblical prophet. To look at Thoreau's role in social protest in any terms other than prophecy in the biblical sense is to fall short of the true dimension. Henry Eulau, professor of political science at Stanford, with the best goodwill in the world, has analyzed it in terms of his discipline. The result is devastating. It appears inconsistent, self-contradictory, ambiguous, and even dangerous.

Thoreau's philosophy should warn us of the dilemma into which he fell and from which he could not escape because he returned time and again, to individual conscience as the "ultimate reality." His thought was full of ambiguity and paradox, and he did not realize sufficiently how contradictory and, in fact, dangerous the moral can be.[4]

The key to "Civil Disobedience," as well as to Thoreau's later defense of John Brown's insurrection, is not some supposed political philosophy but the simple and "dangerous" role of biblical prophet. Hebrew prophecy is no mere verbal exercise in general social or political criticism. It is called forth by specific incidents in the community; for example, the approach of Sennacherib's army or the inequities of class structure in Amos' day. Often the prophet is led to do some act which has parabolic significance and serves as the context in action for the "Word of the Lord." Jeremiah buys a field or wears a yoke. Thoreau expresses this double pattern of the Hebrew prophet, the act and the interpretation of the act. The *Week*, "Civil Disobedience," and *Walden* have this structure. In the first Thoreau takes a journey which suggests a Transcendental interpretation; in the second he refuses to pay his tax and is jailed; in the third he leaves "civilization" for the nearest accessible "wilderness" and then interprets this act for his readers. We are compelled to make up our minds either for or against Thoreau by the challenge of a direct action and are either helped or hindered in this response by the literary work which he provides as a catalyst.[5]

Before analyzing "Civil Disobedience," we should look into his *Journal* and related writings for clues to coming events. It can be noted in advance, however, that nothing adequately prepares us for his position. It is all very similar to Amos, who appeared suddenly in Bethel with a message of doom, asserting that his basic work had been as a herdsman and gatherer of sycamore fruit, but that he now stood where he did because the Lord had commanded him to. If such a review fails to establish clear connection, it will at least bring us up to 1849 in the area of Thoreau's attitudes toward society. "Signing off" from the church in 1841 is really the prototype for signing off from poll taxes in the middle forties.

Thoreau's first public address was at the Concord Lyceum, April 11, 1838, on the topic "Society." From the surviving scraps in the *Journal* it is clear that it was a strong support for his brand of defiant individualism. Much of the effectiveness of *Walden* is gained by Thoreau's use of folk sayings which he alters in some surprising way. In the Lyceum lecture he started the practice by changing the proverb "Man was made for society" to "Society was made for man."[6] In 1841 John and Henry Thoreau debated Bronson Alcott on the question, "Is it ever proper to offer forcible resistance?" with the brothers approving the use of violence when needful.

The appeal to conscience is naturally basic for Thoreau's social ethic. He even extends it to cover the task of the writer.

Good writing as well as good acting will be obedience to conscience. There must not be a particle of will or whim mixed with it. If we can listen, we shall hear. By reverently listening to the inner voice, we may reinstate ourselves on the pinnacle of humanity.[7]

The 1840s were an era of utopian and communitarian experiments, such as Brook Farm at West Roxbury and Fruitlands in the town of Harvard, to mention only two with which Thoreau was acquainted, but he resolutely refused to join any, building his own "one-man community" at Walden Pond. "As for these communities, I think I had rather keep bachelor's hall in hell than go to board in heaven," he wrote in 1841.[8] Within a month he returned to the theme, stalwart in his ideology of individual reform. "The true reform can be undertaken any morning before unbarring our doors. It calls no convention. I can do two thirds the reform of the world myself."[9] For Thoreau social ethics are really personal ethics, in the conviction that one person can leaven the whole lump. Later in 1844 he wrote the article "Herald of Freedom" for the *Dial*, an endorsement of the Abolitionist Nathaniel Rogers, whose weekly paper was read in the strongly Abolitionist Thoreau household. Rogers' strategy centered upon individual moral reform, not upon the political organization of William Lloyd Garrison, who was willing to engage in expedient politics in the hopes of building up voter strength for emancipation. For the Jacksonian *Democratic Review* he wrote an essay on a utopian book by J. A. Etzler, *The Paradise Within the Reach of All Men, Without Labour, by Powers of Nature and Machinery*, faulting it not because of its technology but because the aim was "to secure the greatest degree of gross comfort and pleasure merely." The basis of Thoreau's social ethic was the motivating power of love.

Love is the wind, the tide, the waves, the sunshine. Its power is incalculable; it is many horse-power . . . it can make a paradise within which will dispense with a paradise without. But though the wisest men in all ages have labored to publish this force, and every human heart is, sooner or later, more or less, made to feel it, yet how little is actually applied to social ends.[10]

The churchmen of Concord refused their buildings for a meeting to hear Emerson on the tenth anniversary of West Indian emancipation. Nothing daunted, Thoreau rang the bell in the church steeple to assemble the people to hear the address in the courthouse hall for which he had made the arrangements. That winter the liberal members of the Concord Lyceum were able to outvote the conservative interests, which did not want to have slavery discussed. After Emerson and Thoreau were elected to the governing board, Wendell Phillips was invited to speak on the issue. Thoreau wrote up the occasion for the *Liberator*, March 28, 1845. His attitude toward slavery was to see it as part of the larger picture of man's "un-freedom," whether as wage slavery in the proliferating mills of the North or as self-imposed fear of public opinion. "It is hard to have a Southern overseer, it is worse to have a Northern one; but worst of all when you are yourself the slavedriver."[11]

It is impossible here to discuss "Civil Disobedience" fully; the main purpose is to establish it as a piece of biblically inspired prophecy and to examine this religious dimension. No modern reader can pick it up without feeling that he is being addressed by Thoreau on the "law-and-order" issue and on Vietnam. "Witness the present Mexican war, the work of comparatively a few individuals using the standing government as their tool; for, in the outset, the people would not have consented to this measure."[12] Excessive devotion to law and order often covers acquiescence in injustice. It may lead to militarism and crises of conscience within a nation. With us it has produced Watergate.

It is not desirable to cultivate a respect for the law, so much as for the right. . . Law never made men a whit more just; and, by means of their respect for it, even the well-disposed are daily made the agents of injustice. A common and natural result of an undue respect for law is, that you may see a file of soldiers, colonel, captain, corporal, privates, powder-monkeys, and all, marching in admirable order over hill and dale to the wars, against their wills, aye, against their common sense and consciences, which makes it very steep marching indeed, and produces a palpitation of the heart.[13]

Taking Jefferson's dictum that the government is best which governs least, Thoreau playfully converts it into "That government is best which governs not at all."[14] Lest the reader dismiss him as an anarchist, he soon adds, "But to speak practically and as a citizen, unlike those who call themselves no-government men, I ask for, not at once no government, but *at once* a better government."[15] Most men, he believes, serve the state without questioning it. "Others" —and here he recognizes the unconscious corruption of self-interest in a very profound way—"as most legislators, politicians, lawyers, ministers, and office-holders, serve the state chiefly with their heads; and, as they rarely make any moral distinctions, they are as likely to serve the Devil without *intending* it, as God."[16] Thoreau feels personal shame in being a citizen of a slaveholding government. He takes a dim view of electoral politics because there is really little choice offered the voter. His own refusal to vote is best explained by his discussion of the dilemma of the respectable man: "He forthwith adopts one of the candidates thus selected as the only *available* one, thus proving that he is himself *available* for any purposes of the demagogue."[17]

The patriots of the American War of Independence recognized the right of revolution.

When a sixth of the population which has undertaken to be the refuge of liberty are slaves, and a whole country is unjustly overrun and conquered by a foreign army, and subjected to military law, I think that it is not too soon for honest men to rebel and revolutionize.[18]

The Transcendentalist valuation comes out clearly when he says, "It is not so important that many should be as good as you, as that there be some absolute goodness somewhere; for that will leaven the whole lump."[19] This might be called "the politics of absolute goodness," but it has only to be stated to reveal its problems. It is not really a political program as much as a moral imperative, but an imperative which, interestingly enough, establishes its own relevance in the political order.

Action from principle, the perception and the performance of right, changes things and relations; it is essentially revolutionary, and does not consist wholly with anything which was. It not only divides states and churches, it divides families; ay, it divides the *individual,* separating the diabolical in him from the divine.[20]

Clearly Thoreau is not offering a viable politics of the type desired by Professor Eulau. The God-dimension and the call to secede from the union and Massachusetts are equally apparent in what follows.

I do not hesitate to say, that those who call themselves Abolitionists should at once effectually withdraw their support, both in person and property, from the government of Massachusetts, and not wait till they constitute a majority of one, before they suffer the right to prevail through them. I think that it is enough if they have God on their side, without waiting for that other one. Moreover, any man more right than his neighbors constitutes a majority of one already.[21]

Then follow his direct statements on passive resistance, showing that he is not only interested in demonstrating for justice but wants to prevail in actual fact. The picture of the state presupposed is the democratic one dedicated to humane values, not the totalitarian leviathan.

If the alternative is to keep all just men in prison, or give up war and slavery, the State will not hesitate which to choose. If a thousand men were not to pay their tax-bills this year, that would not be a violent and bloody measure, as it would be to pay them, and enable the State to commit violence and shed innocent blood.[22]

Thoreau introduces his ideal of simplicity in living by remarking that rich men capitulate faster to the state's pressure than do those who have not given the state this advantage over them. He makes a skillful use of the incident of Christ and the tricky Herodians, who asked him whether one might give tribute to Caesar.

Christ answered the Herodians according to their condition. "Show me the tribute-money," said he;—and one took a penny out of his pocket;—if you use money which has the image of Caesar on it, and which he has made current and valuable, that is, *if you are men of the State,* and gladly enjoy the advantages of Caesar's government, then pay him back some of his own when he demands it; "Render therefore to Caesar that which is Caesar's, and to God those things which are God's,"—leaving them no wiser than before as to which was which; for they did not wish to know.[23]

Thoreau has never refused to pay his highway tax, because he wants to be a good neighbor. He supports education, even to the extent, in a *Journal* passage a few years later, of advocating that villages become universities.

This town,—how much has it ever spent directly on its own culture? To act collectively is according to the spirit of our institutions, and I am confident that, as our circumstances are more flourishing, our means are greater. New England can hire all the wise men in the world to come and teach her, and board them round the while, and not be provincial at all.[24]

Some "pure" moralists have faulted him for the following sentence, but his point of view is not inconsistent with his previous assertions. "In fact, I quietly declare war with the

State, after my fashion, though I will still make what use and get what advantage of her I can, as is usual in such cases."[25]

The prophetic dimension of Thoreau's essay, which might be described in New Testament terms as the obligation "to obey God rather than men," comes out again in two ways near the end. First it gives structure to his appeal from people en masse to God, then to those very persons as themselves created by God. "I see that appeal is possible, first and instantaneously, from them to the Maker of them, and, secondly, from them to themselves."[26] The second instance is even more interesting because Thoreau does not introduce the absolutism of the religious dimension at the very first, but allows a preliminary hierarchial structuring of existence with a generous recognition of the good of the American system.

Seen from a lower point of view, the Constitution, with all its faults, is very good; the law and the courts are very respectable; even this State and this American government are, in many respects, very admirable and rare things, to be thankful for, such as a great many have described them; but seen from a point of view a little higher, they are what I have described them; seen from a higher still, and the highest, who shall say what they are, or that they are worth looking at or thinking of at all?[27]

But when Thoreau takes his stand on "the highest" point of view it is unambiguously that of a biblical prophet. Webster's "prudence" is brushed aside because he is one of those who "are wont to forget that the world is not governed by policy and expediency."[28] Thoreau's Puritan inheritance of America as the covenant nation especially called to obey God and therefore especially subject to God's judgments and punishments for disobedience is the perspective of the following remarkable sentences, seldom quoted by recent analysts of the essay.

If we were left solely to the wordy wit of legislators in Congress for our guidance, *uncorrected by the seasonal experience and the effectual complaints of the people, America would not long retain her rank among the nations.* For eighteen hundred years, though perchance I have no right to say it, the New Testament has been written; *yet where is the legislator who has wisdom and practical talent enough to avail himself of the light which it sheds on the science of legislation?*[29]

At this point Thoreau is beyond quoting from Confucius, the *Bhagavad-Gita,* or the *Laws of Menu.* They still will have their place when in the future the discussion is about wisdom, liberality of view, or contemplation, but when he is deeply challenged by injustice and there is an imperative to act he will stand forth in the role of biblical prophet with many of the inheritances of his Puritan forebears.[30] There is still another Puritan presupposition in the last quotation. It is the confidence that the experience of the people and their complaints will correct the legislators. This is the contribution of left-wing Puritanism; namely, that the open church meeting in which all are equally gifted by the Spirit and open to his guidance is to be listened to by the godly magistrate. It is the prophetic source of the dictum that "the voice of the people is the voice of God" and not its perversion later into idolatry by the absolutizing of a democratic majority no longer obedient to biblical presuppositions.[31]

It will be useful at this point to carry forward an analysis of Thoreau's activity and expression on the subject of social ethics, chiefly in his *Journal,* to the time that he was putting the finishing touches on *Walden* for the press and just before another dramatic event called forth his protest in "Slavery in Massachusetts." In the winter of 1851 Congress passed the Fugitive Slave Law, giving slaveholders federal help in tracking down runaway slaves in the North and returning them by force to their masters. A group of Massachusetts citizens in February forcibly rescued Shadrach from the Boston authorities, took him to Concord to the house of Thoreau's neighbor, and successfully sent him to Canada, away from the fiery furnace of slavery. Then in April, the officials of government with 250 troops arrested Thomas Sims and, frustrating an attempted rescue, returned him by ship to Georgia, where he nearly died under the lash. Thoreau's *Journal* exploded for seven pages of denunciation of the government, the press, and the church. "I believe that in this country the press exerts a greater and a more pernicious influence than the church. We are not a religious people, but we are a nation of politicians. We do not much care for, we do not read, the Bible, but we do care for and we do read the newspaper."[32] He rested his position not alone on general principles of justice and humanity but on an argument drawn from the New Testament. This may well make him a pioneer of the Christian theology of liberation which in our day has tried to make it clear to un-comprehending America that by Christ's teaching and action anything done to another human being by way of compassion and justice and love is done to Christ himself, and anything of injustice and inhumanity done to such a person, or even "benign neglect," is done as it were to Christ himself. This radical turning of Christological confession to prophetic activity and not just verbal formulation, as in the orthodox churches, is as threatening to our contemporaries in the areas of racial prejudice, minority rights, compensation, and empowerment of the deprived as it was in Thoreau's day over the issue of slavery, American imperialism, and the injustices done to the Indians. It is, therefore, fascinating to find Thoreau exegeting the parable of Matthew 25 along the lines of a contemporary theologian of liberation.

Of course it makes not the least difference—I wish you to consider this—who the man was,—whether he was Jesus Christ or another, —for inasmuch as ye did it unto the least of these his brethren ye did it unto him. Do you think *he* would have stayed here in liberty and let the black man go into slavery in his stead?[33]

He returned again to his prophetic conviction that judgment awaits unjust nations as well as individuals. "I wish my townsmen to consider that, whatever the human law may be, neither an individual nor a nation can ever deliberately commit the least act of injustice without having to pay the penalty for it."[34] Whereas his position in "Civil Disobedience" might seem to be only peaceful and passive resistance to unjust law, it is clear that he would in 1851 sanction war to remove the evil of slavery. Quietism and militancy were poles in the oscillation of his views on political action. His words are still significant for us as we approach the nation's bicentennial.

So one would say . . . that the vast majority of the inhabitants of the city of Boston . . . were not descendants of the men of the Revolution. . . . But I would have done with comparing ourselves with our ancestors, for on the whole I believe that even they, if somewhat braver and less corrupt than we, were not men of so much principle and generosity as to go to war in behalf of another race in their midst. I do not believe that the North will soon come to blows with the South on this question. It would be too bright a page to be written in the history of the race at present.[35]

This is in its way a prediction of a war for emancipation.

The indignation over the Sims affair was transformed by the following month into a remarkable passage in the *Journal* in which Thoreau records for himself a deepened sensitivity to his fellowmen, an appreciation of the divine aspect of man so powerful as to suggest to Thoreau that it represented a sort of "proof" of God. He relates this deepened insight, so powerful for him existentially, to his previous conviction about the revelations of nature in such a way that the author of *A Week* and of "Civil Disobedience" will henceforth be seen as the same person, whether he is "on the alert to find God in nature, to know his lurking-places,"[36] or to discover him in human beings charged with responsibilities for historical decisions. The passage demands quotation in some fullness. It shows him drawn out of his intense religious individualism toward a more corporate fellow-feeling religiously.

I think that we are not commonly aware that man is our contemporary. . . . Man, the crowning fact, the god we know. While the earth supports so rare an inhabitant, there is somewhat to cheer us. Who shall say that there is no God, if there is a *just* man. It is only within a year that it has occurred to me that there is such a being actually existing on the globe. . . . We have not only the idea and vision of the divine ourselves, but we have brothers, it seems, who have this idea also. Methinks my neighbor is better than I, and his thought is better than mine. . . . We have the material of heaven here. I think that the standing miracle to man is man. . . . The revelations of nature are infinitely glorious and cheering, hinting to us of a remote future, of possibilities untold; but startlingly near to us someday we find a fellow-man. . . . From nature we turn astonished to this *near* but supernatural fact. I think that the existence of man in nature is the divinest and most startling of all facts. . . . Imagine yourself alone in the world, a musing, wondering, reflecting spirit, *lost* in thought, and imagine thereafter the creation of man!—man made in the image of God![37]

In just a few months after this, the evidence is clear that Thoreau passed from the status of law-abiding citizen to resister against and breaker of unjust laws, although he had probably helped long before in the underground railroad.

Henry Williams, a fugitive from Virginia who was trying through an agent to buy his freedom from his master (who was also his father) fled Boston as the police closed in. He arrived in Concord at the Thoreau household with a letter from Lovejoy and Garrison. The Thoreaus hid him until funds could be raised to forward him to Canada. Henry Thoreau bought his ticket and put him on the train after he had determined that there were no police staked out for him. Again in 1853 Thoreau received a fugitive slave in the night and spent the next day bathing his sores, according to Moncure Conway's testimony, prior to sending him along to freedom in Canada.

An interesting passage from the *Journal* for November 10, 1851, compares the proper functioning of politics to the unconscious processes of the body. We only should be aware of politics when the body is diseased or in the throes of indigestion. The Gold Rush of '49 appalled Thoreau. He asked:

Of what significance the philosophy, or poetry, or religion of a world that will rush to the lottery of California gold-digging on the receipt of the first news, to live by luck, to get the means of commanding the labor of others less lucky, i.e. of slaveholding, without contributing any value to society? . . . It makes God to be a moneyed gentleman who scatters a handful of pennies in order to see mankind scramble for them. Going to California. It is only three thousand miles nearer to hell.[38]

The Congressional debate over the Kansas-Nebraska bill in 1854 drew him to reading newspapers again.

This chapter may fittingly be closed with a prayer and meditation remarkable for its quality from August 17, 1851. Its piety, which Thoreau seldom revealed to the world, introduces us to the milieu of *Walden*. We are awakened to the spiritual dimension of his masterpiece, which he was revising again and again, polishing it as smooth as a water-sanded stone. There is a Franciscan quality to the passage.

My heart leaps into my mouth at the sound of the wind in the woods. I, whose life was but yesterday so desultory and shallow, suddenly recover my spirits, my spirituality, through my hearing. . . . Ah, I would walk, I would sit and sleep, with natural piety! What if I could pray aloud or to myself as I went along by the brooksides a cheerful prayer like the birds! For joy I could embrace the earth; I shall delight to be buried in it. And then to think of those I love among men, who will know that I love them though I tell them not! . . . I thank you, God. I do not deserve anything. I am unworthy of the least regard; and yet I am made to rejoice. I am impure and worthless, and yet the world is gilded for my delight and holidays are prepared for me, and my path is strewn with flowers.[39]

5

THE RELIGION
OF *WALDEN*

One of the reasons for the popularity of *Walden* is that the book is so rich in perspectives and accomplishment that readers can find in it at least four different books. Walter Harding has identified these as *Robinson Crusoe*, Gilbert White's *Natural History of Selborne*, *Gulliver's Travels*, and *Pilgrim's Progress*. Although Thoreau had gone to Walden Pond with the intention to write his *Week* and did this, the actual masterpiece that finally flowered from his experience was *Walden*. The version of *Walden* written at the pond, however, passed through six revisions after he had returned to live in Concord, first at the Emersons', when Emerson was away lecturing in England, and then in his parents' house, in which he remained for the rest of his life.[1]

The actual cause of its writing was the questioning Thoreau met from his townsmen, who asked him how he felt being alone and how he made out without what were commonly thought to be the necessary supports for living. He was encouraged to lecture on this topic at the Lyceum, the lecture becoming the nucleus of the first chapter on "Economy." He then proceeded, in the fashion of Crusoe, to solve the basic requirements of existence—food, shelter, fuel, and clothing—in such an interesting story that he hooked both the armchair readers of how-to-do-it books and those dissatisfied with their lot who sought motivation for change and the means to accomplish it in practical living. In the process of his composition, he produced a superb book about nature, the revolution of the seasons, and his animal neighbors which most of his contemporaries, to judge from reviews and the first generation of critics, saw as a richer example of White's nature writing. Some still read it simply in this light, although in recent years many have been finding in it a welcome satire on the morals and manners of mass man in an affluent and acquisitive society, a contemporary version of *Gulliver's Travels*. All these interpretations have their justification in Thoreau's book, but if one probes very far beneath the surface of the questions they raise, particularly the philosophic one of how these three interpretations can possibly coexist without outright contradiction, the reader will be led to a fourth one, *Pilgrim's Progress*, the title already suggested by a comment Thoreau made about Bunyan's classic in the *Week*.

If we trace through the late evolution of the chapter on "Higher Laws" as developed by J. Lyndon Shanley in *The Making of Walden*, we can, as it were, see Thoreau himself, developing and deepening this material as though it provided the organic bond for all the rest he had to say. His own search for the meaning of life that originally sent him to the pond, the asceticism he practiced there in order to simplify the practical art of living, and the later recollection of what it had all really signified followed something comparable in his personal life to the reactions of later generations of readers. At the very least, one might hope that the compilers of Thoreau anthologies would cease and desist from omitting the chapter on "Higher Laws," which in this interpretation becomes the center for understanding the book.

The very conception of "the higher law" was the means by which the Transcendentalist reformers had appealed from the federal Constitution with its recognition and protection of slavery to the still more ultimate law of God. In *Walden* Thoreau succeeded in giving flesh to this spiritual perception by taking it away from the esoteric and abstract perceptions of the movement and by identifying his practical day-to-day life under discipline as a quest for it. It becomes a gospel which he commends to his readers by arranging the very seasons to testify to spiritual rebirth and awakening. Harding has described this dimension of the book.

As earnest as John Bunyan's *Pilgrim's Progress*, it is a guide book to the higher life. On this level it is Transcendentalism in its purest form—a plea that would we but obey that light within us we could attain a fulfillment, a happiness, and a success such as man has never known. And Thoreau in his buoyant optimism believed that man would some day achieve that goal.[2]

Before we accept *Pilgrim's Progress* as *Walden's* classic prototype, however, it should be said that *Walden* might also bear the title of "a forest treatise" or some comparable description of the soul's journey from the literature of Hinduism or, in larger terms, from the Orient so prominent in Thoreau's thought and practice. In his description of how ice cut from Walden Pond reaches Madras, Bombay, and Calcutta in Yankee trading ships, Thoreau acknowledges this influence. "In the morning I bathe my intellect in the stupendous and cosmogonal philosophy of the Bhagvat Geeta, since whose composition years of the gods have elapsed, and in comparison with which our modern world and its literature seem puny and trivial."[3] The decision, however, to choose *Pilgrim's Progress* as the nearest classic reference is fully justified by the facts and represents a development in Thoreau's own religious orientation from the *Week* to *Walden*. It will be recalled that Horace Greeley in his New York *Tribune* review of the *Week* had lectured Thoreau about commenting unfavorably on the Bible, which he supposedly had not studied. Even Greeley, who failed to understand Thoreau's ironic remark, could never have repeated the charge about *Walden*, for the Eastern books are quoted from much less and only when their addition confirms the point Thoreau is making on his own.[4] Furthermore, the style of *Walden*, both in its quotation of biblical passages and its imitation or adaptation of biblical phraseology to give an authoritative note to Thoreau's own teaching, is far more pronounced than in the *Week*. While a quantitative analysis is not necessarily conclusive in itself, it is significant that a by-no-means complete count reveals fifty-six references to the Bible to twenty-four from Oriental and Greek religions in *Walden*. When this fact is added to the Puritan heritage so evident in Thoreau's religious orientation in *Walden*, it is not unduly restrictive to select *Pilgrim's Progress* as the prototype. Christian, however, has been somewhat "de-Bunyanized." He carries a copy of the *Bhagavad-Gita* in his pack, stops longer for contemplation on his pilgrimage, and gazes with an Eastern and somewhat less evangelical joy at the heavenly city.

Meditation was a discipline that Thoreau undertook at

Walden. How much this practice is to be identified or associated with Yoga will be discussed in the later chapter on
mysticism. Here what must be established is the practice of
meditation itself. He began the day with a dip in Walden,
calling it "a religious exercise." Thereafter he often remained
in meditation for hours at a time. The classic description is
in the second paragraph from "Sounds," which describes his
practice and attributes to it substantial personal growth and
insight.

There were times when I could not afford to sacrifice the bloom
of the present moment to any work, whether of the head or
hands. I love a broad margin to my life. Sometimes, in a summer
morning, having taken my accustomed bath, I sat in my sunny
doorway from sunrise till noon, rapt in a revery, amidst the pines
and hickories and sumachs, in undisturbed solitude and stillness,
while the birds sang around or flitted noiseless through the house,
until by the sun falling in at my west window, or the noise of
some traveller's wagon on the distant highway, I was reminded
of the lapse of time. I grew in those seasons like corn in the
night, and they were far better than any work of the hands
would have been. They were not time subtracted from my life, but
so much over and above my usual allowance. I realized what the
Orientals mean by contemplation and the forsaking of works. For
the most part, I minded not how the hours went.[5]

In another passage he describes cleaning his house by putting all his furniture out on the grass and scrubbing the floor
with wet sand until "the morning sun had dried my house
sufficiently to allow me to move in again, and my meditations were almost uninterrupted."[6] Later, in comic relief and
with some spoofing of himself, he writes a dialogue between
"Poet" (his friend Channing, come to get him to go fishing)
and "Hermit" (himself, "just concluding a serious meditation"). When Poet goes to dig worms, Hermit tries unsuc-
cessfully to return to contemplation.

Let me see, where was I? Methinks I was nearly in this frame of
mind; the world lay about at this angle. Shall I go to heaven or
a-fishing? If I should soon bring this meditation to an end, would
another so sweet occasion be likely to offer? I was as near being
resolved into the essence of things as ever I was in my life. . . .
My thoughts have left no track, and I cannot find the path
again. What was it that I was thinking of? It was a very hazy day.

I will just try these three sentences of Con-fut-see; they may fetch that state about again. I know not whither it was the dumps or a budding ecstasy. . . . Well, then, let's be off. Shall we to the Concord? There's good sport there if the water be not too high.[7]

The previous quotations demonstrate the reality of his practice of contemplation and its often Oriental form or structure. It may be helpful to fit this into his sense of vocation and of special guidance, a clear inheritance of the Puritan doctrine of "special providence" previously noted in the *Journal*, but here publicly confessed. It is also a dynamic factor in Thoreau's vocation as a prophet.

Sometimes, when I compare myself with other men, it seems as if I were more favored by the gods than they, beyond any deserts that I am conscious of; *as if I had a warrant and surety at their hands which my fellows have not, and were especially guided and guarded.*[8]

There is no longer in *Walden* such a feeling of difference between a biblical orientation and an Oriental frame of reference as seemed to trouble him in the *Week*. He is far closer to resolving the historical differences between religious cultures into an individual mystical experience common to all. He appears to have appropriated more liberality into his own evaluations, in accordance with his own announced dictum that "with wisdom we shall learn liberality." The following section is critical to his own understanding of the process of spiritual awakening, as well as an indication of how he would reform the exclusive religious situation of Concord were he able.

The solitary hired man on a farm in the outskirts of Concord, who has had his second birth and peculiar religious experience, and is driven as he believes into silent gravity and exclusiveness by his faith, may think it is not true; but Zoroaster, thousands of years ago, travelled the same road and had the same experience; but he, being wise, knew it to be universal, and treated his neighbors accordingly, and is even said to have invented and established worship among men. Let him humbly commune with Zoroaster then, and, through the liberalizing influence of all the worthies, with Jesus Christ himself, and let "our church" go by the board.[9]

Contemplation was one discipline Thoreau practiced by

the pond. Another was simplicity, or voluntary poverty. "None can be an impartial or wise observer of human life but from the vantage ground of what we should call voluntary poverty."[10] With an existentialist commitment very much comparable to Kierkegaard's criticism of the Hegelian philosopher or his satire on the theologian, Thoreau pleads for practical philosophers who will be "the progenitors of a nobler race of men."

There are nowadays professors of philosophy, but not philosophers. Yet it is admirable to profess because it was once admirable to live. To be a philosopher is not merely to have subtle thoughts, nor even to found a school, but so to love wisdom as to live according to its dictates, a life of simplicity, independence, magnanimity, and trust. It is to solve some of the problems of life, not only theoretically, but practically.[11]

A third discipline, closely related to simplicity was a deliberate life-style. It involved among other things religious honesty and authenticity.

I went to the woods because I wished to live deliberately, to front only the essential facts of life. . . . For most men, it appears to me, are in a strange uncertainty about it, whether it is of the devil or of God, and have somewhat hastily concluded that it is the chief end of man here to "glorify God and enjoy him forever."[12]

Reformers, although Thoreau was obviously chief among them, fare ill at his hands in Walden. He finds philanthropy generally misnamed and malpracticed. Thorough individualist that he is, he is convinced that the painful process of reform must take root in the individual. In a paraphrase, his message could be reduced to being good rather than trying to do good. Hitting at symptoms is, he believes, an illusion.

There are a thousand hacking at the branches of evil to one who is striking at the root, and it may be that he who bestows the largest amount of time and money on the needy is doing the most by his mode of life to produce that misery which he strives in vain to relieve. It is the pious slave-breeder devoting the proceeds of every tenth slave to buy a Sunday's liberty for the rest.[13]

In other words, Thoreau was aware of how "reform" could

both actually acquiesce in horrible social ills that were left unchallenged and also serve as an ego crutch for the philanthropist. Community self-help projects are often an affront to the social welfare establishment that feels its power threatened or simply its paternalistic desire to dominate the needy frustrated. "If any thing ail a man . . . he forthwith sets about reforming—the world."[14] Thoreau, in offering this criticism, does not smugly imply that he is above this pathetic situation. "I never dreamed of any enormity greater than I have committed. I never knew, and never shall know, a worse man than myself."[15] Although he protested against the doctrine of original sin, it is significant that he had few illusions about the goodness of the natural man, including himself. He had a hardy Puritan realism about sniffing out evil wherever it might be found. Indeed, it was probably this insight into evil at the core of selfhood that made him skeptical of popular movements for reform and even dogmatic in his insistence that true reform must be centered on the individual.

The confusion about philanthropy, he believed, readily translated itself into wrong attitudes about God and religious life-style. Men and women were taught resignation and hopelessness by an infantile conception of God. True praise of God and heartfelt thanksgiving were seldom found.

Our hymn-books resound with a melodious cursing of God and enduring Him forever. One would say that even the prophets and redeemers had rather consoled the fears than confirmed the hopes of man. There is nowhere recorded a simple and irrepressible satisfaction with the gift of life, any memorable praise of God.[16]

This caricature of true piety upsets people's compass bearings. They cease to see or expect the glory of God in this life and project all divine reality into the next world. Into the vacuum spreads the worship of mammon and power as activities of the pious businessman. Resignation is inculcated as a virtue and joylessness becomes the milieu. It produces a complete caricature of biblical faith. "What Thoreau rejected was the debased 'Christianity' of his time, the Mammonized Puritanism which had become the mere consecration of worldliness, self-righteousness and sentimentality."[17]

With Hebraic prophetic realism, Thoreau wrote, "God himself culminates in the present moment, and will never be more divine in the lapse of all the ages. And we are enabled to apprehend at all what is sublime and noble only by the perpetual instilling and drenching of the reality which surrounds us."[18]

In the first version of *Walden*, as reconstructed by Shanley from Huntington Manuscript 924, Thoreau in 1846–47 linked the two major themes we have been tracing with these concluding sentences: "I think that the universe really needs no patching from us—and its Maker no condolence. Let us remember that God is well."[19] Also, in the earliest version, the paragraph in the final text about the "innocence and beneficence of Nature" concludes with a sentence that Thoreau probably thought too personal to allow to remain: "God is my father and my friend—men are my brothers—but nature is my mother and my sister."[20]

"Higher Laws" was present in the first version only as the beginning of a discussion about the propriety of fishing and hunting. The discussion was expanded in subsequent versions, leading to an analysis of the higher and lower natures in people, the place of the wild, eating habits, and the body as a temple. It is placed just before autumn in the book, as a signal for entering the more reflective period of winter. In the final version it is, in a sense, paired with the "Conclusion" that follows the rebirth of spring and brings "Higher Laws" to fulfillment.

Thoreau begins "Higher Laws" with the confession that once he was tempted to seize a woodchuck and devour him raw, "not that I was hungry then, except for that wildness which he represented."[21] He makes a two-fold analysis, distinguishing an impulse toward a higher spiritual life and one which expresses the primitive.

I found in myself, and still find, an instinct toward a higher, or, as it is named, spiritual life, as do most men, and another toward a primitive rank and savage one, and I reverence them both. I love the wild not less than the good. The wilderness and adventure that are in fishing still recommended it to me.[22]

Thoreau owed his first contacts with the woods to fishing and hunting. No boy, he feels, should be deprived of this recapitulation of the experience of early man, but the mature man puts aside hunting. "No humane being, past the thoughtless age of boyhood, will wantonly murder any creature, which holds its life by the same tenure that he does."[23]

He rarely tastes meat, believing that "every man who has ever been earnest to preserve his higher or poetic faculties in the best condition has been particularly inclined to abstain from animal food, and from much food of any kind."[24] He is confident that as humanity has given up cannibalism so in the future improvement of the race the eating of animals will stop. It may seem strange to some that a chapter supposedly on religion should be a discussion of eating habits, but this simply demonstrates the down-to-earth practicality of Thoreau's concern. There is abundant precedent for this asceticism in Hindu thought and in the apostle Paul. The misconception that Thoreau is a sort of nature boy can be illustrated from this appeal to discipline. "Nature is hard to be overcome, but she must be overcome. What avails it that you are Christian, if you are not purer than the heathen, if you deny yourself no more, if you are not more religious?"[25]

"Our whole life is startlingly moral," he asserts, leading on to discipline of the sex impulse, Victorian for its brevity and generality, foreign to today's counterculture, an open invitation to Freudian explanations, and yet possessing the simplicity of the monastic call to chastity.

The generative energy, which, when we are loose, dissipates and makes us unclean, when we are continent invigorates and inspires us. Chastity is the flowering of man; and what are called Genius, Heroism, Holiness, and the like, are but various fruits which succeed it. Man flows at once to God when the channel of purity is open. By turns our purity inspires and our impurity casts us down. He is blessed who is assured that the animal is dying out in him day by day, and the divine being established.[26]

Toward the end of the chapter, he announces his text, which is really a variant on Paul's passage in Corinthians: "Surely you know that you are God's temple, where the Spirit of God dwells (1 Cor. 3:16, NEB)." Thoreau's version is replete with a jab at building churches. "Every man is the builder of a temple, called his body, to the god he worships, after a style purely his own, nor can he get off by hammering marble instead."[27] Then, as he so often does in *Walden* when he wants to drive his text home, he tells us a parable. Here it is John Farmer, who sat by his door after a hard day's work. He had bathed. (Incidentally, this practice already sets him aside as a somewhat unusual farmer in a day when the bath had not yet established itself in America; perhaps Thoreau might be credited with motivating the movement with its motto that "cleanliness is next to godliness.") John Farmer heard the distant notes of a flute, and the reality of street, village, and state faded away. In the following parable the basis for improvement is a healthy respect for the self. One of Thoreau's misgivings about the traditional doctrine of original sin was that it produced self-hatred rather than self-acceptance.

A voice said to him,—Why do you stay here and live this mean moiling life, when a glorious existence is possible for you? Those same stars twinkle over other fields than these.—But how to come out of this condition and actually migrate thither? All that he could think of was to practise some new austerity, to let his mind descend into his body and redeem it, and treat himself with ever increasing respect.[28]

Thoreau's New England forebears had looked upon the Bay Colony, "a city built upon a hill," as a holy experiment in the keeping of covenant between them and God in which the success of the enterprise might be determined by whatever visitations God should bring. Thoreau identified his experiment in holy living at Walden with theirs and was not at all hesitant in claiming success for it.

I learned this, at least, by my experiment; that if one advances confidently in the direction of his dreams, and endeavors to live the life which he has imagined, he will meet with a success unexpected in common hours. He will put some things behind, will pass an invisible boundary; new, universal, and more liberal laws will begin to establish themselves around and within him; or the old laws be expanded and interpreted in his favor in a more liberal sense, and he will live with the license of a higher order of beings.[29]

Another of the regulative principles of Puritan theology was the doctrine of the perseverance of the saints predestined to salvation. This drive exalted the individual in his quest for perfection. It reappears in Thoreau's search for perfection. He tells the tale of the artist in the city of Kouroo. This wise craftsman "was disposed to strive after perfection" in carving a staff. His patience was without limit; he outlasted a whole dynasty, for the integrity of his quest, without his knowledge, had endowed him with perennial youth. "When the finishing stroke was put to his work, it suddenly expanded before the eyes of the astonished artist into the fairest of all the creations of Brahma. He had made a new system in making a staff, a world with full and fair proportions."[30]

The second parable, this one from New England, is designed to echo the ecstatic cry of the previous chapter that with the coming of spring the Walden that was dead is alive again.

Every one has heard the story which has gone the rounds of New England, of a strong and beautiful bug which came out of the dry leaf of an old table of apple-tree wood, which had stood in a farmer's kitchen for sixty years, first in Connecticut, and afterwards in Massachusetts,—from an egg deposited in the living tree many years earlier still, as appeared by counting the annual layers beyond it; which was heard gnawing out for several weeks, hatched perchance by the heat of an urn. Who does not feel his faith in a resurrection and immortality strengthened by hearing of this?[31]

The first edition of *Walden* had the subtitle *Life in the Woods*. This final parable must have delighted Thoreau, with his love of puns, because it dramatized the theme of life-in-the-wood. In a burst of Transcendentalist fervor and optimism he concludes his masterpiece: "Only that day dawns to which we are awake. There is more day to dawn. The sun is but a morning star."[32]

One of the themes that Thoreau carries further in *Walden* than he did in the *Week* is the attraction of wildness. He recognized in "Higher Laws" that there were in him both an instinct for a higher and spiritual life and an instinct for the wild and that he reverenced them both. Part of the purpose of *Walden* was "to live a primitive and frontier life, though in the midst of an outward civilization."[33] It was, therefore, not an exercise in romantic primitivism such as might have led him to build a wigwam on the slopes of Katahdin. Instead he built a frame house, plastering the walls and shingling the exterior. In the second winter he even substituted a stove for the open fireplace. All of this is a symbol of Thoreau's acceptance of a certain amount of the "benefits and conveniences" of civilization. He accepted the railroad which shattered the isolation of the pond, using its track as his path to his parents' house and Concord. He simply wanted to be sure that the so-called "conveniences" remained tools for leading the good life and did not become masters of people. The task was to keep open to wildness. "Grow wild according to thy nature, like these sedges and brakes, which will never become English hay."[34] Human freedom requires the dimension of wildness. At the beginning of the chapter on "Solitude" he wrote: "This is a delicious evening, when the whole body is one sense, and imbibes delight through every pore. I go and come with a strange liberty in Nature, a part of herself."[35] The ideal life combines the wild of nature and the good of the human community. This is why *Walden* can be called a Transcendental pastoral.[36] It may also explain why for the second edition of *Walden* Thoreau deleted the subtitle. He wanted the emphasis to fall on how we handle life wherever we may be, not on just a guide to woods lore. He most certainly did not want imitators building ten-by-fifteen-foot replicas of his house.

I would not have any one adopt *my* mode of living on any account: for, beside that before he has fairly learned it I may have found out another for myself, I desire that there may be as many different persons in the world as possible; but I would have each one be very careful to find out and pursue *his own* way, and not his father's or his mother's or his neighbor's instead.[37]

The real problem was how to keep the element of wildness from disappearing completely, a threat to the integrity of village life as Thoreau saw it. This disappearance of wildness has been transformed in our day into a famine of deprivation for the city dweller and into the uglification of much of rural America by suburban scrawl and pollution. Thoreau believed that life without some relation to wildness suffered from anemia or deficiency. In our day Americans are just beginning to demand not merely national parks to preserve spectacular scenery and opportunities for recreation but also the preservation of wilderness areas and wild rivers, even if they never "use" them, a new asceticism that would have pleased Thoreau.

Our village life would stagnate if it were not for the unexplored forests and meadows which surround it. We need the tonic of wildness,—to wade sometimes in marshes where the bittern and

the meadow-hen lurk, and hear the booming of the snipe. . . .
At the same time that we are earnest to explore and learn all
things, we require that all things be mysterious and unexplorable,
that land and sea be infinitely wild, unsurveyed and unfathomed
by us because unfathomable. We can never have enough of
Nature. We must be refreshed by the sight of inexhaustible
vigor, vast and Titanic features, the sea-coast with its wrecks,
the wilderness with its living and its decaying trees, the thunder-
cloud, and the rain which lasts three weeks and produces freshets.
We need to witness our limits transgressed, and some life pasturing
freely where we never wander.[38]

Thoreau is telling us here of experiences that would
flower into *The Maine Woods* and *Cape Cod,* his two
classic travel books. His sense of the wild was immeasur-
ably deepened for him by his struggle to reach the top
of Katahdin. He experienced threatening dimensions of
the wild that he had not known on the sunny tops of
Annursnack Hill in Concord or even on Wachusett or Monadnock. The wilderness trip by batteau to Katahdin was his
one major trip away from Walden during his stay at the
pond. It cured him of any sentimental or romantic feelings
about nature he might have had, probably strengthened
his perception that God was to be found in human communities wrestling with historic responsibilities as well as
in nature, and enlarged the dimensions of *Walden* beyond
mere nature writing to an attempt to see life and see it
whole. The experience of terrifying aloneness on Katahdin
drove him down to rejoin his comrades, abandoning the
earlier-mentioned possibility that he might leave them for
further solitary exploration of the range. On his last
Maine trip down the East Branch of the Penobscot to the
east of the mountain, with access there to Chimney Pond
Basin and the Knife-Edge, he had hoped to climb it again,
but when he realized that his companion's feet were not
up to the climb, he significantly did not attempt the mountain alone. Since the experience of Katahdin was so overwhelming for him and so durable in its influence upon his
later views, enough of his description must be quoted to
give the reader its flavor, but it should be read in its entirety.
It shook him to his depths and plunged him into a crisis
of identity. The last sentence in the paragraph is unlike any
that he would write again.

I caught sight of a dark, damp crag to the right or left; the mist driving ceaselessly between it and me. . . . It was vast, Titanic, and such as man never inhabits. Some part of the beholder, even some vital part, seems to escape through the loose grating of his ribs as he ascends. He is more lone than you can imagine. There is less of substantial thought and fair understanding in him, than in the plains where men inhabit. His reason is dispersed and shadowy, more thin and subtile like the air. Vast, Titanic, inhuman Nature has got him at disadvantage, caught him alone, and pilfers him of some of his divine faculty. She does not smile on him as in the plains. She seems to say sternly, why came ye here before your time? . . . Nature was here something savage and awful, though beautiful. . . . Man was not to be associated with it. . . . There was there felt the presence of a force not bound to be kind to man. It was a place for heathenism and superstitious rites,—to be inhabited by men nearer of kin to the rocks and to wild animals than we. . . . What is this Titan that has possession of me? Talk of mysteries!—Think of our life in nature,—daily to be shown matter, to come in contact with it,—rocks, trees, wind on our cheeks! the *solid* earth! the *actual* world! the *common sense! Contact! Contact! Who* are we? *Where* are we?[39]

Thoreau in *Walden* by a process of recollection came to terms with this jarring experience by conflating the instincts of the wild and the good, not canceling out the former but absorbing it ever anew into the maturation of the spiritual dimension of human life. The polarities of the primitive and the civilized man, the unspoiled landscape and nature transformed to pastoral use, would enrich his philosophy. At the end of his second trip into the Maine woods, he virtually says that the wilderness is a nice place to visit but that he would not want to live there.

Nevertheless, it was a relief to get back to our smooth, but still varied landscape. For a permanent residence, it seemed to me that there could be no comparison between this and the wilderness, necessary as the latter is for a resource and a background, the raw material of all our civilization. . . . Perhaps our own woods and fields . . . are the perfection of parks and groves, gardens, arbors, paths, vistas, and landscapes. They are the natural consequence of what art and refinement we as a people have.[40]

Underlying this more developed philosophy of the complementary relations of wilderness and civilization, there is in *Walden* a more comprehensively articulated understanding of the environment than that advanced in the *Week*. Thoreau laments that the farmer in Concord has lost the ancient sense of the sacredness of his vocation. There are no real festivals of thanksgiving. "He knows Nature but as a robber."[41] The sun shines on the cultivated and uncultivated field with equal benevolence. Thoreau has the ecologist's sensitivity for the filling of all the niches in nature with the myriad forms of life. He recognized the ecological pyramid. "Such a man has some right to fish, and I love to see Nature carried out in him. The perch swallows the grub-worm, the pickerel swallows the perch, and the fisherman swallows the pickerel; and so all the chinks in the scale of being are filled."[42] Thoreau moves easily with other forms of life. Chickadees come to him; a sparrow alights on his shoulder; the perch are hypnotized by his flute playing. Yet he recognizes the strangeness of other life as a barrier to communication. He seems to suggest a polarity of immanence and transcendence between God and people on the analogy of the relation between people and insect.

As I stand over the insect crawling amid the pine needles on the forest floor, and endeavoring to conceal itself from my sight, and ask myself why it will cherish those humble thoughts, and hide its head from me who might perhaps be its benefactor, and impart to its race some cheering information, I am reminded of the greater Benefactor and Intelligence that stands over me the human insect.[43]

He has a feeling for the wholeness of nature, partly the result of mystical intuition and partly the result of the kind of observation that was leading Darwin and others to the panorama of organic evolution. Thoreau is fascinated that when the frozen sand in the railroad cut thaws it assumes the shape of a leaf.

You find thus in the very sands an anticipation of the vegetable leaf. No wonder that the earth expresses itself outwardly in leaves, it so labors with the idea inwardly. . . . The Maker of this earth but patented a leaf. What Champollion will decipher this hieroglyphic for us, that we may turn over a new leaf at last? . . . There is nothing inorganic.[44]

This theme he developed in a poorly rhymed poem, but one that identifies the topography of Walden Pond with his whole being. Inanimate nature ceases to be merely inorganic when it becomes part of him and a means of communion with God.

[Its Maker] rounded this water with his hand, deepened and clarified it in his thought, and in his will bequeathed it to Concord. I see by its face that it is visited by the same reflection; and I can almost say, Walden, is it you?

> It is no dream of mine,
> To ornament a line;
> I cannot come nearer to God and Heaven
> Than I live to Walden even.
> I am its stony shore,
> And the breeze that passes o'er;
> In the hollow of my hand
> Are its water and its sand,
> And its deepest resort
> Lies high in my thought.[45]

Thoreau's perception of the interrelationship of all laws of nature and their harmony lays the foundation for a philosophy of holism, increasingly influential in our day as we awaken to the reality of our environmental crisis. There is a passionate passage about man's savage destruction of his environment that needs to be better known than it is. Thoreau's indignation at what a farmer named Flint had done to the pond that bore his name reaches the sustained invective of Amos among the Old Testament prophets. The destruction of the environment is for Thoreau essentially the crime of sacrilege. (It should also be known that Flint had refused to let Thoreau build and live by his pond.)

Flint's Pond! Such is the poverty of our nomenclature. What right had the unclean and stupid farmer, whose farm abutted on this sky water, whose shores he has ruthlessly laid bare, to give his name to it? Some skin-flint, who loved better the reflecting surface of a dollar, or a bright cent, in which he could see his own brazen face; who regarded even the wild ducks which settled in it as trespassers. . . . I go not there to see him nor to hear of him; who never *saw* it, who never bathed in it, who never loved it, who never protected it, who never spoke a good word for it, nor thanked God that He had made it . . . him who thought only of its money value; whose presence perchance cursed all the shores; who exhausted the land around it, and would fain have exhausted the waters within it; who regretted only that it was not English hay or cranberry meadow,—there was nothing to redeem it forsooth, in his eyes,—and would have drained and sold it for the mud at its bottom . . . who would carry the landscape, who would carry his God, to market, if he could get any thing for him.[46]

What is the religion of *Walden?* It is certainly not simple nature mysticism. God is not to be found simply by a retreat into the woods. Nor is God simply the apotheosis of the wild. On the other hand, it is just as wrong to conclude that, because he left Walden, Thoreau became disillusioned with the attempt to find God in nature and was now expecting to find renewal in society and civilization, as suggested by John Pickard. "In a sense the chapter ["Higher Laws"] suggests that the ideal can never be realized in nature and that society and civilization are more suitable to spiritual renewal."[47] Thoreau's position is far more complex than either of these disjunctives suggest. First, there is his strong feeling for the environing structure of human existence composed of what may be called the wild, the civilized, nature, history, and society. Second, if there is a clue to the mysterious bond of union between these seemingly conflicting but really mutually interdependent aspects of reality, it is in the conscience which is not solely autonomous but, to use Tillich's phrase theonomous, related to God. Thoreau's prescription is to wake up, to find renewal both in the recognition and contemplation of this mysterious harmony, but even more in a life of ethical action responsive to it. This will be possible because we are not alone; God will be with us in the struggle. God is environing reality as well as Cosmic Builder.

I delight to come to my bearings,—not walk in procession with pomp and parade, in a conspicuous place, *but to walk even with the Builder of the universe, if I may,*—not to live in this restless, nervous, bustling, trivial Nineteenth Century, but stand or sit thoughtfully while it goes by. What are men celebrating? They are all on a committee of arrangements, and hourly expect a speech from somebody. *God is only the president of the day, and Webster is his orator. . . .* Drive a nail home and clinch it so faithfully that you can wake up in the night and think of your work with satisfaction,—a work at which you would not be ashamed to invoke the Muse. *So will help you God, and so only. Every nail driven should be as another rivet in the machine of the universe, you carrying on the work.*[48]

The year 1854 which finally saw the publication of *Walden* brought with it also his foundation work for a posthumously published essay, "Life Without Principle," which he gave many times as a lecture under various titles and which he prepared for the press in the last few months of his life. In this short and magnificent essay, he blended the distilled essences of *Walden* and "Civil Disobedience." He included in it a statement about his difficulty in communicating his religion to Lyceum audiences that shows his low estimate of what passed as "religion" in the churches.

In some lyceums they tell me that they have voted to exclude the subject of religion. But how do I know what their religion is, and when I am near to or far from it? I have walked into such an arena and done my best to make a clean breast of what religion I have experienced, and the audience never suspected what I was about. The lecture was as harmless as moonshine to them. Whereas, if I had read to them the biography of the greatest scamps in history, they might have thought that I had written the lives of the deacons of their church.[49]

6

"I AM A MYSTIC"

Thoreau's statement "I am a mystic" is supported by his letters, by many entries in his *Journal*, and by the testimony of his contemporaries. It may seem like belaboring the obvious to make the point, but a surprising number of studies of Thoreau deny that he was a mystic or simply choose to ignore the evidence.

Some of the problem may arise from confusion about the word mysticism and from a certain vagueness about the word in popular speech. Dean Inge, in his classic Bampton Lectures on the subject, provided a definition sufficiently broad and yet precise enough to be a useful tool in the analysis of this aspect of Thoreau's religion: "The phase of thought or feeling which we call Mysticism has its origin in that which is the raw material of all religion, and perhaps of all philosophy and art as well, namely that dim consciousness of the *beyond,* which is part of our nature as human beings."[1] On February 9, 1851, Thoreau wrote in his *Journal:*

My desire for knowledge is intermittent; but my desire to commune with the spirit of the universe, to be intoxicated even with the fumes, call it, of that divine nectar, to bear my head through atmospheres and over heights unknown to my feet, is perennial and constant.[2]

This quotation from Thoreau fills the somewhat abstract

terms of Inge's definition, but overflows them in its concreteness and excitement. The richness of Thoreau's profession
is better reflected in a more recent fuller definition of
mysticism than Inge's or than the twenty-six definitions by
others in the appendix to his study.

The crucial aspect of the mystical consciousness is in its intense
realization of meaningful patterns in the universe, life, and history
so that the meanings so apprehended glow with a sublime fire
in the inner soul and give to the person so favored an ineffable
sense of the wonder, beauty, glory, and unity of the Ultimate—
that Being which is alike the concern of philosopher and mystic.[3]

Bronson Alcott, in two passages in his *Journals,* caught
the unique flavor of Thoreau's mysticism.

He is less thinker than observer; a naturalist in tendency but of a
mystic habit, and a genius for detecting the essence in form and
giving forth the soul of things seen. . . . His mysticism is alike
solid and organic, animal and ideal. He is the mythologist of these
last days.[4]

Thoreau's friend Thomas Cholmondeley, who had sent him
the library of Eastern books, wrote Thoreau from Rome
on December 16, 1856, mentioning his mystical dimension:
"What you are engaged in I suspect to be Meditations on
the Higher Laws as they show themselves in Common
Things."[5]
    It is possible to be much more specific about Thoreau's
mysticism than this testimony from his friends. In a letter
to Isaac Hecker in 1844, after his return from Mount Greylock and from his walking trip with Channing to the
Catskills, he turned down Hecker's invitation for a trip to
Rome.

But the fact is, I cannot so decidedly postpone exploring the
Farther Indies, which are to be reached you know by other routes
and other methods of travel. I mean that I constantly return from
every external enterprise with disgust to fresh faith in a kind of
Brahminical Artesian, Inner Temple, life. All my experience, as
yours probably, proves only this reality.[6]

What Thoreau meant by a "Brahminical" life is that he

was following Hindu disciplines of meditation, concentration, and asceticism, in particular, Yoga. Unfortunately for our understanding of Thoreau, most Americans associate this word with special exercises in breathing and posture, if not special acts of self-torture like staring at the sun. Yoga properly means union and, in a derived way, the path to that union. There are many paths in Yoga: Jnana (knowledge), Raja (will), Hatha (courage), Mantra (speech), Karma (works), and Bhakti (love, worship). Thoreau, who never liked systems, can hardly be imagined as following one particular method; he took what he liked in the eclectic way observed in our discussion of the *Week*. In the famous letter of November 20, 1849, to H. G. O. Blake he twice professed, although in a qualified way, his devotion to Yoga after two quotations from Hindu sources.

"Free in this world, as the birds in the air, disengaged from every kind of chains, those who have practiced the *yoga* gather in Brahma the certain fruit of their works."

Depend upon it that rude and careless as I am, I would fain practise the *yoga* faithfully.

"The yogin, absorbed in contemplation, contributes in his degree to creation: he breathes a divine perfume, he hears wonderful things. Divine forms traverse him without tearing him, and united to the nature which is proper to him, he goes, he acts, as animating original matter."

To some extent, and at rare intervals, even I am a yogin.[7]

Earlier Thoreau had written in his *Journal* his approval of Hindu ascetic practices, sounding every bit the Puritan of iron discipline. "One may discover the root of a Hindoo religion in his own private history, when, in the silent intervals of the day or the night, he does sometimes inflict on himself like austerities with a stern satisfaction."[8] What we often find in his *Journal* is not so much the direct expression of a mystical state, as we do, say, in Pascal, but the carefully recollected re-living, as a literary craftsman, of the previous primary experience now transformed in memory by the magic of words. This may account for the fact that so many have failed to understand that he was a mystic. He described the process very closely in one entry.

Our ecstatic states, which appear to yield so little fruit, have this value at least: though in the seasons when our genius reigns we may be powerless for expression, yet, in calmer seasons, when our talent is active, the memory of those rarer moods comes to color our picture and is the permanent paint-pot, as it were, into which we dip our brush. Thus no life or experience goes unreported at last; but if it be not solid gold it is gold-leaf, which gilds the furniture of the mind. It is an experience of infinite beauty on which we unfailingly draw, which enables us to exaggerate ever truly.[9]

He asks at one point whether it would not be a luxury to spend an entire day in a swamp up to his neck in water, amid cranberry vines and moss and sweet fern, conversing with a leopard frog and hearing the mosquitoes and the bittern. His distillation of this mystical rapport with nature is expressed in a stanza from "The Thaw."

> Fain would I stretch me by the highway side,
> To thaw and trickle with the melting snow,
> That mingled soul and body with the tide,
> I too may through the pores of nature flow.[10]

The purpose behind the nature mysticism is to know God and to communicate his revelation to humankind. The poetry often catches this note of consecration to the task and is a surer guide to Thoreau's religious depths than has yet been pointed out by the critics.

> I've searched my faculties around
> To learn why life to me was lent
> I will attend his faintest sound
> And then declare to man what God hath meant.[11]

On September 7, 1851, he wrote, "My profession is to be always on the alert to find God in nature, to know his lurking-places, to attend all the oratorios, the operas, in nature. . . . To watch for, describe, all the divine features which I detect in Nature."[12]

Rudolph Otto's *Mysticism East and West* is a masterly study of Sankara and Eckhart to demonstrate the underlying common characteristics of mysticism the world over and through the ages as well as the special identity of each mystic in terms of his religious and cultural background. This polarity of a common base to mysticism and yet an irreducible particularity for every mystic is a method of description especially helpful for analyzing Thoreau's mysticism. There is little evidence in his writings that he really understood or knew the Western mystical tradition in its great exponents and how similar it was to the mystical writings of the East, which he knew in part and quoted with enthusiasm. This limitation in his reading is unfortunate because he would have found in the West some mystics who shared the basic attitudes and disciplines which he admired in the East, but who developed at the same time a world-affirming mysticism to which he would have responded heartily. There was much in the acosmic, or world-denying, character of certain types of Eastern mysticism that displeased him. If, for example, he could have read, among his well-liked seventeenth-century English metaphysical poets and writers, Thomas Traherne's great *Centuries of Meditations,* he would have found a kindred spirit. While he read Ralph Cudworth among the Cambridge Platonists, showed the influence of Sir Thomas Browne, and admired Herbert, Vaughn, and Quarles, he could not have known Traherne's mystical writings for they were not discovered until the 1920s.

One of the delights in Thoreau's mysticism is his down-to-earthness. A simple event in nature can charm him into a mystical experience, such as putting up a box for blue-birds in the yard and waiting to see next spring whether the birds will find and use it. There is something very home-spun, almost Franciscan, in the simple joy of his poem "The Bluebirds."

> And I wandered forth o'er the steamy earth,
> And gazed at the mellow sky,
> But never before from the hour of my birth
> Had I wandered so thoughtfully.
>
> For never before was the earth so still,
> And never so mild was the sky,
> The river, the fields, the woods, and the hill,
> Seemed to heave an audible sigh.
>
> I felt that the heavens were all around,
> And the earth was all below,
> As when in the ears there rushes a sound
> Which thrills you from top to toe.
>
> I dreamed that I was an waking thought—

A something I hardly knew—
Not a solid piece, nor an empty nought,
But a drop of morning dew.

'Twas the world and I at a game of bo-peep,
As a man would dodge his shadow,
An idea becalmed in eternity's deep—
'Tween Lima and Segraddo.

Yes, the bluebird found Thoreau's box and awakened him from his mystical rapture.

The bluebird had come from the distant South
To his box in the poplar tree,
And he opened wide his slender mouth,
On purpose to sing to me.[13]

A common structural feature of mysticism is the three ascending levels of experience: purgation, contemplation (or illumination), and union. It is possible to find illustrations of all these stages in Thoreau's writings, but he seems never to have made this catalog his own tool for exposition. His selection of quotations from the Oriental mystics for the *Dial* can often, however, be arranged under these three headings. In fact, he shows little interest in the analysis of mysticism as a phenomenon; it was enough for him that it "worked."

The stage of purgation has already been obvious in his writings, particularly in the *Week,* in which he proposed to purify the senses until they would lead him directly to God, to lead "a *purely* sensuous life."[14] F. O. Matthiessen has explained the extraordinary quality of sensuous awareness in Thoreau's writings by saying that he thought with his body. He had an acute sense of smell, often depending upon it for night walks when sight was less helpful. Pages could be quoted to this effect. Likewise his sense of touch helped him keep the path at night and, translated into his dreaming, produced "the dream about Rough and Smooth" which recurred over a period of many years. Yet he had a feeling about not probing into other life with careless hands, especially with respect to plants. His essay "Wild Apples" carries his enthusiasm for tasting these wildlings after autumn frosts and freezings have given way to winter thawing. Probably few who experiment will agree that they are superior, as he claimed, to the pineapple, but all can agree on the emphasis he placed on taste as a sheer human delight and even as a means for identifying certain plants. Channing, intrigued by his friend's keenness of taste, said that he had an "edible religion." His sense of sight was tremendously developed, although he felt like an amateur when he accompanied his Indian guides. He was fond of pointing out the difference between mere "looking at" and real "seeing," as, for example, in his poem "Inspiration," previously discussed. He would have agreed with Robert Frost that observation includes both sight and insight. He placed special emphasis upon the beatitude that the pure in heart would *see* God. There are interesting parallels in Thoreau's feeling for the disciplined senses as avenues to God in some of the statements of Jonathan Edwards, the great nature mystic among the New England Puritan theologians. At the same time that he stressed intentionality in the direction of the senses, Thoreau also understood the need to let go, to abandon oneself to being led by experience itself. Here again he acts out a common principle in the mystical way. The following endorsement of walking is not without mystical overtones, as his etymology of "saunter" brings out.

I have met with but one or two persons in the course of my life who understood the art of taking walks daily,—not [to] exercise the legs or body merely, nor barely to recruit the spirits, but positively to exercise both body and spirit, and to succeed to the highest and worthiest ends by the abandonment of all specific ends,—who had a genius, so to speak, for sauntering. And this word "saunter," by the way, is happily derived "from idle people who roved about in the country [in the Middle Ages] and asked charity under pretence, of going à la Sainte Terre," to the Holy Land, till, perchance, the children exclaimed, "There goes a *Sainte-Terrer*," a Holy-Lander. They who never go to the Holy Land in their walks, as they pretend, are indeed mere idlers and vagabonds.[15]

It was, however, the fifth of the senses that meant the most to Thoreau, the sense of sound. Although he had little knowledge of classical music and made naïve comments in this field, he loved the sounds of earth, including the whistling of the wind in the newly installed telegraph line past Walden Pond. In one of his earliest essays, "The Service," he portrays the hero stepping to sphere music.

One of his best-known lines (from the Conclusion to *Walden*) is about a person marching to the sound of a different drummer. Thoreau writes much about the Pythagoreans and their belief in the music of the spheres. It is clear that music brought him the experience of ecstasy. He liked to float at evening in his boat, playing on his flute.

The strains of the aeolian harp and of the wood thrush are the truest and loftiest preachers that I know now left on this earth. . . . I would be drunk, drunk, drunk, dead drunk to this world with [it] forever. He that hath ears, let him hear. The contact of sound with a human ear whose hearing is pure and unimpaired is coincident with an ecstasy. Sugar is not so sweet to the palate, as sound to the healthy ear; the hearing of it makes men brave.[16]

Silence, the deliberate suspension of all sound, however, was the climax of the process of purifying the senses. There is evidence for the position in the essay on silence included near the end of the *Week,* in many references throughout his *Journal,* and also in his letters, particularly in a letter of August 8, 1854, to Blake. Thoreau is describing to his disciple a technique in a meditation conducted while walking which aimed at shutting out the world and which was rewarded by the discovery that sound was musical.

The other evening I was determined that I would silence this shallow din; that I would walk in various directions and see if there was not to be found any depth of silence around. . . . The falling dews seemed to strain and purify the air, and I was soothed with an infinite stillness. I got the world, as it were, by the nape of the neck, and held it under in the tide of its own events, till it was drowned, and then I let it go down stream like a dead dog. Vast hollow chambers of silence stretched away on every side, and my being expanded in proportion and filled them. Then first could I appreciate sound, and find it musical.[17]

The disciplining of the senses, the curbing of instincts in the interest of a higher life ("Chastity is perpetual acquaintance with the All"[18]), and the pursuit of a simple life-style were all stages in preparation for mystical experience and growth into a higher form through constant rebirth. Thoreau liked the analogy of the grub that advanced from coarser stages until it emerged from the cocoon a beautiful butterfly in a more spiritual medium. He speculated about his own metamorphoses, extending the lines forward to immortality and suggesting at times lines backward in a sort of transmigration. His picture of organic evolution drew richness from this comparison.

Some men's lives are but an aspiration, a yearning toward a higher state, and they are wholly misapprehended, until they are referred to, or traced through, all their metamorphoses. We cannot pronounce upon a man's intellectual and moral state until we foresee what metamorphosis it is preparing him for.[19]

Thoreau returns again and again to love as the motivating factor for purification. He had much of the spirit of Augustine's dictum that if one loved God he might then do as he wished, the death to all attempts to live in terms of codes or legalism. "Do nothing merely out of good resolutions. Discipline yourself only to yield to love, suffer yourself to be attracted. . . . There must be the copulating and generating force of love behind every effort destined to be successful."[20] Then rising to a crescendo in his poem "The Hero," he writes four lines that express the primacy of love and the thirst for being that leads one beyond knowledge.

> Forever to love and to love and to love
> Within him, around him—beneath him above,
> To love is to know, is to feel, is to be,
> At once 'tis his birth and his destiny[21]

Solitude assures that the path of purification will remain open, but its discipline does not leave Thoreau feeling lonely. In his walks abroad he had, as it were, an unseen friend, "some grand, serene, immortal, infinitely encouraging, though invisible, companion."[22] In one of his didactic letters to Blake, he drove home his point about solitude.

It is not that we love to be alone, but that we love to soar, and when we do soar, the company grows thinner & thinner till there is none at all. It is either the Tribune on the plain, a sermon on the mount, or a very private *extacy* [sic] still higher up. We are not the less to aim at the summits, though the multitude does not ascend them.[23]

The second stage in the mystical ladder, contemplation, has been abundantly illustrated from his writings already.

In general, students of mysticism distinguish between that type of contemplation which burrows within to find in the innermost depths of selfhood identity or union with the One and the type that intuits behind the varied phenomena of the outer world the presence of the One. Professor Stace has described these as the "introvertive" and "extrovertive" types.[24] At times they are found in the same mystic, for the obvious reason that "self" and "world" are themselves already unifying constructs on the road toward the all-embracing unity of God, but each mystic can usually be classified without much of a problem under one or the other of the alternatives. While there are some passages in Thoreau that may be interpreted as introvertive, the overwhelming weight of the evidence is on the extrovertive side. Thoreau is "the nature mystic" par excellence. This definition needs no further qualification once it is understood that each person is properly part of nature, for Thoreau may be said to have humanized nature.

Nature must be viewed humanly to be viewed at all; that is, her scenes must be associated with humane affections, such as are associated with one's native place, for instance. She is most significant to a lover. A lover of Nature is preeminently a lover of man. If I have no friend, what is Nature to me? She ceases to be morally significant.[25]

With such a wealth of passages available it is difficult to choose one to be representative of the whole, but there is an entry from Christmas Day 1851 that shows much thought on how a sunset, which can be described scientifically in terms of water vapor and optics, can through the agency of the imagination become revelatory of the deepest mysteries. The section almost suggests Coleridge's analysis.

I witness a beauty in the form or coloring of the clouds which addresses itself to my imagination, for which you account scientifically to my understanding, but do not so account to my imagination. It is what it suggests and is the symbol of that I care for, and if, by any trick of science, you rob it of its symbolicalness, you do me no service and explain nothing. I, standing twenty miles off, see a crimson cloud in the horizon. You tell me it is a mass of vapor which absorbs all other rays and reflects the red, but that is nothing to the purpose, for the red vision excites me, stirs my blood, makes my thoughts flow, and I have new and indescribable fancies, and you have not touched the secret of that influence. If there is not something mystical in your explanation, something unexplainable to the understanding, some elements of mystery, it is quite insufficient. . . . What sort of science is that which enriches the understanding, but robs the imagination? . . . If we knew all things thus mechanically merely, should we know anything really?[26]

One of the watersheds in interpretations of Thoreau is the view of some who believe that after *Walden* Thoreau began to decay. They interpret the immense amount of quantitative analysis of natural phenomena in the later *Journal* as a waning of artistic power, philosophical insight, and religious vitality, concluding that he died essentially a disillusioned or disappointed man.[27] The other view, while acknowledging a different character to the later *Journal* and aware that in the last couple of years his waning health made new writing impossible, refutes such extreme statements. It sees a certain triumph of joy and integrity throughout the whole life. For this study of Thoreau's religion, the crucial question becomes: Although he described himself as a mystic in 1853, did he not cease in point of fact really to be a mystic as the years advanced? The answer, I am convinced, must be that despite less articulate discussion of his mysticism in the later *Journal* there is evidence of continuity with what went before. If there is any movement away from mysticism, it is in the direction of a strengthened role as a biblical prophet, but all this is so involved in his Transcendentalism that we are really discussing shifts in emphasis rather than some fundamental change along the lines of the "catastrophe" school of interpretation. As late as October 4, 1859, he could still be writing along the lines of his earlier *Journal:*

It is only when we forget all our learning that we begin to know. . . . If you would make acquaintance with the ferns you must forget your botany. . . . You have got to be in a different state from common. Your greatest success will be simply to perceive that such things are, and you will have no communication to make to the Royal Society. If it were required to know the position of the fruit-dots or the character of the indusium, nothing could be easier than to ascertain it; but if it is required that you be affected by ferns, that they amount to anything, signify anything, to you, that they be *another sacred scripture and revelation to you,* helping to redeem your life, this end is not so surely accomplished.[28]

The last entry on this subject occurs a little more than a year before he stopped writing his *Journal*. It is particularly interesting because he writes with such approval of the Old Testament, which earlier at times he had criticized, but which now he seems to have made the vehicle for his faith in creation without mentioning in this period the Eastern books at all.

In science, I should say, all description is postponed till we know the whole, but then science itself will be cast aside. . . . Which are the truest, the sublime conceptions of Hebrew poets and *seers*, or the guarded statements of modern geologists, which we must modify or unlearn so fast?[29]

The third stage of mysticism is usually described as the unitive experience or vision. Thoreau experienced many aspects of this reality. There is a remarkable passage that draws many threads together from June 22, 1851, a summer memorable for the intensity and sustained quality of his mystical experience and a period of the greatest number of biblical allusions in his *Journal*. The emphasis falls upon the disciplined preparation, the sense of being allured, of loving, of serenity, of joy, of being "clarified" and "calmed healthily," and of "unconscious obedience." There is an effortless revelation of the depths of selfhood, a hearing of a music unheard by others, and, finally, the very personal communion of feeling blessed by his Maker. It is a rich transcript of a transforming experience.

After a hard day's work without a thought, turning my very brain into a mere tool, only in the quiet of evening do I so far recover my senses as to hear the cricket, which in fact has been chirping all day. In my better hours I am conscious of the influx of a serene and unquestionable wisdom which partly unfits, and if I yielded to it more rememberingly would wholly unfit me, for what is called the active business of life, for that furnishes nothing on which the eye of reason can rest. What is that other kind of life to which I am thus continually allured? which alone I love? Is it a life for this world? Can a man feed and clothe himself gloriously who keeps only the truth steadily before him? who calls in no evil to his aid? Are there duties which necessarily interfere with the serene perception of truth? Are our serene moments mere fore-tastes of heaven,—joys gratuitously vouchsafed to us as a consolation,—or simply a transient realization of what might be the whole tenor of our lives?

To be calm, to be serene! There is the calmness of the lake when there is not a breath of wind; there is the calmness of a stagnant ditch. So it is with us. Sometimes we are clarified and calmed healthily, as we never were before in our lives, not by an opiate, but by some unconscious obedience to the all-just laws, so that we become like a still lake of purest crystal and without an effort our depths are revealed to ourselves. All the world goes by us and is reflected in our deeps. Such clarity! obtained by such pure means! by simple living, by honesty of purpose. We live and rejoice. I awoke into a music which no one about me heard. Whom shall I thank for it? The luxury of wisdom! the luxury of virtue! Are there any intemperate in these things? I feel my Maker blessing me.[30]

Another quality of the unitive stage in mysticism is to be brought out of the temporal flux into the experience of eternity, a process which brings to light the immortality of the mystic. In *Walden* Thoreau had said that God culminated in the present, a statement comparable to the widespread mystical emphasis upon the "Eternal Now." This is only partly the Platonic contrast between Eternity and Time, because it is also somewhat akin to Paul Tillich's distinction between *chronos*, mere clock time, and *kairos*, the moment that has become "timely"; that is to say, ripe for decision and action, pregnant with the eternity of God himself. In *Walden* also Thoreau understood because of this process that his identity included that of ancient thinkers in their common devotion to the divine.

The oldest Egyptian or Hindoo philosopher raised a corner of the veil from the statue of the divinity; and still the trembling robe remains raised, and I gaze upon as fresh a glory as he did, since it was I in him that was then so bold, and it is he in me that now reviews the vision.[31]

The unitive experience not only transcends time, it overcomes the separations and strangeness of space, leading to communion with forms of life other than human, even to fellowship with inanimate matter. Thoreau described a rain in *Walden:*

Every little pine needle expanded and swelled with sympathy and befriended me. I was so distinctly made aware of the presence of something kindred to me, even in scenes which we are accustomed to call wild and dreary, and also that the nearest of blood to me and humanest was not a person nor a villager, that I thought no place could ever be strange to me again.[32]

In a significant letter to Blake, Thoreau counsels letting things alone and then applies the same principle to the soul's relation to God, carrying the recommended "distance" through so thoroughly that he hesitates to call God "God." Behind all this there is also the suggestion of the ineffability of God, the mystic's approach to the divine by the negative way of canceling out all positive ascriptions. Note, however, that he retains the personal form of the relative pronoun "whom" rather than the impersonal "what."

Let God alone if need be. Methinks, if I loved him more, I should keep him,—I should keep myself rather,—at a more respectful distance. It is not when I am going to meet him, but when I am just turning away and leaving him alone, that I discover that God is. I say, God. I am not sure that that is the name. You will know whom I mean.[33]

We have been examining the mystical aspect of Thoreau's religion in terms of its structure and its relations to mysticism in general. Even in the midst of this technical detail, the reader may have had his own religious experience awakened at some point by the artistry of Thoreau's words and the integrity of his quest. One of the joys of reading his *Journal* is to be led by him into a meeting with God through sharing his skillful description of some aspect of nature. His depth and enthusiasm can be transferred to the alert reader who recognizes dimensions in some past experience that up until this time remained on the level of unconsciousness but are now given articulate expression. "Yes, that's the way it really was!" exclaims the reader, becoming aware of the spiritual dimension in the experience for the first time. Or the reader may feel that he has been newly sensitized so that when he himself meets next the kind of experience in nature Thoreau has described he will look upon it with a new awareness. He will be open to allow the experience to become transparent to God's revelation of himself in the world he has made. It is the poet and the articulate nature mystic rather than the dry-as-dust natural theologian who can enrich our experience in this area. The following passage has been carefully selected both to communicate to the reader Thoreau's experience of finding God in nature and to help us understand the dimensions of the experience. Thoreau by recollection gave new and deepened dimensions to an experience recalled from his past. One of the anticipatory pleasures in reading his *Journal* is to find him often a few days or sometimes weeks after an event returning to it with renewed but deeper insight. The following description of seeing a rainbow has this double time phase. Presupposed also is a strongly biblical understanding of creation and even the Genesis story of the covenant God setting his bow in the heavens. It all comes alive through the writer's imagination and sense of wonder in such a way that one could wish it could be used in special services of worship to help lead churchgoers and others into an encounter with God in the created order.

June 22 [1852], 8 P.M.—Up the Union Turnpike.

We have had a succession of thunder-showers today and at sunset a rainbow. How moral the world is made! This bow is not utilitarian. Methinks men are great in proportion as they are moral. After the rain He sets his bow in the heavens! The world is not destitute of beauty. Ask of the skeptic who inquires, *Cui bono?* why the rainbow was made. While men cultivate flowers below, God cultivates flowers above: he takes charge of the parterres in the heavens. Is not the rainbow a faint vision of God's face? How glorious should be the life of man passed under this arch! What more remarkable phenomenon than a rainbow, yet how little it is remarked![34]

And then, six weeks later, recollection transforms the experience further and leads his readers into new insight, melding biblical and Greek perspectives into what if developed philosophically (which Thoreau characteristically does not do) might produce an argument for God on the basis of beauty.

The rainbow, after all, does not attract an attention proportionate to its singularity and beauty. Moses [?] was the last to comment on it. It is a phenomenon more aside from the common course of nature. Too distinctly a sign or symbol of something to be disregarded. What form of beauty could be imagined more striking and conspicuous? An arch of the most brilliant and glorious colors completely spanning [the] heavens before the eyes of men! Children look at it. It is wonderful that all men do not take pains to behold it. At some waterfalls it is permanent, as long as the sun shines. Plainly thus the Maker of the universe sets the seal to his covenant with men. Many articles are thus clinched. Designed to impress man. All men beholding it begin to understand the significance of the Greek epithet applied to the world,— name for the world,—*Kosmos,* or beauty. It was designed to impress man. We live, as it were, within the calyx of a flower.[35]

He never lost the sense of wonder; it was a perpetual fountain of youth for him, although he worried about losing it in his later years. Seven years later he wrote again about the rainbow, "If men were to be destroyed and the books they have written [were to] be transmitted to a new race of creatures, in a new world, what kind of record would be found in them of so remarkable a phenomenon as the rainbow?"[36]

7

"I AM
A TRANSCENDENTALIST"
(PROPHET)

Thinking over the difficulty of making his position under-
standable to the Association for the Advancement of Science
which had sent him the questionnaire, Thoreau wrote in his
Journal for March 5, 1853, "Now I think of it, I should have
told them at once that I was a transcendentalist. That would
have been the shortest way of telling them that they would
not understand my explanations."[1] The reader who has
followed in a previous chapter the description of the sources
of Transcendentalism in the philosophies of many countries
distilled into a special New England blend may be pardoned
for regarding the product as somewhat anemic. It may,
therefore, come as a surprise that Thoreau called John
Brown after his insurrection at Harpers Ferry "a Transcendentalist." Plainly for Thoreau it was not a bloodless category.
"A man of rare common-sense and directness of speech,
as of action; a transcendentalist above all, a man of ideas
and principles,—that was what distinguished him."[2] Later,
in the eulogy read for him at North Elba at the burial of his
Transcendentalist hero, Thoreau further defined the esoteric
word. "The North, I mean the *living* North, was suddenly
all transcendental. It went behind the human law, it went
behind the apparent failure, and recognized eternal justice
and glory."[3]

The most satisfactory simple definition of Transcendentalism, with the authority also of Thoreau behind it, is "belief
in the Higher Law of God." Thoreau so eloquently and un-

compromisingly took his position on the New Testament saying that we must obey God rather than man that he is best described in the biblical category of a prophet. This dimension was already clear in his essay "Civil Disobedience"; it becomes the warp and woof of "Slavery in Massachusetts," put together from his 1851 notes on the Sims affair and brought to incandescence by Massachusetts seizing another slave, Anthony Burns, in 1854 and shamefully returning him to captivity. Thoreau delivered it first as a speech before three thousand at an antislavery convention in Framingham at which William Lloyd Garrison burned a copy of the Constitution. Printed first in the *Liberator* on July 21, 1854, it was reprinted August 2 by Horace Greeley in the New York *Tribune*, America's most widespread newspaper, reaching one of the largest audiences Thoreau was probably to have in his lifetime. The essay contains thirteen direct or indirect references to God, about one per page, and the references are not conventional but the revolutionary leaven itself. Here are some of the references:

1. "Does any one think that justice or God awaits Mr. Loring's decision?" (Edward G. Loring was the United States Commissioner who ordered Burns returned.)

2. He charges the governor and the United States government with "robbing a poor innocent black man of his liberty for life, and, as far as they could, of his Creator's likeness in his breast."

3. Massachusetts stands convicted. "The Commissioner on her case is God, not Edward G. God, but simple God." Then, like an Amos or an Isaiah or a Jeremiah, he adds, "I wish my countrymen to consider, that whatever the human law may be, neither an individual nor a nation can ever commit the least act of injustice against the obscurest individual, without having to pay the penalty for it."

4. The Justices of the Supreme Court, recognizing no authority but the Constitution, become mere inspectors of the murderer's tools. "There was a prior case on the docket, which they, as judges appointed by God, had no right to skip."

5. Thoreau advises a judge in Massachusetts "to resign his office, and get his living innocently, whenever it is required of him to pass sentence under a law which is merely contrary to the law of God."

6. The following passage, partly in biblical idiom, is pure prophecy. "The question is, not whether you or your.

grandfather, seventy years ago, did not enter into an agreement to serve the Devil, and that service is not accordingly now due; but whether you will not now, for once and at last, serve God,—in spite of your own past recreancy, or that of your ancestor,—by obeying that eternal and only just Constitution which He, and not any Jefferson or Adams, has written in your being."

7. The principle of majority rule becomes a travesty when applied to the higher law. The irony is biting. "The amount of it is, if the majority vote the Devil to be God, the minority will live and behave accordingly,—and obey the successful candidate, trusting that, sometime or other, by some Speaker's casting-vote, perhaps they may reinstate God."

8. Then, finally, piling crime upon crime, he charges idolatry and blasphemy. "Thus we steadily worship Mammon, both school and state and church, and on the seventh day curse God with a tintamar from one end of the Union to the other."[4]

This atmosphere of prophetic denunciation is so unusually prevalent and so absolute in spurning every possible political relativism that it is difficult to comment on the "political theory" of such an essay. Whereas passive resistance was the message of "Civil Disobedience," here it is plainly defiance of the law, boycott of offending newspapers, criticism of oppressive churches, dissolution by Massachusetts of her union with the slaveholder, and, returning to the individual as the base for reform and defiance of injustice, dissolution by each citizen of his union with the state "as long as she delays to do her duty." There is even the suggestion of a more radical stance to come in the future. "[Fame] praises till she is hoarse the easy exploit of the Boston tea party, but will be comparatively silent about the braver and more disinterestedly heroic attack on the Boston Court-House [to rescue Burns], simply because it was unsuccessful!"[5]

Thoreau complains that the country has directly assaulted him. Earlier slavery could be said to be a Southern problem, but under the Fugitive Slave Act every Northerner was transformed into a slave catcher. His indefinite sense of loss at last is clarified; he has lost a country. "I cannot persuade myself that I do not dwell *wholly within* hell. The site of that political organization called Massachusetts is to me morally covered with volcanic scoriae and cinders, such as Milton describes in the infernal regions."[6] His walks are spoiled. "I walk toward one of our ponds; but what signifies the beauty of nature when men are base?"[7]

He did, however, see the white water lily bloom out of the muck and he smelled its fragrance. Nature had not agreed to any Missouri Compromise. Then, like a true Transcendentalist, his confidence in man restored by nature, he triumphantly concludes his sermon, for that is what it is. "The foul slime stands for the sloth and vice of man, the decay of humanity; the fragrant flower that springs from it, for the purity and courage which are immortal."[8]

Leo Stoller's *After Walden: Thoreau's Changing Views on Economic Man* is an important study of the area indicated by the title. In *A Week* the two brothers had rowed hastily past the huge mills being constructed at Manchester, New Hampshire. They were an excrescence on the landscape. Thoreau was troubled by the condition of the textile workers, particularly the girls from New England farms. When they were not working long shifts, they were concentrated in dormitories where they could be "protected from vice." The railroad, he said, had been built using the bodies of Irishmen as sleepers to carry the rails. He found clothing for little Johnny Riordan, the son of a shanty by the tracks. He felt the Irish should have the right to salvage dead wood for their use from the Concord woodlots, whose owners never cleared them. In *Walden* he saw the early working of the capitalist system in the textile mills. "I cannot believe that our factory system is the best mode by which men may get clothing . . . since, as far as I have heard or observed, the principal object is, not that mankind may be well and honestly clad, but, unquestionably, that the corporations may be enriched."[9] Against the rising colossus of industrialism, however, because of his sheer individualism, he could offer only the handicraft system of the past, in what looked increasingly to his contemporaries and even apparently to himself as more and more an ineffectual and romantic dream. Drawn into the family business of making pencils, Thoreau greatly improved the product and invented simple machines for handling the plumbago more efficiently. Had he exploited these opportunities, especially when plumbago began to be more used in various printing processes, he might have become, as someone incongruously remarked, "the graphite king of America" and thus have fulfilled Emerson's regret, so curiously expressed in the funeral eulogy, about his lack of ambition. "Wanting this, instead of engineering for all America, he was the captain of a huckleberry party."[10] In later life he seems to have accepted the increased impact of technology upon the industrial system, judging by his responses to visiting a gigantic gingham mill in Clinton and also a steel mill. He seems to have concluded that it was not possible to return to Walden. But his prophetic feeling for the injustice of the profit-centered system and his cold fury at its inhumanity flared up in the *Journal*.

Yesterday I walked under the murderous Lincoln Bridge, where at least ten men have been swept dead from the cars within as many years. I looked to see if their heads had indented the bridge, if there were sturdy blows given as well as received, and if their brains lay about. But I could see neither the one nor the other. The bridge is quite uninjured, even, and straight, not even the paint worn off or discolored. . . . Boucaniers of the Fitchburg Railroad, they lie in wait at the narrow passes and decimate the employees. . . . The Vermont mother commits her son to their charge, and when she asks for him, again the Directors say: "I am not your son's keeper. Go back beneath the ribs of the Lincoln Bridge."[11]

Next year in 1857 when the economic life of the country was turmoiled by a depression, with attendant business failures, bank closings, and large-scale unemployment, Thoreau was confirmed in his criticism of the idol with clay feet. Again he quarried from the Bible in pronouncing judgment.

If our merchants did not most of them fail, and the banks too, my faith in the old laws of the world would be staggered. . . . Does it not say somewhere, "The Lord reigneth, let the earth rejoice"? If thousands are thrown out of employment, it suggests that they were not well employed. Why don't they take the hint? It is not enough to be industrious; so are the ants. What are you industrious about?[12]

There is a disappointing lack of material in the *Journal* between the Anthony Burns case and the events surrounding John Brown, but the way is prepared for Thoreau to support Brown (whom he will meet for the first time in 1857) from a letter of Thoreau's to Cholmondeley in England. What is most interesting in this letter, dated October 20, 1856, is

Thoreau's support for irregular territorial governments as "most divine." Just as he would discard tradition-twisted religion for fresh, authentic revelation, so the rough-and-ready local revolutionary forces seemed superior to those with the tradition of the nation behind them and their legacy of political compromises. There is alienation and distance in the choice of the third person plural pronoun rather the first person plural.

They are on the eve of a Presidential election, as perhaps you know, and all good people are praying that of the three candidates Fremont may be the man; but in my opinion the issue is quite doubtful. As far as I have observed, the worst man stands the best chance in this country. But as for politics, what I most admire now-a-days, is not the regular governments but the irregular primitive ones, like the Vigilance Committee in California and even the free state men in Kansas. They are the most divine.[13]

Thoreau's family entertained John Brown at their home in 1857, and Thoreau again saw the leader of Ossawatomie the following night at the Emersons. Brown visited Concord again, just before his raid on Harpers Ferry, but did not communicate his plans to anyone, even to Frank Sanborn, his chief contact in Concord. The first reaction to Brown's insurrection at Concord as well as in the nation at large was completely negative and condemnatory. The abolitionists vied with each other to dissociate themselves from what Garrison called "a misguided, wild, and apparently insane effort." Spurning the advice of the town radicals that the time was not favorable for discussion, Thoreau announced a meeting and delivered on October 30, 1859, "A Plea for Captain John Brown." He began by saying that he actually knew little about Brown but was prepared to speak for his act and his character. He hoped Brown would not be hung. He invited supporters to speak up, but he seemed to have given him up as already dead. He called Brown old-fashioned "in his respect for the Constitution, and his faith in the permanence of this Union."[14] He praised Brown as a Puritan and said it would be in vain to kill him, for he had really died some time ago in Cromwell's time and since reappeared.

[The Puritans] were a class that did something else than celebrate their forefathers' day, and eat parched corn in remembrance of that time. They were neither Democrats nor Republicans, but men of simple habits, straightforward, prayerful; not thinking much of rulers who did not fear God, not making many compromises, not seeking after available candidates.[15]

When he described Brown as a "volcano with an ordinary chimney-flue," he certainly pictured his own response to the events. Quoting and endorsing Brown's speeches, he made this cleverly expressed tribute: "It was like the speeches of Cromwell compared with those of an ordinary king."[16] Appropriating one of Lincoln's metaphors made famous the previous year, Thoreau said:

There is hardly a house but is divided against itself. . . . The curse is the worship of idols, which at length changes the worshipper into a stone image himself; and the New Englander is just as much an idolater as the Hindoo. This man was an exception, for he did not set up even a political graven image between him and his God.[17]

Then his wrath turned against the churches, but the result is more blather than effective condemnation. "A church that can never have done with excommunicating Christ while it exists! . . . Take a step forward, and invent a new style of out-houses."[18]

Thoreau, now cast in the role of defender of the old-time religion, takes issue with the press for claiming that Brown's sense of being appointed to free the slave was proof of his "insanity." "They talk as if it were impossible that a man could be 'divinely appointed' in these days to do any work whatever; as if vows and religion were out of date as connected with any man's daily work."[19]

Thoreau invests Brown with many of the descriptions of Christ, coming surprisingly close to presupposing doctrines of vicarious sacrifice and the redemptive nature of suffering. "He took up his life and he laid it down for [all the others]."[20] "Some eighteen hundred years ago Christ was crucified; this morning perchance, Captain Brown was hung. These are the two ends of a chain which is not without its links. He is not Old Brown any longer, he is an angel of light."[21] He seems to have sensed that Brown dead would be more valuable than Brown alive. Within two years the boys of the North, setting forth for battle, would be singing "John Brown's Body." Now, the first person to defend

Brown publicly in Concord and nearly so in the country, Thoreau put the whole matter in a nutshell: "It was his peculiar doctrine that a man has a perfect right to interfere by force with the slaveholder, in order to rescue the slave. I agree with him."[22]

Thoreau repeated his plea in Worcester at a meeting arranged by his friend Blake, but before he could appear there he was asked to substitute at Tremont Temple in Boston for the scheduled speaker, Frederick Douglass. Douglass, implicated by some in the Brown raid, had fled to Canada. The speech was widely commented on, but the New York *Tribune* called it "foolish" and observed with considerable truth that "editors like those of *The Tribune* and *The Liberator*, . . . while the lecturer was cultivating beans and killing woodchucks on the margin of Walden Pond, made a public opinion strong enough on Anti-Slavery grounds to tolerate a speech from him in defense of insurrection."[23] There is a homespun Concord reaction to the speech worthy of quotation because it typifies the unwillingness of people to hear a statement drawn from biblical prophecy. What is heard instead, whether it is about Vietnam or minority peoples in our day or about slavery in his day, is a shocking criticism of political rulers who are naïvely regarded with a patriotic piety bordering on stupidity and idolatry. The letter is by Minot Pratt on the day of Thoreau's plea.

The lecture was full of Henry's quaint and strong expressions: hitting the politicians in the hardest manner and showing but little of that veneration which is due our beloved President and all the government officials, who are laboring so hard and so disinterestedly for the welfare of the dear people. The church also, as a body, came in for a share of whipping, and it was laid on right earnestly.[24]

Thoreau, with others, spoke at services in Concord on December 2, 1859, commemorating John Brown, who had been hung on that day. That evening a counter gathering burned Brown in effigy. Within a short time Francis Merriam, one of the fugitives from Brown's attack force, appeared in Concord, distraught and seeking help. Sanborn, telling Thoreau that the fugitive's name was "Mr. Lockwood" as a cover in case Thoreau was summoned to testify before the Senate inquiry on the raid, assigned him the task of driving Merriam to the South Acton station for an escape to Canada. Merriam, confused and willful, got out of Emerson's borrowed wagon on the way, but somehow, by persuasion or simple force, Thoreau delivered him to the station. A few months later five federal marshals in disguise tried to carry Sanborn off in their carriage but were thwarted by a rising of citizens, Thoreau among them. Judge Hoar immediately issued a writ of habeas corpus and the Concord deputy sheriff with the citizens took Sanborn by force from the marshals, who were then chased out of town. Thoreau volunteered to sleep in Sanborn's house to protect his sister, should federal forces return that night.

Then on July 4, 1860, at a memorial service at North Elba in the Adirondacks, Thoreau's eulogy "The Last Days of John Brown" was read. Now there was some support from the clergy.

The more conscientious preachers, the Bible men, they who talk about principle, and doing to others as you would that they should do unto you,—how could they fail to recognize him, by far the greatest preacher of them all, with the Bible in his life and in his acts, the embodiment of principle, who actually carried out the golden rule? All whose moral sense had been aroused, who had a calling from on high to preach, sided with him.[25]

He took the opportunity, however, to lash out again against the churches. If Emerson called it "droll" to see Thoreau in church, the picture of his conducting liturgical researches into Anglican prayer books is even more fantastic, especially when reported in a eulogy.

When I looked into a liturgy of the Church of England, printed near the end of the last century, in order to find a service applicable to the case of Brown, I found that the only martyr recognized and provided for by it was King Charles the First, an eminent scamp. . . . What a satire on the Church is that![26]

Thoreau believed that everything done against Brown had really turned out in his favor. By providence a slave-woman with her child stood by the way between his prison and the gallows. He stooped and kissed the child. "On the day of his translation, I heard, to be sure, that he was *hung,* but I did not know what that meant. . . . He is more alive than ever he was. He has earned immortality."[27]

Thoreau wrote a letter to Charles Sumner on July 16, 1860, congratulating him for a speech in Congress on slavery in which Sumner emphasized the moral as against the merely political side of slavery. Although there is scanty evidence of Thoreau's attitude toward the Civil War, owing in large part to his failing health, the few letters written, and the discontinuing of his *Journal*, the letter to Sumner is a clue. Thoreau distrusted the temporizing of politicians, including Lincoln at the beginning of his administration, but he responded much more favorably with support for the Union whenever there was recognition of the moral imperative that demanded emancipation. He lectured his friend Alcott for his confidence in Lincoln at the time of the President's inauguration. He wrote the Abolitionist and family friend Parker Pillsbury on April 10, 1861, two days before Fort Sumter was fired upon, "Blessed were the days before you read a president's message. Blessed are the young for they do not read the president's message. Blessed are they who never read a newspaper, for they shall see Nature, and through her, God."[28]

When the war actually came, Thoreau strongly supported it, forgetting the old Abolitionist strategy of disunion. He had found again the country he had reported losing in "Slavery in Massachusetts." Sanborn held that Thoreau believed "from the beginning that it would prove a war for emancipation, which he foresaw and predicted."[29] When Moncure Conway visited Concord shortly after the Union debacle at Bull Run in late July, he reported that "optimism had fled even from the home of Emerson. Thoreau, sadly out of health, was the only cheerful man in Concordia; he was in a state of exaltation about the moral regeneration of the nation."[30] This last statement about Thoreau's "exaltation about the moral regeneration of the nation" has been left unexplained by his biographers, but the reason for this response, certainly not detectable as yet in the national consciousness, must have been due to his reading Lincoln's now largely forgotten but amazing Proclamation on Bull Run. Thoreau doubtless read more into it in terms of emancipation than was yet in the mind of Lincoln; with his feeling for the Puritan heritage, he could find in it the same prophetic biblical idiom that he had used in his reform essays and speeches, only now more intensified. He could conclude that a morally regenerated nation would abandon its political expediency and have to emancipate its slaves. Lincoln's Proclamation demands quotation here in part.

And whereas, when our own beloved Country, once, by the blessing of God, united, prosperous and happy, is now afflicted with faction and civil war, it is peculiarly fit for us to recognize the hand of God in this terrible visitation, and in sorrowful remembrance of our own faults and crimes as a nation and as individuals,—to humble ourselves before Him, and to pray for His mercy,—to pray that we may be spared further punishment, though most justly deserved; that our arms may be blessed and made effectual for the re-establishment of law, order and peace, throughout the wide extent of our country; and that the inestimable boon of civil and religious liberty, earned under His guidance and blessing, by the labors and sufferings of our fathers, may be restored in all its original excellence.[31]

Thoreau had written in his *Journal* as early as 1851 that a conflict would be too glorious a thing to expect. In "The Last Days of John Brown" he spoke of "a slight revival of old religion" and hoped that it would lead to a more generous and intelligent act than that of the founding fathers, namely, "a revolution in behalf of another and an oppressed people."[32] He was again disappointed that the government could not come clean with a pure intention for the war. In December 1861 Alcott reported that Thoreau "does not conceal his impatience with the slowness of the present administration and its disregard of honor and justice to the free sentiments of the North."[33] Thoreau died about six months before Lincoln's preliminary proclamation of emancipation. According to Channing, he had interiorized the struggle, for "the country's misfortunes in the Union war acted on [his] feelings with great force; he used to say he 'could never recover while the war lasted.' "[34]

There is one aspect of the message of the biblical prophets that was profoundly uncongenial to Thoreau. He bristled at the word repentance. Traditional development of the biblical conception of repentance has yielded a three-fold progression: contrition or sorrow for one's sins, confession of guilt to God, and amendment of life. Thoreau dismissed the first two stages as being essentially wasteful and substituted for the whole process the third stage, amendment of life. Partly his opposition stemmed from his own Unitarian religious heritage, which was on the one hand critical of the sacramental systematizing of repentance and on the other hand profoundly hostile to its substitute, the revivalist technique of "convicting the sinner" as a preliminary to his "conversion to salvation." It must be admitted that on Thoreau's side behind *metanoia*, the New Testament word for repentance, stands the Hebrew word *shuv*, the primary significance of which is to "turn away from toward" amendment of life. In a sense, Thoreau on this topic belongs with the wisdom literature of the Old Testament rather than the prophets or the priests, but there is in him beyond all this a personal uncomfortableness or even disgust with repentance. He seems to feel that it compounds the offense to dwell upon it and that repentance is wasted motion. He wants instead to concentrate upon future behavior in accordance with a lofty ideal.

Jan. 9 [1842]. Sunday. One cannot too soon forget his errors and misdemeanors; for [to] dwell long upon them is to add to the offense, and repentance and sorrow can only be displaced by somewhat better, and which is as free and original as if they had not been. Not to grieve long for any action, but to go immediately and do freshly and otherwise, subtracts so much from the wrong. Else we may make the delay of repentance the punishment of the sin. But a great nature will not consider its sins as its own, but be more absorbed in the prospect of that valor and virtue for the future which is more properly it, than in those improper actions, which by being sins, discover themselves to be not it.[35]

Another reason for Thoreau's distaste for repentance stemmed from the particular quality of his mysticism. He found it actually cut the person off from fellowship with God. In his earlier years he preferred what he felt to be the Hindu way.

Their religious books describe the first inquisitive and contemplative access to God, the Hebrew bible a conscientious return, a grosser and more personal repentance. Repentance is not a free and fair highway to God. A wise man will dispense with repentance. It is shocking and passionate. God prefers that you approach him thoughtful, not penitent, though you are the chief of sinners. It is only by forgetting yourself that you draw near to him.[36]

Thoreau was consistent in his dislike for repentance anywhere. In *A Week* he quoted from the *Gulistan* of Sadi but carefully cut from the quotation a section on repentance.

It is unfortunate that Thoreau missed the therapy that is part of the biblical understanding of repentance. Had he been able to open himself fully to God in this area, it is quite possible that his life might have shown more grace at times than it did. An illustration is the burning of the woods for which he and Edward Hoar were responsible on an April day near Fairhaven Pond in 1844. Foolishly kindling a fire on a stump to cook their fish, the friends could not beat out the flames as they spread into the dry, dead grass and on into the woods. Thoreau, exhausting himself in beating the fire and then in running for help, watched it from the cliffs. "It was a glorious spectacle, and I was the only one there to enjoy it." Actually, he was profoundly distressed, but by unconvincing rationalization attempted to explain away to himself his guilt in five pages of his *Journal* written six years after the event.

Hitherto I had felt like a guilty person,—nothing but shame and regret. But now I settled the matter with myself shortly. I said to myself: "Who are these men who are said to be the owners of these woods, and how am I related to them? I have set fire to the forest, but I have done no wrong therein, and now it is as if the lightning had done it." . . . Some of the owners, however, bore their loss like men, but other some declared behind my back that I was a "damned rascal," and a flibbertigibbit or two, who crowed like the old cock, shouted some reminiscences of "burnt woods" from safe recesses for some years after. I have had nothing to say to any of them.[37]

He reported the loss as "over a hundred acres or more," whereas the *Concord Freeman* reported three hundred acres and more than two thousand dollars' damage. He was lucky not to have been prosecuted and may have escaped it because his companion was the son of Concord's leading citizen.

Although Thoreau may have overestimated his own ability to conquer evil in himself by simple decision to do better, he must not be represented, as he has been by some, as unaware of his own sinfulness. Of the many *Journal* entries on this point, a representative one is from February 10, 1852.

Now if there are any who think that I am vainglorious, that I set myself up above others and crow over their low estate, let me tell them that I could tell a pitiful story respecting myself as well as them, if my spirits held out to do it; I could encourage them with a sufficient list of failures, and could flow as humbly as the very gutters themselves; I could enumerate a list of as rank offenses as ever reached the nostrils of heaven; that I think worse of myself than they can possibly think of me, being better acquainted with the man.[38]

There is a Pauline streak in Thoreau as he expresses himself about sin and the impact of evil on the self. He sees the devil always at work even in his good acts, marvels at the togetherness of good and evil, wonders whether sin is really a part of himself, and senses one side of the self as always standing apart and observing the participant self. "The good which I want to do, I fail to do; but what I do is the wrong which is against my will; and if what I do is against my will, clearly it is no longer I who am the agent, but sin that has its lodging in me (Rom. 7:19-20, NEB)." Thoreau simply does not exhibit the easy optimism of Emerson on the subject of evil and good. Although Thoreau rejected the doctrine of the fall of man and of original sin, he is more in agreement with his Puritan heritage on the actual corrupting power of evil in persons and history than Emerson is, but he did share a belief in the American Adam, an "image contrived to embody the most fruitful contemporary ideas . . . of the authentic American as a figure of heroic innocence and vast potentialities, poised at the start of a new history."[39] Thoreau even undertook to update the New England Primer by adding two lines of his own:

I believe that Adam in paradise was not so favorably situated on the whole as is the backwoodsman in America. You all know how miserably the former turned out,—or was turned out,—but there is some consolation at least in the fact that it yet remains to be seen how the western Adam in the wilderness will turn out.

> In Adam's fall
> We sinned all.
> In the new Adam's rise
> We shall all reach the skies.[40]

In "Life Without Principle" he made clear his objection to the traditional doctrine of the fall of man by an imaginative use of the very imagery of the doctrine. "Thus men will lie on their backs, talking about the fall of man, and never make an effort to get up."[41] He put the responsibility just where he felt it belonged in a bit of doggerel:

> Man Man is the Devil
> The Source of all evil.[42]

Thoreau speaks so often of the goodness of external nature that many interpreters have assumed he also applied this without qualification to man. Norman Foerster in his classic *Nature in American Literature* understood the problem.

If Thoreau imputed "natural goodness" to external nature, it is clear that he also imputed "natural depravity" to man, i.e., to the fluctuant life of instinct and desire that relates man to the flux of external nature. The very thing that is good in nature is thus evil in man, unless governed by the supernatural in man. "I am impure and worthless," he writes repeatedly with quite the Puritan accent. "Did you ever remember the moment when you were not mean?"[43]

The existence of evil, however, did not for Thoreau cast a gloom upon the whole of existence. He had such strongly developed powers of acceptance that Emerson, mistaking a part for the whole, could call him a Stoic in the funeral eulogy. In response to a direct question from Blake, he revealed without protective explanation much about this side of his constitution.

You ask if there is no doctrine of sorrow in my philosophy. Of acute sorrow I suppose that I know comparatively little. My saddest and most genuine sorrows are apt to be but transient regrets. The place of sorrow is supplied, perchance, by a certain hard and proportionably barren indifference. I am of kin to the sod, and partake largely of its dull patience,—in winter expecting the sun of spring. In my cheapest moments I am apt to think that it is not my business to be "seeking the spirit," but as much its business to be seeking me. I know very well what Goethe meant when he said that he never had a chagrin but he made a poem out of it. I have altogether too much patience of this kind. I am too easily contented with a slight and almost animal happiness. My happiness is a good deal like that of the woodchucks.[44]

A dimension of his life only hinted at in the preceding paragraph, with its mention of patience, but one which also accounts for his remarkable equanimity, is his strong faith in immortality. This faith was a corollary of his Transcendental philosophy as well as a personal victory attained through struggle when deprived early of his closest human companion, his brother. It was won anew through later experiences of bereavement of friends and relatives.

One day, walking through the Deep Cut on the railway, he felt the telegraph conveying to him "a message from heaven." Perhaps he missed the initial words, which may have been, "Calling all Transcendentalists." What he heard was the following: "Bear in mind, Child, and never for an instant forget, that there are higher planes, infinitely higher planes, of life than this thou art now travelling on. Know that the goal is distant, and is upward, and is worthy of all your life's efforts to attain to."[45] The strenuousness of the moral ideal coupled with the disproportionate transiency of life was for Immanuel Kant and the Transcendentalists a "proof" of immortality. Thoreau's particular emphasis was to reject the sharp division between this world and the next and to understand that immortality was present in the here and now. His chief criticism of the churches of his day was that they depreciated the value of this life by insisting upon a resignation to ills and evils in this one in the hope of a better existence in the next world, "pie-in-the-sky-when-you-die." As a replacement he offered immortality now, the present transformation of the temporal and finite by the eternal and the infinite, much in the spirit of the Johannine mystical faith that "this is life eternal, that they might know thee the only true God (John 17:3, KJV)." He gave a special twist to the line of the English romantic poet.

Heaven lies about us, as in our infancy. There is nothing so wild and extravagant that it does not make true. It makes a dream my only real experience, and prompts faith to such elasticity that only the incredible can satisfy it. . . . It is a life unlived, a life beyond life, where at length my years will pass. I look under the lids of Time.[46]

But before this faith could be personally appropriated by him out of his Transcendentalist background, he had to win through to it on the other side of the death of his brother John. There is a long silence in the *Journal*, following John's death on January 11, 1842, as Thoreau struggled in mind and body to come to terms with the shattering event. He was even confined to bed with a sympathetic syndrome of lockjaw. "My soul and body have tottered along together of late, tripping and hindering one another like unpracticed Siamese twins."[47] A letter in early March to Lucy Brown shows the continuing struggle. Thoreau asks what right he has to grieve since he has not ceased to wonder. The clue to the meaning of his question is the therapy to be found in nature.

Only nature has a right to grieve perpetually, for she only is innocent. Soon the ice will melt, and the blackbirds sing along the rivers which he frequented, as pleasantly as ever. The same everlasting serenity will appear in this face of God, and we will not be sorrowful, if he is not.[48]

Then, welding his philosophy to his deepening faith, he writes very concretely about his brother.

I do not wish to see John ever again—I mean him who is dead—but that other whom only he would have wished to see, or to be, of whom he was the imperfect representative. For we are not what we are, nor do we treat or esteem each other for such, but for what we are capable of being.[49]

To his friend Emerson, also at this time in grief at the death of his son Waldo, Thoreau writes ten days later about the serenity and persistence of nature. "How plain that death is only the phenomenon of the individual or class. Nature does not recognize it, she finds her own again under new forms without loss. Yet death is beautiful when seen to be a law, and not an accident—it is as common as life."[50] The mature expression of his faith after this bereavement comes out on March 14, 1842: "Life is grand, and so are its environments of Past and Future. Would the face of nature be so serene and beautiful if man's destiny were not equally so? . . . Love never stands still, nor does its object. It is the revolving sun and the swelling bud."[51] Many years later, following his father's death, he remarks that we partially die ourselves in the death of friends and relatives.

Thoreau's way of speaking of eternal life is not to invent a transcendent furniture for a distant heaven but to purify or refine our present relationships with nature. There is a question of how much is "eschatological fact" and how much simply symbol in the following passage, not printed in the Walden edition of the *Journal*. It is a poetic rendering of an ecologist's paradise.

The future will no doubt be a more natural life than this. We shall be acquainted and shall use flowers and stars, and sun and moon, and occupy this nature which now stands over and around us. We shall reach up to the stars and planets fruit from many parts of the universe. We shall *purely* use the earth and not abuse it—God's in the breeze and whispering leaves and we shall then hear *him*. We live in the midst of all the beauty and grandeur that was ever described or conceived. We have hardly entered the vestibule of nature. It was here, be assured, under these heavens that the gods intended our immortal life should pass—these stars were set to adorn and light it—these flowers to carpet it.[52]

It is with this fanciful yet serious strain of celestial music that we should associate the sentence about the Chesuncook pine which, as mentioned earlier, James Russell Lowell deleted from his essay. ("It is as immortal as I am, and perchance will go to as high a heaven, there to tower above me still."[53]) Similarly, statements about or allusions to the transmigration of souls have convinced a number of students of Thoreau that he held this doctrine, but again it is difficult to decide whether the statement is offered as a poetic flight of the imagination or whether the close sense of identification and continuity with all forms of life is not better explained as a consequence of his general mysticism than as a carefully articulated doctrine of transmigration of souls metaphysically mapped out.[54] Much of what Thoreau says about the conditions of immortality is really imaginative thinking, designed not to feed our speculation about a future state but to give new urgency to our enjoyment of this life, to eternalize it by the quality of our participation.

I can see nothing so proper and holy as unrelaxed play and frolic in this bower God has built for us. The suspicion of sin never comes to this thought. Oh, if men felt this they would never build temples even of marble or diamond, but it would be sacrilege and profane, but disport them forever in this paradise.[55]

Thoreau's sense of relationship to the circle of the seasons was very close, so intimate that every spring not only renewed his body but also built up his soul in immortality. We are to understand *Walden* not merely as a fable of the renewal of life but also as the gospel of an eternal life. In the *Journal* for the spring of 1856 he visits the Deep Cut again.

I am reassured and reminded that I am the heir of eternal inheritances which are inalienable, when I feel the warmth reflected from this sunny bank. . . . The eternity which I detect in Nature I predicate of myself also. How many springs I have had this same experience! I am encouraged, for I recognize this steady persistency and recovery of nature as a quality of myself.[56]

Thoreau's firm faith in immortality appears in a paragraph from *Cape Cod* about the wreck of the brig *St. John* from Galway, Ireland, on the rocks near Cohasset. He says it is hard to part with one's body, but "no doubt, it is easy to do without it once it is gone." He concludes the passage with typical Transcendentalist optimism: "A just man's purpose cannot be split on any Grampus or material rock, but itself will split rocks till it succeeds." The location of the wreck gave him an opportunity to link it with his characteristic feeling for migration westward.

[The owners of these dead bodies] were coming to the New World, as Columbus and the Pilgrims did,—they were within a mile of its shores; but, before they could reach it, they emigrated to a newer world than ever Columbus dreamed of, yet one of whose existence we believe that there is far more universal and convincing evidence—though it has not yet been discovered by science—than Columbus had of this; not merely mariners' tales and some paltry drift-wood and sea-weed, but a continual drift and instinct to all our shores. I saw their empty hulks that came to land; but they themselves, meanwhile, were cast upon some shore yet further west, toward which we are all tending, and which we shall reach at last, it may be through storm and darkness, as they did.[57]

This analysis of Thoreau's belief in immortality may fittingly be closed with a short poem of his. He had the ability to state so often in a poetic nugget the religious conviction which he felt deeply but never was willing to spell out in a carefully argued and metaphysically tight way.

> Light hearted, careless, shall I take my way,
> When I to thee this being have resigned,
> Well knowing where upon a future day,
> With usurer's craft, more than myself to find.[58]

8

"I AM
A NATURAL
PHILOSOPHER"
(ECOLOGIST)

In his imagined reply to the questionnaire from the Association for the Advancement of Science in 1853 Thoreau refused to classify himself as a scientist, although he claimed that he probably stood as near to nature as any of them and was as good an observer as most. Largely because his friend Blake published selections from his journals in four books named for each of the seasons, Thoreau's reputation at first was that of a naturalist. This oversimplification inevitably engendered a counter criticism. Bradford Torrey, for example, criticized his bird identifications. He apparently mistook the hermit for the wood thrush. Defenders leaped forward to excuse his mistakes on the grounds that he did not have proper bird glasses and adequate identification guides like the Roger Tory Peterson series. The truth of the matter is that he was not, strictly speaking, a scientist at all, despite the overwhelming catalogs of observations in the later *Journal,* some of which are still valuable to scientists in various habitat studies. He himself sensed the difference when he deliberately chose to call himself a "natural philosopher" rather than either "naturalist" or "scientist." His friend Ellery Channing chose an apt title for his biography of Thoreau in the phrase *Poet-Naturalist.* Had Bronson Alcott written a biography he might, judging from phrases in his *Journals,* have called him the Mystic-Scientist, which would have been equally suggestive.

Today another title could be given him, that of "ecologist." Learned articles have already hailed Thoreau as an ecologist because of his pioneering discoveries about the succession of forest trees, his observations about climate with respect to flora and fauna, and his limnological data about water currents, depths, inversions, and relation to fish. Articles apparently just as learned have appeared to refute these claims and to debunk his ecological work as inadequately scientific, largely because it was not sufficiently quantified by statistical analysis or because he lacked the special tools of analysis that have since evolved. It is, however, clear that Thoreau had a pioneering feeling for habitat studies and anticipated in some degree out of philosophical speculation and keen observation some of the conclusions of Darwin about organic evolution. His relation to Darwin, incidentally, has often been incorrectly stated. *Journal* entries refer to *The Voyage of the Beagle,* which he read, but which apparently interested him more in terms of anthropological data than as a harbinger of the *Origin of Species* of 1859. When the latter appeared, he quickly obtained a copy and filled six pages in one of his commonplace books with notes from it. He told Sanborn that he liked the book very much, supported it when Emerson told him of Agassiz's objections to it, but did not show in his *Journal* entries thereafter any direct influence on him of its theories. His acceptance of the "development theory," stimulated by his readings in geology, is evident from the following passage, dated October 18, 1860:

I think that we are warranted only in supposing that the former [a pool in Beck Stow's swamp] was stocked in the same way as the latter, and that there was not a sudden new creation,—at least since the first; yet I have no doubt that peculiarities more or less considerable have thus been gradually produced in the lilies planted in various pools, in consequence of their various conditions, though they all came originally from one seed.

We find ourselves in a world that is already planted, but is also still being planted as at first. We say of some plants that they grow in wet places and of others that they grow in desert places. The truth is that their seeds are scattered almost everywhere, but here only do they succeed. Unless you can show me the pool where the lily was created, I shall believe that the oldest fossil lilies which the geologist has detected (if this is found fossil) originated in that locality in a similar manner to these of Beck Stow's. We see thus how the fossil lilies which the geologist has .

detected are dispersed, as well as these which we carry in our hands to church.

The development theory implies a greater vital force in nature, because it is more flexible and accommodating, and equivalent to a sort of constant *new* creation.[1]

The choice of the name ecologist as a description for Thoreau cannot be justified if the word is narrowly taken to mean the particular scientific discipline today, but if the word is used in its more generally descriptive sense and in terms of its etymology, as the "study of the household or environment," Thoreau richly deserves the description. Perhaps we should call him an "ecological philosopher" or a "mystic ecologist." Thoreau had difficulty communicating his position, and so shall we in describing it. It is just the full-orbed complexity of his position that we today find so attractive as an antidote for the excessively myopic concentration, narrow specializations, and technical analyses that threaten us with the loss of meaning for the whole. Modern holism as a movement in philosophy owes much to his inspiration. His vision of the unity of human experience will be increasingly recognized in the future. His way of indicating the problem of communication was to stress his philosophical purpose. The entry about the questionnaire from the Association for the Advancement of Science concludes with this line; "If it had been the secretary of an association of which Plato or Aristotle was the president, I should not have hesitated to describe my studies at once and particularly."[2]

His ecological philosophy had as a base at least two major components: (1) a mystical sense of the oneness of all life through reciprocal interrelationships and (2) a sensitivity toward all of nature, organic and inorganic, and a desire for fellowship with all things. Its motivating force was a sense of wonder coupled with love. It was this perpetual sense of wonder that drew him to the writings of the old naturalists. He had the same enthusiasm for rocks and their solidity that characterizes Teilhard de Chardin's "Hymn to Matter." Water fascinated him; the two books published in his lifetime are built around rivers and ponds. In *Cape Cod* we hear always in the background the booming of the surf on the beach. In *The Maine Woods* he describes the lakes as civilizing the wilderness even as its streams and rivers became his highways for travel. "I should wither and dry up if it were not for lakes and rivers. I am conscious that my body derives its genesis from their waters, as much as the muskrat or the herbage on their brink."[3] A sense that the levels of development in nature were recapitulated in him kept him out-of-doors, for the sake, as he put it, of the mineral, the vegetable, and the animal in him. We have observed earlier his imaginative treatment of the thawing sand in the Deep Cut and the conviction it brought him that there was nothing that was not organic. The earth itself had spirit somewhat comparable to Henri Bergson's development much later of the *élan vital*. He was interested in the relation of animals to plants and used Gray's *Botany* to spin out four pages of analogies between human beings and plants. He felt especially close to lichens, seeing in them signs of immortality "not known to the divines."

As a Sunday entry in his *Journal,* he copied a curious quotation from G. Segger's *The True Messiah; or the Old and New Testaments, examined according to the Principles of the Language of Nature:*

Examine animal forms geometrically, from man, who represents the perpendicular, to the reptile which forms the horizontal line, and then applying to those forms the rules of the exact sciences, which God himself cannot change, we shall see that visible nature contains them all; that the combinations of the seven primitive forms are entirely exhausted, and that, therefore, they can represent all possible varieties of morality.[4]

He is obviously looking for a comprehensive method for explaining reality. Both the Pythagorean concern for mystical geometry and for the harmony of celestial sphere music inspired him. Another example describes motion in a Transcendentalist way. "But the subtlest and most ideal and spiritual motion is undulation. . . . The two waving lines which express flight seem copied from the ripple.—There is something analogous to this in our most inward experiences. In enthusiasm we undulate to the divine spiritus—as the lake to the wind."[5]

He quotes from Darwin's description of the primitive inhabitants of Tierra del Fuego, in particular of an old man who cut off thin slices of putrid whale blubber, muttered over them, and gave them to his group, which maintained a profound silence during the ritual. Thoreau's speculation would probably have surprised Darwin. "This was the only evidence of any religious worship among them. It suggests that even the animals may have something divine in them and akin to revelation,—some inspirations allying them to man as to God."[6]

His feeling for the earth as a mother, the special delight of his Freudian analyzers, was confirmed by his study of the way it seemingly nursed the turtle eggs deposited in it. Another analogy that was meaningful for him in his attempt to describe the unity of the cosmos was the flower. "The heavens and the earth are one flower. The earth is the calyx, the heavens the corolla."[7] With his sense of the unity pervading the cosmos, he was outraged that the only study of insects made by the state of Massachusetts was entitled *Insects Injurious to Vegetation*. His reaction shows clearly both the religious dimension of his thought and his criticism of science as an inadequate account of reality.

This is the way we glorify God and enjoy him forever. Come out here and behold a thousand painted butterflies and other beautiful insects which people the air, then go to the libraries and see what kind of prayer and glorification of God is there recorded. Massachusetts has published her report on "Insects Injurious to Vegetation" and our neighbor the "Noxious Insects of New York." We have attended to the evil and said nothing about the good. This is looking a gift horse in the mouth with a vengeance. Children are attracted by the beauty of butterflies, but their parents and legislators deem it an idle pursuit. The parents remind me of the devil, but the children of God. Though God may have pronounced his work good, we ask, "Is it not poisonous?"

Science is inhuman. Things seen with a microscope begin to be insignificant. So described, they are as monstrous as if they should be magnified a thousand diameters. Suppose I should see and describe men and houses and trees and birds as if they were a thousand times larger than they are! With our prying instruments we disturb the balance and harmony of nature.[8]

When Thoreau saw a great bird, gliding far above the cliffs at Fairhaven, possibly an eagle, he asked why it was that we feel just like intruders into the domain of bird and beast. Most of his contemporaries and most of ours did not and do not share that feeling; nature for them is merely something to be conquered, something destined to be harnessed for use. This view has been justified religiously by appeal to the verse in Genesis that supposedly makes us the subduers of all "lesser" life. Thoreau believed in and acted upon the principle that we are not the whole, but simply a part of nature.

It appears to me that . . . man is altogether too much insisted on. The poet says the proper study of mankind is man. I say, study to forget all that; take wider views of the universe. That is the egotism of the race. . . . Man is but the place where I stand, and the prospect hence is infinite. It is not a chamber of mirrors which reflect me. When I reflect, I find there is other than me.[9]

His righteous anger blazed up at a farmer who sent a hired man to chop down his fencerows and in the process unknowingly cut down two or three very rare Celtis trees, not found elsewhere in Concord. "I would as soon admit a living mud turtle into my herbarium. If some are prosecuted for abusing children, others deserve to be prosecuted for maltreating the face of nature committed to their care."[10]

Thoreau was pressing toward the principles of forest management in his study of "The Succession of the Forest Trees," an essay he finally prepared for the Middlesex Agricultural Society in September of 1860. He advocated that towns preserve some tracts "forever wild," an anticipation of the idea of National Parks and, more particularly, of the more recently recognized wilderness areas and wild rivers. He was quite willing to use the instruments of government for the general welfare, to provide such things as public libraries, community colleges, adult continuing education, town museums, and art galleries. He said that it was in accordance with the spirit of our institutions to act collectively. By this, however, he was not abandoning his defiant individualism; he was only providing an area for the common action corporately of concerned individuals. One of his most poignant passages about the conservation of wildlife sprang from his view of the interrelationships between all aspects of nature, including us, and a mystical sense of reverence for the magnificence of the whole. The loss of species meant for him literally a suicidal drive. He is our first theologian of the wilderness, for he understood, as most in the Judeo-Christian tradition had forgotten, that "the Almighty is wild above all," drawing upon Trench's curious derivation "that a wild man is a willed man."[11]

But when I consider that the nobler animals have been extermi-
nated here,—the cougar, panther, lynx, wolverene, wolf, bear,
moose, deer, the beaver, the turkey, etc, etc,—I cannot but feel
as if I lived in a tamed and, as it were, emasculated country. . . .
Is it not a maimed and imperfect nature that I am conversant with?
As if I were to study a tribe of Indians that had lost all its
warriors. . . . When I think what were the various sounds and
notes, the migrations and works, and changes of fur and plumage
which ushered in the spring and marked the other seasons of the
year, I am reminded that this my life in nature, this particular
round of natural phenomena which I call a year, is lamentably
incomplete. I listen to [a] concert in which so many parts are
wanting. . . . Primitive Nature is the most interesting to me.
I take infinite pains to know all the phenomena of the spring, for
instance, thinking that I have here the entire poem, and then, to
my chagrin, I hear that it is but an imperfect copy that I possess
and have read, that my ancestors have torn out many of the first
leaves and grandest passages, and mutilated it in many places. I
should not like to think that some demigod had come before me
and picked out some of the best of the stars. I wish to know an
entire heaven and an entire earth.[12]

Every philosopher has the problem of defining the relations between a person and others, person and nature, person and God. Emerson, for example, simplified his options
by centering all reality in the self in terms of a thoroughgoing idealism. Emerson's person saw nature as his own
construct and, looking within himself, found a core of identity with the Over-Soul in a fairly consistent pantheism.
Most people think that this was Thoreau's basic position, or
his position with only slight modifications. But the God of
Thoreau is far more than the universe become self-conscious
in us. In spite of some youthful language that appears at
times to be borrowed from Emerson, Thoreau cannot be
called an idealist in the Emersonian sense. To use technical
philosophical language, Thoreau is really a critical realist.
He accepts the "givenness" of nature, other selves, and God
and does not attempt to reduce their existence to some activity of the self. Most people are naive realists, accepting
the complete independence of nature, other persons, and,
if indeed their analysis goes this far, God. At times, however, they wonder how these discrete entities, like stones
in a box, can possibly be related to each other. Thoreau,
while accepting the existence of these separate realities,

does not confer completely objective independence on each of them. Rather he sees them as intimately related to each other. The key notes of his philosophy are relationship, interdependence, and reciprocity. When he finds that nature is deeply moral, he does not believe that he is making up moral ideas or ideals and then projecting them upon a supposedly neutral nature. He is convinced, on the other hand, that there are values objectively resident in nature, but which need correlation with the knowing self to effect the recognition of their beauty or their moral significance. Values for Thoreau have both subjective and objective aspects. It has been clear throughout our analysis of Thoreau that contrary to majority opinion today in our culture, that sets person over against nature (if not in actual adversary relation, at least in a potential one in terms of a theory of knowledge), Thoreau held that people are part of the reality designated nature. In order, however, to be able to discuss people in terms of their environment, he, like anyone else, had at times to use language that in differentiating between nature and person seemed to separate, but the seeming separation is legitimate only for the preliminary purposes of analysis. In order to have some terms for analysis, we shall write a diagram of relationship between the four terms: God (Nature↔Person [or the Self] ↔ Other People). The first term to be examined more fully is nature.

Nature for Thoreau is therapy for tired and despairing people. It is joy, happiness, communion with God. It builds up the body and renews the spirit. It preserves moral and intellectual health. He believes that we can also come close to nature through reading, since books of natural history make "the most cheerful winter reading."

In society you will not find health, but in nature. You must converse much with the field and woods, if you would imbibe such health into your mind and spirit as you covet for your body. Society is always diseased, and the best is the sickest. There is no scent in it so wholesome as that of the pines, nor any fragrance so penetrating and restorative as that of everlasting in high pastures. . . . To the soul that contemplates some trait of natural beauty no harm nor disappointment can come. The doctrines of despair, of spiritual or political servitude, no priestcraft nor tyranny, was ever [sic] taught by such as drank in the harmony of nature.[13]

Like a true Transcendentalist, Thoreau not merely looked at nature but, in looking at her, looked through and beyond her to richer meanings. He wanted the scientific fact to flower into a moral truth, to become the vehicle for communion with the Maker of nature. Nature for the spiritually awakened person could become a language for expressing what was deepest within people. Historically mythology developed to accomplish this very thing, but what was even more significant was that the individual could mythologize his existence. He would not make it "untrue," in the commonly received meaning of "myth," but just the opposite— he would make it communicable to all because universalized beyond the private self into the experience of nature that was common to all. In *Walden* Thoreau wrote a mythology of human existence communicated in part, at least, by the symbolism of nature as a universalizing agent. We have seen that Alcott called him, with real perception, "the mythologist of these last days." The following entry in Thoreau's *Journal* was stimulated by his seeing the willows bordering the Turnpike just outside Concord. It is decisive for understanding his literary work as well as his religious orientation.

He is the richest who has most use for nature as raw material of tropes and symbols with which to describe his life. If these gates of golden willows affect me, they correspond to the beauty and promise of some experience on which I am entering. If I am overflowing with life, am rich in experience for which I lack expression, then nature will be my language full of poetry,—all nature will *fable,* and every natural phenomenon be a myth. The man of science, who is not seeking for expression but for a fact to be expressed merely, studies nature as a dead language. I pray for such inward experience as will make nature significant.[14]

In attempting to describe the relationship between nature and people, Thoreau oscillates between two poles: one the utter necessity for the presence of people to make nature significant, and the other the need to keep their presence from overwhelming the essential apartness of nature. The first pole can be illustrated from an early entry in the *Journal* that shows more Emersonian influence than his later expression of the same point would reveal. "We are one virtue, one truth, one beauty. All nature is our satellite, whose light is dull and reflected. She is subaltern to us,—an episode to our poem, but we are primary and radiate light and heat to the system."[15] Still another way of expressing the first pole was Thoreau's insistence that the appreciation of nature involved more than an isolated relation between it and the solitary individual. That individual had to be drawn out of himself into social intercourse before nature could be fully appreciated. "If I have no friend, what is Nature to me?" Here we see the organic tie in Thoreau between nature and society that makes *A Week* and "Civil Disobedience" clearly the unified products of the same mind and not the gyrations of a Jekyll-and-Hyde. "[Nature] is most significant to a lover. A lover of Nature is preeminently a lover of man."[16]

The second or opposite pole in the relationship between person and nature is the need to keep from overwhelming and tainting nature. Thoreau seemed at times to be conscious that he was himself in danger of moralizing nature. "The moral aspect of nature is a jaundice reflected from man."[17] In a memorable passage that supplies Thoreau's corrective to his first point, he indicates that nature is untainted by the wretched institutions that corrupt the need for society. He finds gladness and freedom in nature.

I love Nature partly *because* she is not man, but a retreat from him. None of his institutions control or pervade her. There a different kind of right prevails. In her midst I can be glad with an entire gladness. If this world were all man, I could not stretch myself, I should lose all hope. He is constraint, she is freedom to me. He makes me wish for another world. She makes me content with this. None of the joys she supplies is subject to his rules and definitions. What he touches he taints. In thought he moralizes. One would think that no free, joyful labor was possible to him.[18]

It is in the context of this relationship between nature-person-society that the significance of Thoreau's passion for wildness, which we have examined before, becomes evident. Wild nature is the guarantee that nature has not been invaded and violated to such a degree that nature would lose its restorative and renewing influence upon people. Also, a proper human respect for wildness is the best criterion of the disfunctional development of social institutions. *Walden* achieves much of its undoubted effectiveness as a critique of social institutions by exhibiting Thoreau's simplified life at the pond as a deliberate return to the primitive levels of human existence before the institutional-ized expression of the need for food, shelter, clothing, etc., could develop the monstrous structures of political, eco-nomic, cultural, social, and religious life that really enslave people rather than liberate them. For Thoreau wildness is not an optional extra but a requirement for existence. As he put it, "in Wildness is the preservation of the World."[19] He said that wildness was a civilization other than our own. The following passage from the year he published *Walden* estab-lishes the category of wildness as an infinite expectation of the self to such a point that it becomes a means for com-munion with God.

We soon get through with Nature. She excites an expectation which she cannot satisfy. The merest child which has rambled into a copsewood dreams of a wilderness so wild and strange and inexhaustible as Nature can never show him. The red-bird which I saw on my companion's string on election days I thought but the outmost sentinel of the wild, immortal camp,—of the wild and dazzling infantry of the wilderness,—that the deeper woods abounded with redder birds still; but, now that I have threaded all our woods and waded the swamps, I have never yet met with his compeer, still less his wilder kindred. The red-bird which is the last of Nature is but the first of God.[20]

It is clear from this exposition of the organic interrelated-ness of nature, self, and society that nature is not an op-tional extra for technological man, if his hobby tends in that direction, but the very lifeblood of his existence. On the other hand, it cannot be isolated from its relation to other people, as it has been in the "cult of nature" that has led many to flee urban living to pursue a detached existence in suburbia, a sentimental flight from responsibility and reality. Thoreau would not have recognized many self-styled dis-ciples of his today who invoke his name without understand-ing the complexity of his position. "I like better the surliness with which the woodchopper speaks of his woods, handling them as indifferently as his axe, than the mealy-mouthed en-thusiasm of the lover of nature."[21] The ideal relationship be-tween person and nature is sacramental, a form of commun-ion. Berry-picking at Fairhaven stimulated reflection on this.

Wines of all kinds and qualities, of noblest vintage, are bottled up in the skins of countless berries, for the taste of men and animals.

To men they seem offered not so much for food as for sociality, that they may picnic with Nature,—diet drinks, cordials, wines. We pluck and eat in remembrance of Her. It is a sacrament, a communion.[22]

And yet, even this communion is meant to point one on to a higher one, to a relationship to God.

May not my life in nature, in proportion as it is supernatural, be only the spring and infantile portion of my spirit's life? . . . My spirit's unfolding observes not the pace of nature. The society which I was made for is not here. . . . I am enamored of the blue-eyed arch of heaven.[23]

For Thoreau the extended lines of the web of interrelationships denoted by the diagram "Nature↔Self↔Other People" meet in God, but even this geometrical picture of the extension of lines would falsify the immediacy of God in nature, in the self, and in other people. God is the supporting foundation as well as the purposive realization of these realities. Just as Thoreau's philosophy sought to avoid describing nature, self, and other people as separate stones in a box, so his theism avoids the same pitfall by intimately relating God to his creation. Emerson's method of doing this was pantheism. Thoreau's was his inherited theistic frame from the Judeo-Christian tradition reshaped to express greater emphasis upon the immanence of God. It is this last tendency that accounts largely for the verdict of many of his contemporaries and critics that he was a pantheist. It is significant that he himself never initiated the word pantheism as a description of his position, although he accepted it once in a very tentative fashion in a letter to Greeley protesting the censoring of his essay *A Yankee in Canada* by George William Curtis, the editor of *Putnam's Monthly Magazine.* "I am sorry that my manuscript should be so mangled, insignificant as it is . . . since I was born to be a pantheist— if that be the name of me, and I do the deeds of one."[24] This letter, of course, could not have been known to many of his contemporaries; they either accepted the judgment of Horace Greeley's review of the *Week,* which we examined earlier, and the remarks of James Russell Lowell, or they felt they verified the term by their own reading of his writings. Critics in later periods have followed both these lines and, once the letter to Greeley became known, may have felt they had Thoreau's own word to support their conclusion.

Three other factors may have influenced a number of those who call him a pantheist. One would be confusion of his position with Emerson's, since the latter's essay on *Nature* was known to have influenced him greatly in his youth. A second may be his early interest in Hinduism, with its often pantheistic ethos. The third factor may be a strange confusion of terms, a situation that might have appealed to Thoreau's fondness for puns, arising from his partly tongue-in-cheek statement in the *Week* that he was constant at the shrine of Pan. Technically, this would make him a "Pan-theist," not necessarily a "pantheist," for here the word "pan" is derived from the Greek meaning "all," not from the proper name of the mythological deity of the woods. The truth of the matter is that Thoreau had no metaphysical interest in clarifying the type of theism or pantheism which he may have held. It was sufficient for him just to state his belief in God's relation to nature, self, and other people, often in very poetic and imaginative ways, without going on to attempt to reconcile these intuitions or inferences in a consistent philosophical or theological position. But having said this, it is significant that what he did say carries some very important philosophical wisdom that we must attempt to analyze with accuracy. Pantheism, moreover, in his day was considered by the orthodox as a dangerous heresy. There is a greater tolerance today, as the writings of Bishop John Robinson should prove, in some Christian circles for panthe-ism as a possible option for expressing some aspects of the Christian understanding of God. The problem, however, has been a long one in terms of contentiousness. The Christian mystics, particularly Eckhart and Jacob Boehme, have often been charged with pantheism by their critics. Jonathan Ed-wards, often thought by many today the very exemplar of Puritan orthodoxy, was criticized as pantheistic by some of his contemporaries because he, like Thoreau, found God intimately in the created order of existence. In our own day the Jesuit Pierre Teilhard de Chardin was hounded by his critics for his view of God which he occasionally called "Christian pantheism." Some have probably used this term pantheism somewhat loosely in pointing to Thoreau's feeling of validity to all religions.

Pantheism, however, is essentially the belief or theory that God and the universe are identical. Three major types of pantheism have been described as (1) the pantheism of identity, illustrated classically by Spinoza's phrase God or

Nature *(Deus sive Natura)* and less clearly by Emerson, (2) the pantheism of correlation, demonstrated by Hegel's statement that God without the world is not God, and (3) the pantheism of continuity, typified by the neo-Platonic picture of the primal divine substance spilling down a series of levels in which it becomes progressively less ethereal until it reaches the substantial but derived divinity of the human soul. The critics of pantheism have felt that it destroyed the personality of God, lost the unique particularity of the self by merging it in the all like a drop of water in the ocean, destroyed man's ethical struggle against an evil apparently accepted as a necessary part of the all, and reduced personal immortality to the mere survival of soul substance. The real issue about pantheism, philosophically or theologically, is whether it is justifiable to replace the transcendence of God by the immanence of God without remainder.

Careful study of Thoreau's *Journal* proves that he is not a pantheist despite his quotations from Hinduism and his highly imaginative names for God. The evidence from the *Journal* is supported by his poems, in which his own piety often comes out still more clearly. To be sure, the poetry, while difficult to date, is mainly from his early period. There is, however, a consistent view of God that emerges from his writings that recognizes that God is more than the sum of the complex formula "Nature↔Self↔Other People." God for Thoreau is never simply identical with nature, as many self-styled Thoreauvians claim. Moreover, God is never identical with the self, a view often found in Emerson. Thoreau accepted the doctrine of creation too thoroughly for that. God is the transcendent creator. His language on this point, as well as his conceptual framework, was borrowed from the Judeo-Christian tradition. God remains God over and beyond his intimate association and presence in all the orders of his own making. "The red-bird which is the last of Nature is but the first of God." "If Nature is our Mother, is not God much more?"[25]

What is of primary interest to us, however, is not Thoreau's preservation of the transcendence of God, although this point in itself refutes the claim that he is a pantheist and makes him unlike Emerson, but the exciting and creative way in which he expresses the immanence of the transcendent God in his created universe. Christians have generally limited the Genesis word that God created humanity "in his own image" to its human reference and then used it as a means for asserting our unique stature over all the rest of the creation, with supposedly the right to "lord it over" the rest. Thoreau deliberately again and again uses "image of God" to mean, in addition to its human reference, other created beings and even what we might call inanimate objects. The striped bream in Walden's glaucous water is, Thoreau says, another image of God. "The bream, appreciated, floats in the pond as the center of the system, another image of God."[26] Thoreau will occasionally use "the face of God" in a similar sense. What he is really trying to communicate is that God is like the world he has made, just as he is like the person he created. Likeness, however, is not identity. This should not seem strange, because to be like one is to be like the other, both by the creative action of God sharing in the structural correspondence or relationship of creation. Another way of expressing this is to say that God holds us as individuals responsible both for our relation to nature and our relation to other people because of the created web of interrelationships binding nature, self, and other people from the very start. Again, there is no conflict in Thoreau's being the author of the *Week* and of "Civil Disobedience," because God is the author of these interrelated facets of his being that have responded in awareness to the diagram God (Nature↔Self↔Other People). Thoreau has got his feet down through the sphagnum and muck to rock bottom.

This understanding of reality brings more light to the previously discussed statements of Thoreau that "man is the crowning fact, the god we know," and that God must exist given the reality of "one *just* man." Thoreau is telling us that while we must seek fulfillment in nature, we do rise above the subhuman structures of nature to become for our own awareness the best possible clue to the character of God. This correspondence is realized when it is understood that a *just* man points to God. Thoreau might have said a *loving* person, in terms of this dimension in his thought, but here he has clearly laid the basis not only for holding the individual person responsible before God but also for holding him morally responsible before and to other people. Humanity for Thoreau is a universal organism and not merely a social one. Thoreau believes in the God-given nature of human community in spite of his perpetual warfare against all the institutional embodiments of corporate life. These he regards as deficient and corrupted expressions of the responsible self.

This is the place to underscore the kind of relationship which Thoreau believed should exist between the responsible self and God. It must be a mature one, based upon one's deep self-respect and ethical action, not upon a fawning on God that really substitutes for infantile dependency, the despairing piety of resignation, or the useless self-flagellation of a repentance that has not the intention to struggle heroically. In a passage that immediately suggests Dietrich Bonhoeffer to a contemporary reader, Thoreau defines the right relationship between the person and God.

As my own hand bent aside the willow in my path, so must my single arm put to flight the devil and his angels. God is not our ally when we shrink, and neuter when we are bold. If by trusting in God you lose any particle of your vigor, trust in Him no longer. When you trust, do not lay aside your armor, but put it on and buckle it tighter. . . . I cannot afford to relax discipline because God is on my side, for He is on the side of discipline. . . . And there is more of God and divine help in a man's little finger than in idle prayer and trust.[27]

The timidity of the orthodox scandalized Thoreau. In his comment about atheism he comes close to the type of criticism pressed home by some of the death-of-God theologians. "Nothing is so much to be feared as fear. Atheism may comparatively be popular with God himself."[28] Behind his statement about Pan's shrine is his feeling that paganism was more humane in orientation than the caricature of Christianity which he knew, people who began their prayers with "Now I lay me down to sleep," wanted nothing to change, and were totally unconcerned about their responsibilities to their fellows. The institutional church had sold its soul to materialism. Thoreau himself loved the material world, particularly the little oases of wildness, with "something akin to reverence." People just did not understand what idolatry was all about; it was a spirit of mind, not just the worship of sticks and stones.

It would imply the regeneration of mankind, if they were to become elevated enough to truly worship sticks and stones. It is the sentiment of fear and slavery and habit which makes a heathenish idolatry. . . . If I could, I would worship the parings of my nails. . . . I would fain improve every opportunity to wonder and worship, as a sunflower welcomes the light. The more thrilling, wonderful, divine objects I behold in a day, the more expanded and immortal I become.[29]

The preceding quotation is not pantheism, but the biblical prophetic attack upon idolatry satirically raised to the nth degree.

The intimate correlation between God and person that overcomes all the spacial images used to express transcendence and immanence comes out in the following sentence, which must have pleased Thoreau because of the double meaning possible in his use of the preposition "without," both of which possibilities he probably meant to underline. "We check and repress the divinity that stirs within us, to fall down and worship the divinity that is dead without us."[30] He believed that there was such a structure as necessity in life, but that we were free to work out our responses to it as agents of God. His many comments on this theme can be represented by a section of a letter which he wrote to Isaiah Williams on March 14, 1842, and which helps to explain his Delphic remark two years before to the effect that necessity was a sort of Eastern cushion on which he reclined.

'Tis true, as you say, "Man's ends are shaped for him," but who ever dared confess the extent of his free agency? Though I am weak, I am strong too. If God shapes my ends—he shapes me also—and his means are always equal to his ends. His work does not lack this completeness, that the creature consents. *I* am my destiny. Was I ever in that straight that it was not sweet to do right? And then for this free agency I would not be free of God certainly—I would only have freedom to defer to him. He has not made us solitary agents. He has not made us to do without him. . . . I believe that what I call my circumstances will be a very true history of myself—for God's works are complete both within and without—and shall I not be content with his success?[31]

Something of the imaginative power of Thoreau as well as his reliance often on biblical presuppositions can be seen from the various names he uses for God over the period covered by the *Journal*. They bear the authenticity of living revelation to him, although some of the titles also show the mediating power of tradition. From an early passage of 1850 to the last book of the *Journal*, there is a continuity of dedication to openness before God and to whatever God under whatever name will reveal. "I like Brahma, Hari, Buddha, the Great Spirit, as well as God," he wrote in 1850, curiously assuming that the word God was somehow the special possession of his culture in contradiction to the very context of his remark.[32] He put his meaning more clearly in the last book of the *Journal*, as he described the conventionally religious of his day. "They accept no god as genuine but the one that bears a Hebrew name. The Greenlander's *Pirksoma* (he that is above), or any the like, is always the name of a false god to them."[33] In the *Week*, Thoreau had expressed reservations about "the personality of God," a subject for which a lectureship had to his regret been endowed by the Earl of Bridgewater. Thoreau's reservation was that the conception limited the majesty of God. He did not wish a subhuman conception of God, but a superhuman understanding. Nevertheless, it is interesting that most of Thoreau's names imply the possibility of personal relations, as do most of his poems, often much more intimate on these matters than his prose.

Thoreau used these names for God, although in some cases it is necessary to know the context to understand the title: the Great God, the Spirit itself, Divinity, My Maker, the Something, the great Assessor, the Great Teacher, Jehovah, the Author and Ruler of the Universe, the Almighty, Universal Intelligence, the Greater Hare, the Lord, the All, Great Artist, Artist of the World, He who Creates, Supreme Being, Creator, the Divine, the Great Mower, the Scene-shifter, the Universal Soul, the Unnamed, Father, Landlord, the Giver, Director of lightning, the great Master, the Highest, and Benefactor. In addition, there are more mythological references to God, such as the reference in *Walden* to "an old settler and original proprietor, who is reported to have dug Walden Pond, and stoned it, and fringed it with pine woods; who tells me stories of old time and of new eternity."[34]

If the sources of these names are arranged chronologically, an interesting trend emerges. The more picturesque titles are early; the more biblical ones, although found scattered throughout, become dominant in his later writing. This is confirmation statistically in a rough way for the conclusion of this whole study of Thoreau—namely, that as he matured his categories became more biblical owing to the increasing expression that he gave to his Puritan heritage. The Bible which shaped his style and which he used to invest his own ideas with an authority for his readers also became, although probably he was never fully aware of it, more meaningful to him to express authentically his developing religious faith. Whenever he appears to disparage the Bible in later life, it is usually because he does not want a person to misuse it by substituting the experience of others for his own experience. Professor Harding's perceptive comments on the Bible and his style could be paraphrased to refer to the Bible and his own faith.

And finally, perhaps more than any other English work, the King James Bible exerted a profound influence on Thoreau's style. Although he often belittled his knowledge of the Scriptures and declared he was more familiar with the Oriental Bibles, his familiarity with the King James Bible is obvious on almost every page he wrote. His allusions to the Bible are frequent, and the word choice and sentence structure of the King James Bible are integral parts of his style.[35]

There are over five hundred references to the Bible in Thoreau. The book quoted most often is the Gospel of Matthew, with its reporting of and emphasis upon the words of Christ (about 116 references). Genesis (about fifty-eight references) with its story of creation is second. As might be expected from his religious orientation, there are many references to the wisdom literature of the Old Testament with about twenty-seven quotations from the Psalms. Also from the wisdom literature comes his single most quoted text: "Remember now thy Creator in the days of thy youth (Eccles. 12:1, KJV)." There are also a substantial number of quotations from the Hebrew prophets which, along with the words of Christ, provided the foundation for him as a prophet and Transcendentalist reformer. There are a surprising number of Pauline quotations, for a person for whom the decisive categories of redemption were not especially meaningful. He liked Paul's understanding of the body as a temple of the spirit, as our closest tie to nature. Thoreau has the capacity to sensitize the reader of the Bible to its ecological depth, a dimension sadly neglected in the Christian tradition. An obvious illustration is his *Journal* entry for January 24, 1860, after he had watched six tree sparrows feeding on the bare ground near a moraine.

Solomon thus describes the return of spring (Song of Solomon, 2:10-12):

"Rise up, my love, my fair one, and come away.

For, lo, the winter is past, the rain is over and gone;

The flowers appear on the earth; the time of the singing of birds is come, and the voice of the turtle is heard in our land."[36]

At another time he appropriated the structure of Psalm 103 to express his own prayerful sense of thanksgiving to God for wildness. "Ah, bless the Lord, O my soul! bless him for wildness, for crows that will not alight within gunshot! and bless him for hens, too, that croak and cackle in the yard!"[37] Here he was simply writing his New England Bible, praising God out of his own direct experience and not from the differing flora and fauna of Palestine.

We have seen before how his passage about the rainbow was enriched by his associating with it the Noachian covenant. Another illustration of the way the Bible pre-forms his experience of nature is his seeing the color scarlet and remembering Isaiah 1:18 ("though your sins be as scarlet"): "In the dry ditch, near Abel Minott's house that was, I see cardinal-flowers, with their red artillery, reminding me of soldiers,—red men, war, and bloodshed. Some are four and a half feet high. Thy sins shall be as scarlet. Is it my sins that I see?"[38]

This illustration is the clue to something far more exciting about Thoreau's use of the Bible than reading nature occasionally through some particular passage in it. Paul Elmer More made a very fruitful suggestion many years ago in an essay on Thoreau that deserves to be carried far beyond the point at which he left it. More wrote that Thoreau "went out to find the God of history in nature, in as much as man is but a part of the whole."[39] The potential validity of this observation should be clear from the analysis thus far made of the diagram of relationships: God (Nature ↔ Self ↔ Other People, or History). The particular view of history in More's phrase the "God of history" which Thoreau held unconsciously was the biblical view of the Israelites as a wandering people of God, except that instead of their being Israelites they turned out to be the Puritans in their migration to New England, their settlement of the wilderness, their trials, covenants, temptations, captivities in Babylon, idolatries, and reformations. His enthusiasm for the Puritan founders needs no documentation. Part of the effect of Cape Cod is that the grandeur of the sea and the isolation of the beaches is looked at through the eyes of the early settlers of the Cape and the still earlier voyages of discovery. In the mysticism that is so prominent in the *Week,* with its intense Oriental flavor and sources, there is also the running commentary on the early settlers and their tribulations which is meant to have its religious significance also. His nature mysticism, in other words, is not "pure" nature mysticism, but a nature observed through the glasses of a Puritan historical heritage. There is no mystery, as many literary critics would seek to claim, about the profoundly moral quality which he finds in nature and which he understands to be a corollary of the beauty of nature. Thoreau was simply a latter-day Puritan, liberated from its narrowness but still reading reality through its prism. The Puritans in their turn were simply latter-day Israelites claiming the promised land in a new kingdom of God. Because of Thoreau's Puritan heritage, biblical phrases not only helped him stylistically to communicate his message to people whose fathers and grandfathers had been nurtured on the Bible, they helped him also to understand the faith that was in him and provided him a major category for experiencing nature. We might paraphrase and expand More's quotation to read: "Thoreau went out to find the God of biblical history in nature, inasmuch as he was a loyal son of the Puritans who in turn were sons of the biblical people of God on pilgrimage." It is probably the biblical dimension of his thought that kept Thoreau from accepting outright a pantheistic view of nature. It is instructive to read again Wordsworth's "Lines on Tintern Abbey" to see how nature read in a different context could yield pantheism. One simply cannot emphasize too much the significance of the Bible to Thoreau, for style and man in him are blended in a rare integrity, but it is doubtful that Thoreau himself understood the full dimensions of this influence.

His intimate friend Ellery Channing reported in his pioneer biography that one of Thoreau's unfulfilled desires at the time of his death was to have been able to study the Bible more thoroughly than he had.[40] Channing also said that no one had left a better unfinished life. Emerson said in his funeral oration that the scale of his studies would have required longevity. One might add that the manner of his death befitted his life and drew its concerns and interests into a serene witness to his integrity, joyfulness, and courage. In answer to a letter from Myron Benton he wrote on March 21, 1862, "You ask particularly after my health. I *suppose* that I have not many months to live; but, of course, I know nothing about it. I may add that I am enjoying existence as much as ever, and regret nothing."[41] The wracking cough grew worse; his features took on the hollow appearance of one being destroyed by tuberculosis. When he sensed that the end was not far off, he had his bed brought downstairs where he could pass his last hours among the family that had meant so much to him. The family friend Parker Pillsbury inquired, "You seem so near the brink of the dark river that I almost wonder how the opposite shore may appear to you." He replied in his famous words, "One world at a time."[42] To his orthodox Aunt Louisa, who asked whether he had made his peace with God, he answered pleasantly, "I did not know we had ever quarrelled, Aunt."[43] Bronson Alcott recorded, "I always think of Thoreau when I look at a sunset. . . . He said to me in his last illness, 'I shall leave the world without regret.'—that was the saying either of a grand egotist or of a deeply religious soul."[44] When Edmund Hosmer told him he had seen a spring robin, Thoreau said, "Yes! This is a beautiful world, but I shall see a fairer."[45] He worked to the very end on his manuscript for *The Maine Woods,* his last distinctly heard words being appropriately "Moose" and "Indians."[46] The end came peacefully on the morning of May 6, 1862. Emerson insisted upon a funeral in the First Parish Church. In the eulogy he referred to Thoreau's religion, perceiving that the poetry was the key to it.

His biography is in his verses. His habitual thought makes all his poetry a hymn to the Cause of causes, the Spirit which vivifies and controls his own . . . in these religious lines:—

> "Now chiefly is my natal hour
> And only now my prime of life;
> I will not doubt the love untold,
> Which not my worth nor want have bought,
> Which wooed me young, and wooes me old,
> And to this evening hath me brought."

Whilst he used in his writings a certain petulance of remark in reference to churches or churchmen, he was a person of a rare, tender and absolute religion, a person incapable of any profanation, by act or by thought. Of course, the same isolation which belonged to his original thinking and living detached him from the social religious forms. . . . Thoreau was sincerity itself, and might fortify the convictions of prophets in the ethical laws by his holy living. . . . He thought that without religion or devotion of some kind nothing great was ever accomplished.[47]

9

THOREAU
AND THE RELIGIOUS
SITUATION TODAY

Thoreau, I believe, must be recognized as one of the great
American mystics and creative religious thinkers. He is the
theologian of creation, the apostle of wilderness, and the
prophet of social action undertaken by the concerned individual. For too long he remained the inspiration for a cult
of nature lovers, many of whom apparently loved nature
more than their fellow human beings. Now he has become
a preserve for some aesthetes who show no real interest in
his basic message but only in his skill as a literary craftsman.
My plea is not now to inaugurate some third circle of theologians or religious people who will concern themselves solely
with his religious significance. It is, however, just the religious dimension in Thoreau that gives meaning and pro-
portionality to his whole authorship. My claim is that the
nature lover will find in Thoreau's religion compassion for
his neighbor, that the student of Thoreau's style will be led
on to the larger reality which Thoreau represents, and that
religious people will be drawn out of their ghettos into a
joyous celebration of God in the midst of his incredibly
beautiful and meaningful creation. In order, however, for
the churches to appreciate this dimension in Thoreau, they
must emerge from their cultural isolation and their inhibi-
tions about nature, accept the work of those in other fields
who have been the real pioneers, and acquire a new awareness and spirituality to be open to his message. For many
this will be a difficult and probably insurmountable task,

167

because of Thoreau's negative attitudes to much that they hold dear. His criticism of organized religion, justified as it was on nearly every count, was still so harsh that it alienated religious people from him. The churches have for too long pretended that Thoreau did not exist. They have isolated themselves from God's created order to the extent that they now find themselves without foundations or a coherent understanding of their responsibilities as the ecological crisis has exploded for all humankind.

The interest of young people in Thoreau is possibly a harbinger of future movement by the churches in his direction. To be sure, the Thoreau who emerges as the hero of the present counterculture is more the projection of wish and ideology than the real Thoreau, but at least one current in this confused flood of almost mass approval of Thoreau is the wholesome search for genuinely authentic religious experience. It is an incredible fact, but a true one, that fewer and fewer young people are finding within the mainline churches, whether Catholic or Protestant, the experience of God they so deeply desire. There is dry rot at their very heart. Either they have half baptized American materialism and are building up organizations in imitation of American business methods or they have so completely identified their mission with helping the helpless in a sort of churchly political program that they are indistinguishable from the usually more effective community agencies or the ideologically more assured secular political groups. God, wonder, worship, and religious experience have largely disappeared from their flat lives.

The mysticism of Thoreau, so appealing to many of the younger generation, is something that needs to be fostered and nourished within the churches. The sanity of his this-worldly mysticism with its disciplines will prove a strong defense against much of the bizarre occultism and tawdry religious fakers who crowd the scene. His mysticism is a healthful bulwark against the bogus or instant mysticism of the drug culture. I debated whether to choose the word eco-mystic as a subtitle for this book, simply to emphasize that Thoreau's mysticism is not an esoteric hobby that withdraws him from communication with other people, but the very opposite, a sense of the oneness of the whole of reality over all its ranges that concentrates meaning for the individual, liberates him from the seemingly endless dissipation and dispersion of modern life, and inspires him to struggle forward and upward. There are, of course, problems in Thoreau's mysticism. He is so much of an individualist that he fails to understand the corporate dimension in religious experience. He does not seem to realize the degree to which the religious books of humankind are not chance products of individual mystics but, to an amazing degree, the corporate responses of individuals within their special historical traditions. He himself, as we have seen, looked at nature through the glasses of his Puritan heritage far more than he was aware of, even when the documents before him were those of the Eastern religions and, in particular, his much-loved *Bhagavad-Gita*. The very fact that his mysticism of nature is one profoundly shaped by his bringing the God of history, even the God ultimately of the biblical tradition, to his mystical contemplation of nature should build a bridge to the pastors of this land. Their seminary training occurred unfortunately in an era when it was thought necessary by many of their teachers to exalt the God of history by running down the God of nature. At last the suicidal nature of this pedagogical device is becoming obvious, in part because of the ecological crisis and a new awareness engendered by it in the seminaries as well as by corrective trends within biblical scholarship, themselves probably responses ultimately to the issue of the environment. Because we have seen that Yahweh must be the lord of nature and not simply of wandering Arameans in isolation from their relation to nature, there is no reason why we have to worship the baals instead of the Lord. A nature mysticism that is isolated from the God of history is a limited exercise. Thoreau's historically mediated mysticism, to the degree that it was influenced by his Puritan heritage (even if unconsciously, most of the time), may be an excellent place for many churchmen to begin to reestablish contact religiously with the world outside the walls of the church building or the seminary ghetto. I have chosen the word begin advisedly, because Thoreau is not equipped to lead on to the deepest areas that many of the Christocentric mystics of the West have reached. However, one must begin somewhere, and the down-to-earth quality of Thoreau's mysticism will have more credibility for the beginner than the strange summits of the classic Christian mystics.

Thoreau's animosity against tradition has both positive and negative elements within it. He rightly saw that most people have never been led on beyond their religious traditions to direct, personal experience of the divine. They have been sold "God's old clothes" and they desperately cling to them as securities, making from them, as he said so well, scarecrows to frighten children. The churches have in our generation become more sensitized to the psychology of development and more careful in religious nurture, although even here bureaucratic empires of religious educators have risen and fallen largely because they were unable to deliver the reality of authentic religious experience in the maze of their methodologies. Thoreau would heartily have endorsed Luther's dictum that everyone has got to do his own believing, as he must his own dying.

The understanding of tradition in nearly all churches is far more appreciatively critical than it was in Thoreau's period. The Consultation on Church Union, for example, has written a definition of tradition so close to that of the Second Vatican Council that many Roman Catholics have endorsed it. "By Tradition (with a capital "T") we understand the whole life of the church insofar as it is guided and nourished by the Holy Spirit. . . . Living Tradition is a continually flexible reality."[1] In this definition the mystical element predominates, although it must be confessed that purity in verbal formulations does not automatically produce the reality toward which it points. Otherwise, the Consultation on Church Union would become a revitalizing force rather than something stopped nearly dead in its tracks by creeping bureaucracy, whether of the denominational headquarters or of the local congregation. Mysticism is the raw material of all religion. Without it the institutional mills may continue to grind, but they will not produce meal. In spite of his excessive religious individualism, Thoreau at times seemed to find a place for the corporate religious dimension. He spoke of the churches as empty powder mills, yet with enough dust of truth on their walls that, if you introduced a spark, they would blow up instantly. But even these seeming recognitions are limited. Many have wondered why Thoreau, with his strong predisposition to silence and its uses, should not have been more drawn to the Quakers than he actually was. The answer surely is that the Friends *organized* their corporate silence, *organized* their expectation of revelation, and *organized* their philanthropy. For Thoreau organization was treason to spiritual religion. "In religion there is no society."[2] When his friend Ricketson wrote him less than a year before his death of his conversion to the Quakers, Thoreau replied,

"I scarcely know what to say about it, unless that judging by your account, it appears to me a change which concerns yourself peculiarly, and will not make you more valuable to mankind."[3]

Thoreau brings a distinct contribution to the present discussion about God. Misunderstood by most of his orthodox contemporaries, who judged him a pantheist, and by many of his friends, who assumed that his view had to be identical with Emerson's, Thoreau actually held a relational view of theism that was many years ahead of its time. He ought to be included, for example, in Bishop Robinson's excellent study *Exploration into God*. Thoreau was dissatisfied with the kind of theism that made God "a great big person up or out there." "Do you presume to fable of the ineffable? Pray, what geographer are you, that speak of heaven's topography? Whose friend are you, that speak of God's personality?"[4] The objections are in part mystical—respect for the absolutely indescribable nature of deity, in part religious—a reduction of the mystery of Godhead to the idol of man's self-projection of his personality, and in part philosophical—a suspicion that the geographer has unduly simplified his task. The reference to the geographer is especially helpful, since much current discussion about God-talk uses by way of analogy the problem of representing a circular or spheroidal globe by a map projection onto a two-dimensional sheet of paper. Since the advent of the air age and particularly of circumpolar flight, most of us have been ridding ourselves of the picture acquired early in school of the Mercator projection with its representation of an immense Greenland, Baffinland, and the northern reaches of Siberia. The Mercator projection was fine for the equator and passable for the mid-temporate zone, but a disaster for the arctic. We have been remapping the arctic in our minds in terms of great circles to give ourselves credible evidence that Moscow and London are about equidistant from San Francisco. Newer map projections have helped to decrease the distortion. Likewise, the older picture of God projected as "a personal being out there" has been losing ground. It once symbolized by the images of space the transcendence of God, but now it tends in a view of an expanding universe to push God so far to the edges that he ceases to have real meaning for us in the center of our lives where the really important things take place. Many orthodox cling tenaciously to the older projection in fear of losing the reality represented but end up, in Thoreau's words, holding only "God's old clothes." The usual theism of Christian theologians in the past was properly critical of the deist projection, with its view of God as the watchmaker who had wound the machine up in the beginning and then, to mix the metaphor, seemingly retired as an absentee landlord. The excessive transcendence of deism was modified by an emphasis on God's immanence, although unfortunately the projection chosen suggested that God "intervened" every now and then in the system as a sort of deus ex machina, or god of the gaps. But the gaps in our knowledge or power have been closing with remarkable rapidity. Bertrand Russell pointed out that fishermen who depend on sailboats are more religious than those who have prospered enough to afford motor boats. Increasing secularization and technology have made the old projection of the god of the gaps intolerable or unneeded. With this shrinking of field has come a loss in the sense of the reality of God. He is for many a disposable item. This was the cultural development behind the bluster some years ago about the "death of God" movement that was dismissed for the next fad by the magazines which create our instant theology of the week before the terms of the debate could be sufficiently clarified for productive thinking. Thoreau sensed the inadequacy of what we may call the Mercator projection of God's personality. "It is remarkable that almost all speakers and writers feel it to be incumbent on them, sooner or later, to prove or to acknowledge the personality of God."[5] Emerson was even more articulate than his friend Thoreau on the point, probably because of his professional theological education. Emerson chose the consistent alternative, the complete immanence of God, or pantheism. Thoreau, on the other hand, kept the transcendence of God but brought God so intimately into the world that most thought him a pantheist. Note the retention, however, of transcendence in the following quotations: "By usurer's craft . . . we strive to retain and increase the divinity in us, when infinitely the greater part of divinity is out of us."[6] "If Nature is our mother, is not God much more?"[7]

Thoreau was doubtless unaware that a technical term had been forged in controversy on the continent before his college days by K. C. F. Krause which fitted his position exactly. That term has now established itself in religious philosophy as a projection that avoids the opposite alternatives of transcendence and immanence by combining the two. It is called panentheism, and it is defined in *The Oxford Dictionary of the Christian Church* as "(Gk, *pan,* 'everything'; *en,* 'in'; *theos,* 'God') the belief that the Being of God includes and penetrates the whole universe, so that every part of it exists in Him, but (as against pantheism) that His Being is more than, and is not exhausted by, the universe."[8]

It is only the term panentheism that is really new. The conception reaches back at least to Paul, who stated it in an eschatological way in 1 Corinthians 15:28 that God may become everything in everyone. It is really the position of Teilhard de Chardin, who tried to baptize the term "pantheism" to the scandal of many hyperorthodox.

A very real "pan-theism" if you like (in the etymological meaning of the word) but an absolutely legitimate pantheism—for if, in the last resort, the reflective centers of the world are effectively "one with God," this state is obtained not by identification (God becoming all) but by the differentiating and communicating action of love (God all *in everyone*). And that is essentially orthodox and Christian.[9]

We have examined with some thoroughness the relational diagram that expresses Thoreau's thought: God (Nature↔Self↔Other People). Thoreau wants to understand the reality of God in terms of relationship to the other words in the equation, not as an isolated deity, but at the same time he does not want to lose the identity of God within these structures by some pantheistic formula of equivalence to one of the triad or even to the sum of the triad. It is his insistence upon the relationship that leads to such a statement as this from his superb essay on "Walking": "The highest that we can attain to is not Knowledge, but Sympathy with Intelligence."[10] This attitude also explains Thoreau's paradoxical comment that atheism may be comparatively popular with God, as well as a comment from his reading of Ralph Cudworth, the Cambridge Platonist. "Dr. Cudworth does not consider that the belief in a deity is as great a heresy as exists."[11] Thoreau wanted people to experience God directly, not to substitute for this an intellectual concept of theism.

Thoreau's images of the relationship of God to his creation are more organic than mechanical, more humane than simply masculine-monarchial. He did not think through this problem in a critically self-conscious way, but his images are suggestive of how he might have proceeded had he ever felt the need to do this. Contemporary philosophers of religion and theologians who are particularly sensitive to this issue of the organic relationship are increasingly turning to the type of process theology developed by Alfred North White-head, or by Charles Hartshorne, or implied by Teilhard de Chardin. This philosophy was, however, hardly an option to Thoreau, for it could only really come into its own after a thorough acceptance of organic evolution, a movement just gathering momentum in his day and one that in its earliest phases captured his imagination. There are suggestions in Thoreau that he was feeling toward some such philosophy. Although he used traditional Platonic language at times, contrasting the eternal and the temporal, it is clear that he was dissatisfied with its dualism and sought a way of making "one world" out of the previous two. I think we may see him calling for a process understanding of reality in his statement that God culminates in the moment. Teilhard's choice of the phrase *milieu divin* as the title for one of his basic books that sets forth his Christocentric mysticism of convergence became the despair of his English translators, who finally had to leave it as *The Divine Milieu*. The French term is richer than the English "field," because it denotes both a center of attraction as well as the field of attraction. We might do worse than compile some of Thoreau's passages from the *Journal* under the title "The Divine Eco-field" or "The Divine Environment," but unfortunately these titles in English carry an impersonal connotation that would falsify the intense personal quality of Thoreau's relationship to God. The problem today is to keep the intimate personal world of the Bible without erecting an idol of "a personal being" out there. God is superpersonal, not impersonal or subpersonal, but our language projections of the personal tend today to dissociate God from his creation. If process thought can retain the biblical element of God's transcendence while at the same time express more meaningfully his immanental presence in his universe, it will have become a valuable new mapping projection.

Thoreau can hardly be called a Christian theologian, be-cause he does not share the basic faith in God's incarnating and redeeming activity in Jesus Christ that the Christian theologian tries to explicate as the center of his under-standing of reality. Thoreau, however, is a far more adequate Christian theologian of creation than many who are more orthodox than he is on such themes as redemption and eschatology. Thoreau can help the Christian community to recover the freshness of insight into God as creator that characterizes the psalmists and the writer of Job, for example, but which has been dulled almost out of recognition in the dry-as-dust discussions by Christian theologians on natural revelation or natural religion. One gets the impression that numerous theologians seeking to refine and define "their concept of nature" have never been out-of-doors in their lives, or, if they have, that they sense no connection between the magnificence of "nature" and their professional discipline of defining concepts. Many services of worship conducted within the walls of our churches would be exposed for their anemia if held out-of-doors. Our hymns in general fail to express the wonders of the American scene. They employ the biblical images of a flora or fauna appropriate to a dry land like Palestine or are borrowed from the English countryside. A knowledge of Thoreau would inspire people to produce authentic hymns describing our own encounters with God-self-others in the agonies now of our ecological crisis. He would renew for many the lost sense of wonder which they knew as children, but which has been bred out of them in the artificialities and commercialism of modern life and its reflection in the churches. It is doubtful that the liturgical worship of the churches can preserve or, as is needed in most cases, revive its vitality without authentic experiences of wonder and of communion with mystery.

There is a passage from "The Allegash and East Branch" in *The Maine Woods* which brings out this sense of wonder in Thoreau. Camped near Mount Kineo on Moosehead Lake with his Indian guide Joe Polis, Thoreau awakened in the dead of night to see a whole log of moosewood aglow with white phosphorescence.

I little thought that there was such a light shining in the darkness of the wilderness for me. . . . I was in just the frame of mind to see something wonderful, and this was a phenomenon adequate to my circumstance and expectation, and it put me on the alert to see more like it. I exulted like "a pagan suckled in a creed" that had never been worn at all, but was bran new, and adequate to the occasion. I let science slide, and rejoiced in that light as if it had been a fellow-creature.

With more reflection on the incident, he concluded that it was of the kind that gives birth to religion.

One revelation has been made to the Indian, another to the white man. I have much to learn of the Indian, nothing of the missionary. I am not sure but all that would tempt me to teach the Indian my religion would be his promise to teach me *his*. Long enough I had heard of irrelevant things; now at length I was glad to make acquaintance with the light that dwells in rotten wood.[12]

Thoreau has the ability to help the reader discover and take joy in the wonder of life.

There is a whole philosophy of religious education for adults as well as for children symbolized in Thoreau's most frequently quoted verse from the Bible and his commentary on it: "Remember thy Creator in the days of thy youth; *i.e.,* lay up a store of natural influences. Sing while you may, before the evil days come. He that hath ears, let him hear. See, hear, smell, taste, etc., while these senses are fresh and pure."[13]

Some of the passages from Thoreau's *Journal* in which he sees God in nature might be printed in the parish bulletin to help people develop awareness. Special services built around natural phenomena with an interpretive reading from Thoreau might be developed. There are many possibilities for enriching people's religious experience of nature through family camping, conservation workshops, slide shows, corporate meditations out-of-doors, lectures, and courses. We have already examined two representative passages of this type, one describing a sunset and another a rainbow. The second was enriched by the biblical presuppositions that Thoreau brought to the experience from the Genesis account of the rainbow as the sign of God's covenant. One of the joys of reading Thoreau is to discover his depth of reflection after the original stimulus has passed. In another passage he describes these experiences in the deeper dimension of mystical insight and religious reflection. His conclusion is that while we cannot see all of God in nature, it would be ridiculous for us not to recognize thankfully that part of him graciously revealed there, namely, his "face."

Ideas that soar above the earth cannot be seen all round, but ever have one side turned toward the heavens. They are moonshine, are they? Very well, then, do your night travelling when there is no moon to light you; but I will be thankful for the light that reaches me from the star of least magnitude. I will be thankful that I see so much as one side of a celestial idea, one side of the rainbow and the sunset sky, the *face* of God alone.[14]

Thoreau has been criticized not only for the woods-burning episode but, more justly, for his rationalizations and unresolved guilt feelings about it that characterize the *Journal* passage six years after the event. He had the power, however, at times of redeeming an evil situation by letting it become transformed in his myth-making imagination. The following description of the northern lights written one year after the offensive passage in the *Journal* is a jewel of writing in itself, but it has been enriched and made possible by the traumatic experience of the humiliating fire that got away from him. One who is sustained by a tradition that saw the revelation of God in the Mosaic burning bush can have his faith imaginatively expanded by inner sympathy with Thoreau's vivid description of a forest fire in heaven.

The northern lights now, as I descend from the Conantum house, have become a crescent of light crowned with short, shooting flames,—or the shadows of flames, for sometimes they are dark as well as white. . . . Now the fire in the north increases wonderfully, not shooting up so much as creeping along, like a fire on the mountains of the north seen afar in the night. The Hyperborean gods are burning brush, and it spread, and all the hoes in heaven couldn't stop it. It spread from west to east over the crescent hill. Like a vast fiery worm it lay across the northern sky, broken into many pieces; and each piece, with rainbow colors skirting it, strove to advance itself toward the east, worm-like, on its own annular muscles. It has spread into their choicest wood-lots. Now it shoots up like a single solitary watch-fire or burning bush, or where it ran up a pine tree like powder, and still it continues to gleam here and there like a fat stump in the burning, and is reflected in the water. And now I see the gods by great exertions have got it under, and the stars have come out without fear, in peace.[15]

The ecological wisdom of Thoreau is the direct result of his insight into the coinherence of reality. *Walden* is really an experiment in and demonstration of human ecology. His philosophy of holism, or of an organic oneness differentiated through interdependent realities, is a rich and dynamic view of existence, but the most remarkable thing about it all is that the complexity grasped does not atrophy the person's responsibilities but rather sharpens them in a heightening of individual action. It provides the needed corrective to that aggressively masculine determination to subject, conquer, and exploit nature that has brought the Western world to the brink of self-destruction. It communicates the certainty that nature awakens, heals, and renews the human spirit through sympathetic relationship rather than through domination. Thoreau is the semisecularized, latter-day Francis of Assisi, bidding us expand the horizons of our love. The New Testament is unexcelled in its plea for love as the creative ground of relationship between people. The parables of Jesus break open all the legal and religious systems by which people before him chose to narrow the circle of human obligation to love one's fellows, but unfortunately the love ethic in Christian tradition has been largely limited to people. What the ecological crisis of our day is plainly demonstrating to us, and what Thoreau so well anticipated, is that neighbor love needs to be expanded to include all the creation, inanimate as well as animate. The parable of the good Samaritan with its decisive question, "Who is my neighbor?" leads to the wider answer of Francis of Assisi in his "Canticle of the Sun" and on to Thoreau's recognition of the kinship of all created reality. Even Albert Schweitzer's magnificent "reverence for life" needs to be expanded to include matter, the foundation of all life, as Teilhard de Chardin does in his "Hymn to Matter." There may be those who will argue that this expansion of field makes love into a sentimental thing. Not so! There is nothing more hardheadedly realistic than a love that nourishes respect for, and preservation of, the universe in which our lives are cast. Love or perish. Martin Buber's "I-Thou" analysis of our meeting other selves can be developed, as he himself suggests, to apply to our relations with subhuman nature. Some of the most moving passages in Thoreau are his attempts to get near other life—to the bream, to the loon, to the fox, to the wet lichens—although he recognizes the strangeness of that other life. It disturbed him that the horse had been made a beast of burden without our trying to communicate anything higher in the process. His speculation from reading Darwin's account of the natives of Tierra del Fuego that animals might have a rudimentary religion is a link in the chain that stretches from Francis' ecstatic faith in preaching to the birds or admonishing the wolf of Gubbio. We are here only at the beginning of exciting discoveries in animal behavior that should extend far beyond teaching dolphins to recover lost torpedoes. A special study could be appropriately made of Thoreau's understanding of "love" and of its circles of application. The poetry provides much insight here, as does the development of his hunger for mystical experience. The linchpin that translates the diagram God (Nature↔Self↔Other People) into fruitful action is love.

> Not once for all, forever, blest,
> Still to be cheered out of the west
> Not from his heart to banish all sighs
> Still be encouraged by the sun rise
> Forever to love and to love and to love
> Within him, around him—beneath him above
> To love is to know, is to feel, is to be
> At once 'tis his birth and his destiny.[16]

Another area in which Thoreau can contribute today is his concern for social reform but, at the same time, his conviction that the key to it all is the concerned individual. Here the pragmatism of his actions against injustice in society outruns his ideology of the individual. The great divorce in America between the fundamentalist churches and the liberal churches and even between groups within the same denomination is the debate between those who press for personal conversion and those who advocate social action. The gospel has been bifurcated into a supposedly personal gospel and a social gospel, with the absurd conviction that never the twain shall meet. Discussions about participation in and the shaping of Campaign Key '73, a mission of revival of national scope, illustrated the problem. No individual can undergo an authentic conversion to the Lord Jesus Christ in some hidden area of personal ethics where the Savior reigns without that person's whole attitude to the business order, his political orientation, and his attitude toward the deprived persons in society being profoundly converted also. To attempt to use verbal conversion to Christ as a bulwark for protecting the established order is about as crooked a game as ecclesiastics can be discovered playing. The fundamentalist who might be prepared to call Thoreau as an ally against the "social gospel" because of Thoreau's individualism needs to hear him say, as he wrote to Blake, "When we are weary with the burden of life, why do we not lay down this load of falsehoods which we have volunteered to sustain, and be refreshed as never mortal was? . . . God reigns, *i.e.*, when we take a liberal view,—when a liberal view is presented to us."[17] On the other hand, if, in opposition to this shallow "conversion" or ideological exploitation of Christian conviction, the mainline churches concentrate upon social action to the extent that they cease to work for individual conversion and become in effect another political party with only a slight religious cast, they are committing suicide. Thoreau's suspicion that the reformer engages upon his campaigns because he has a stomachache or some complaint is not as captious as it may sound at first hearing. To locate the evil "out there" in some structure of society can be a means for avoiding the evil at the center of the self. He wrote to Emerson in England about a peace meeting at Concord at which many signed a pledge to "treat all mankind as brothers henceforth." He professed skepticism: "I think I shall wait and see how they treat me first."[18]

Personal conversion and social action are not mutually exclusive but, quite simply, steps one and two of a lifelong process of bringing Christian perspectives to bear on all areas of existence. Thoreau's defiant protest on behalf of the individual needs to be heard by the liberal churches that have vastly underrated the power of the genuinely concerned individual to act as Thoreau really did for social reform. Thoreau's keen detection of the dishonesties and contradictions to the gospel of Christ in the organized churches needs to be heard by the organizers of campaigns of revival. He expressed his skepticism about the prayer meetings of businessmen.

But Thoreau's relevance goes well beyond the divisions between those who stress personal conversion and those who stress social action. It extends to the very understanding of the teaching of Christ himself. Thoreau's gospel of poverty—or simplicity, as he called it—is far closer to the New Testament than anything in the life of conservative or liberal church people suggests today. American materialism, or affluence, to use its more socially acceptable synonym, is never seriously challenged in church activity today, in plain contradiction to the teaching of Christ. At a time when the well-off American begins to grumble about high taxes in a country which hardly tries to raise its minorities above the poverty line, not alone to face its obvious human responsibilities in a world in which the rich become richer each year and the poor poorer, Thoreau's message of the simple life which is in conformity with the gospel needs to be heard. At a time when Americans who comprise about 6 percent of the world's population consume some 60 percent of the world's resources, the life-style of greater simplicity exhibited by Thoreau needs to be creatively adapted to our changed circumstances from his day. Thoreau's concern for the extirpation of slavery and over the injustices suffered by the Indians and the Irish arose not merely from considerations of common humanity but from a theological understanding of the meaning of the parable of the sheep and the goats in Matthew 25. The act of clothing the naked or feeding the hungry is done as if to Christ himself on the principle that "inasmuch as ye have done it unto one of the least of these my brethren, ye have done it unto me (Matt. 25:40, KJV)." On this text and others like it, the contemporary theology of liberation has found New Testament foundation. One of the greatest contributions Thoreau has to offer to our mass society today, and even to some of the utopian dreams of followers of the social gospel, is his defiant enmity to the institutions of society. It may appear excessive at times, but at the end of our era in 1984, to pick George Orwell's symbolic date, his enmity toward institutionalized society as such may be at last seen to be the humane act of a friend, standing up for the individual against even the most benign group forces that tend to engulf him under the conditions of modern life. Stanley Hyman correctly chastizes Thoreau as a "nut reformer" when he lectures his Irish neighbor in *Walden* about abstinence from tea, coffee, and meat, but he ends with a solid tribute: "At his best, he is the clearest voice for social ethics that ever spoke out in America."[19]

Thoreau is really a strong advocate of basic Christian values which became real for him as he discarded the religious establishment of his day and lived freshly from certain biblical insights. He saw clearly the limitations of science on the very threshold of its cultural triumph in the West and was too much of a disciplined son of the Puritans to be led astray by a cult of freedom that recognized no obligations or responsibilities. Because of these qualities there is a special timeliness to his message for us today, a relevance described with precision by Norman Foerster in the conclusion to his classic *Nature in American Literature,* but perhaps even truer for our cultural situation today than when Foerster wrote fifty years ago.

Thoreau brought together much that is perennially vital in the leading traditions of the Western world—the classical and the Christian—at the very time when they were being assailed with all the weapons of modern science and of the natural man bent on utter emancipation, and he did this, oddly enough, while seeking "to find God in nature." His relative failure in this quest, and his fresh perception of the residuum of truth in the old traditions, are of the deepest interest in our own day, when men are not only questioning the old traditions but also beginning to question the two forces that assailed these traditions—the forces of science and romanticism.[20]

We have already discussed in the second chapter his life-long criticism of the churches. Sometimes he becomes a common scold and reveals simply a Pavlovian syndrome when he is reminded of the institutional church, but most of the time his criticism is right on target and often uses the words of Christ to point out the hypocrisy, cowardice, and prejudice of church people. Church folk build such solid ghettos of self-righteousness and such cozy country clubs for themselves that they just do not hear the increasing criticism of the disenchanted who have dropped out or of the secularists who were not even attracted to join them. The following passage is as devastatingly true of church life today as in Thoreau's time. What is more, the judgment derives from the Gospel saying about the salt that has lost its taste.

Who are the religious? They do not differ much from mankind generally, except that they are more conservative and timid and useless, but who in their conversation and correspondence talk about kindness of Heavenly Father. Instead of going bravely about their business, trusting God ever, they do like him who says "Good sir" to the one he fears, or whistles to the dog that is rushing at him. And because they take His name in vain so often they presume that they are better than you. Oh, their religion is a rotten squash.[21]

Thoreau was even more severe with ecclesiastical leaders than with laity. After all, these professionals ate off their religion. His indignation about a law-and-order bishop needs to be heard today.

I heard the other day of a meek and sleek devil of a Bishop Some-body, who commended the law and order with which Burns was given up. I would like before I sit down to a table to inquire if there is one in the company who styles himself or is styled Bishop, and he or I should go out of it. I would have such a man wear his bishop's hat and his clerical bib and tucker, that we may know him.[22]

Churchmen were unfortunately quick to retaliate against their critic. Since it was easy to write him off as unorthodox, the churches insulated themselves against his message. The chill hostility of his own generation was transmitted in time into the indifference inherited by contemporary church people. Henry Salt, a pioneer English biographer, quotes an evaluation of Thoreau made by the *Church Quarterly Review:*

While the descriptions of scenery are extremely beautiful, and the notes about animal life and plants are most interesting, yet the man himself is thoroughly selfish, quite out of sympathy with men and their sufferings, barbaric, if not animal, in his tastes, and needlessly profane.[23]

The pioneering of Emerson and Thoreau in making the sacred books of the East known to Americans has already been discussed. Thoreau's knowledge of these religions was limited, and he chose from their writings what he wanted and forgot the rest. His eclectic principles of choice turn out on the whole to be various predispositions and values from his Puritan heritage, but he stands as a symbol to the churches of a task of living dialogue with the world's religions that they have yet to begin with seriousness. His enthusiasm for compiling the "ethnical scriptures" of humankind defines the direction that this dialogue should follow —namely, an inquiry into the human religious dimension as such. The Second Vatican Council in its documents has moved forward in a promising way and there have been conferences of representatives of the various religions of the world to find bases of cooperation for peace, but the task has barely begun in the consciousness of the average churchgoer, not alone in those separated from organizational religion. This ecumenical venture will profit by dialogue both with humanists and with communists, who deny the validity of the religious quest. Such dialogue will center upon the human condition as such, but it cannot fail but be useful in defining what religion is all about. Thoreau's use of ascetic disciplines and development of mystical experience, particularly through the *Bhagavad-Gita,* should be helpful to all in deepening the actual reality of religious experience so tragically atrophied in the mainline churches today. Thoreau does not talk about religion, he speaks from authentic experience.

When I revolve it again in my mind, looking into the west at sunset, whether these ordinances of the Hindoos are to be passed by as the whims of an Asiatic brain, I seem to see the divine Brahma himself sitting in an angle of a cloud, and revealing himself to his scribe Menu. . . . They are not merely a voice floating in space *for my own experience is the speaker.*[24]

Thoreau's principles of selection will need critical scrutiny in the growing dialogue, and none of the participants, if it is to be truly ecumenical dialogue, will be asked to abandon his religious convictions. As we have seen before, Thoreau's excessive religious individualism would soon have brought him into conflict with the Eastern religions whose scriptures he admired, if he had actually lived in their countries and had experienced the corporate and organized impact of those faiths. More and more young people are choosing faiths largely of their own creation. Thoreau will stand to them as a sign that the problems of tradition, the principles of selection, the place of the institutional element in religion, and the perils of self or group idolatry must all be faced. His approach, we can venture, would be very open to the theology of secularization in our day that is so misunderstood in the churches and outside, but his acceptance of its cultural analysis would not imply his agreement that man had outgrown religion. He was too much of a mystic for that, "God-propped" as he said. To Marston Watson at Plymouth, who wanted him to read something suitable for a religious meeting on a Sunday, he replied, showing an appreciation of the secular and of its relation to the holy:

At present I have nothing to read which is not severely heathenish, or at least secular,—which the dictionary defines as "relating to the affairs of the present world, not holy"—though not necessarily unholy; nor have I any leisure to prepare it. My writing at present is profane, yet in a good sense, and, as it were, sacredly, I may say; for, finding the air of the temple too close, I sat outside.[25]

Another area in which Thoreau can make a major contribution is in the theological interpretation of American culture. Richard Niebuhr's classic *Kingdom of God in America* and Sidney Ahlstrom's recent *Religious History of the American People* are distinguished studies in this field. The United States, more than any other major power, has had a unique relation with nature as part of its social history, but this fundamental experience of the virgin continent has not really been analyzed in great depth theologically. Hans Huth's *Nature and the American* and Roderick Nash's *Wilderness and the American Mind* are important contributions, but they are only obliquely relevant to this task. Thoreau, because of his theology of nature and his sensitivity to the Puritan tradition, is particularly articulate here. He is also the theologian of wilderness and deserves special study along the lines suggested by George William's *Wilderness and Paradise in Christian Thought.* Someone might draw from his writings and develop a book that might be entitled *The Idea of the Wild* on the analogy of Rudolph Otto's classic *The Idea of the Holy* which might deepen Otto's findings, for Thoreau, as we have seen, held that "the Almighty is wild above all."[26] Had Thoreau lived to write his interpretation of the Indian from the massive notes in eleven volumes from his reading on this subject, he might have articulated even more clearly than he did a theology of wildness. The signs of things to come, as well as a basic shift in emphasis from the Orient to the Indian, are symbolized by his *Journal* entry for February 3, 1859, about the Indians.

If wild men, so much more like ourselves than they are unlike, have inhabited these shores before us, we wish to know particularly what manner of men they were, how they lived here, their relation to nature, their arts and their customs, their fancies and superstitions. They paddled over these waters, they wandered in these woods, and they had their fancies and beliefs connected with the sea and the forest, which concern us quite as much as the fables of Oriental nations do.[27]

This passage became even more of a final leaving-taking of the Oriental religions than Thoreau could have known when he wrote it; it is the last reference in the *Journal* to the religions of the Orient which at one time had so much concerned him. The cutoff point in his correspondence for references to the religions of the East is earlier still. There is still to be written as part of the long overdue theological understanding of American culture a comparison of Thoreau and

John Muir on their theological attitudes toward nature, the one deeply steeped in the Puritan tradition of New England and the other shaped by the Calvinism of Scotland, through his early days there and through the chastening of a father who can only be called a religious fanatic.

Thoreau, it must be recalled, was in revolt from rationalistic Unitarianism and not in the first instance from the Puritanism that had itself led to the Unitarian movement. Thoreau loved the heroic and disciplined figures of the old worthies and recognized a holy vocation of their descendants to carry further their "errand into the wilderness" to the deeper exploration of selfhood in American destiny. "If Columbus was the first to discover the islands, Americus Vespucius, and Cabot, and the Puritans, and we their descendants, have discovered only the shores of America."[28] Thoreau would have agreed with Dag Hammarskjold that the longest journey is the journey within.

At the same time that Thoreau believed in an individual vocation, he was skeptical of the group sense of vocation that produced the "manifest destiny" of his era. Had something of his healthy reservation on this score entered more into the life of the American people, we might not have thrown ourselves with such self-righteous justification and unconscious imperialism into a Vietnamese civil war, all supposedly to make South Vietnam safe for a democracy which it has never known. In this bitter Asiatic crusade that has divided our nation, nothing perhaps better expressed its essentially demonic meaninglessness than the American officer who explained that in order to save the village it was necessary to destroy it.

I am struck by the fact that, though any important individual experience is rare, though it is so rare that the individual is conscious of a relation to his maker transcending time and space and earth, though any knowledge of, or communication from, "Providence" is the rarest thing in the world, yet men very easily, regarding themselves in the gross, speak of carrying out the designs of Providence as nations. How often the Saxon man talks of carrying out the designs of Providence, as if he had some knowledge of Providence and His designs. Men allow themselves to associate Providence and designs of Providence with their dull, prosaic, every-day thoughts of things.[29]

Thoreau felt that John Brown was an individual called to his work but was amazed that most of his contemporaries could not see him in this light. Thoreau was often impatient with Lincoln's slow movement toward emancipation, but had he known of it, he would have been fascinated with Lincoln's swearing a vow and making a covenant with God before Antietam. It is instructive to compare men as different as Lincoln and Thoreau, but the comparison leads to a discovery which has not yet been accorded its true weight in a theological understanding of the American experience. Although Lincoln in later life attended church with considerable regularity, he resolutely refused to join any of the competing denominations of his day. Thoreau, as we have seen, simply dismissed the organized churches. Both Lincoln and Thoreau, however, had a profound knowledge of the Bible and a personal religious faith deeply nourished on biblical presuppositions. They were both dependent on the tradition of Calvinism to a degree greater than they realized. What this suggests is that historically some of the profoundest religious thinking has been done in America quite apart from the hundreds of competing little (or big) denominations through an inherited common tradition of biblical wisdom that remained after the institutional element in church organization had largely discredited itself by the self-contradictions inherent in the denominations. It suggests that there is still a tremendous reservoir, although perhaps less than in Lincoln's and Thoreau's day, of a lay and ecumenical respect for biblical reality that is struggling to find expression through literature, education, art, and other facets of culture rather than in the organized churches. As an illustration, I believe the initial enthusiastic response of lay people to the Consultation on Church Union in the early 1960s tapped these resources for a brief time, before the movement was largely smothered by the organized churches and their bureaucracies. Still another illustration would be the rise of university departments of religious studies that have bypassed the denominations and yet are seedbeds for the nurture of students in biblical (and other) religious tradition. Thoreau and Lincoln can help to lead us toward the pulse of this American phenomenon, a churchless biblical ecumenism. Thoreau's religion showed areas of development which need not be summarized here and which this largely chronological study has made clear. The evidence of serenity in his later years refutes the picture of him as despairing and uncreative. He had Bonhoeffer's piety of sturdy self-reliance in a faith seeking greater maturity and authenticity, not imitative disciples. "God can not give us any other than self-help."[30] While, as Channing reports, he had an aversion for metaphysics, he still had clear, although not completely harmonized, ideas of that environmental complex, which for purposes of analysis has been diagramed as God (Nature↔Self↔Other People, History). He has already been recognized as one of our greatest literary artists. He deserves recognition as one of America's major religious thinkers. Whether in the categories of this study as *mystic, prophet,* and *ecologist* or in his own terms as "mystic, transcendentalist, and natural philosopher, to boot," he is remarkable for the range of his perception of the interrelated aspects of reality and even more of his courageous consistency in molding a life-style to express them. Emerson's funeral address is a noble document and becomes richer with rereading, but the lesser-known tribute of Thoreau's friend Bronson Alcott which appeared in the *Atlantic Monthly* as he lay dying is extraordinarily perceptive, even for our situation today. Sophia, Thoreau's sister, said that Alcott "best understood his religious character."

He, of all men, seems to be the native New-Englander, as much so as the oak, the granite ledge, our best sample of an indigenous American. . . . Of our moralists he seems the wholesomest and the best republican citizen in the world. . . . Perhaps a little over-confident sometimes, and stiffly individual, dropping society clean out of his theories. . . . His works are pieces of exquisite sense, celebrations of Nature's virginity, exemplified by rare learning and original observations. . . . He has been less of a householder than most, has harvested more wind and storm, sun and sky. . . . I think his religion of the most primitive type, and inclusive of all natural creatures and things, even to "the sparrow that falls to the ground," though never by shot of his. . . . Persistently independent and manly, he criticizes men and times largely. . . . The world is holy, the things seen symbolizing the Unseen. . . . Seldom has a head circumscribed so much of the sense of Cosmos as this footed intelligence.[31]

The last words should be Thoreau's. A few stanzas from "Inspiration" ignite his personal faith and, kindling in our own tinder, light up his timeliness for us today.

> But now there comes unsought, unseen,
> Some clear, divine electuary,

And I who had but sensual been,
    Grow sensible, and as God is, am wary.

I hearing get who had but ears,
    And sight, who had but eyes before,
I moments live who lived but years,
    And truth discern who knew but learning's lore.

I hear beyond the range of sound,
    I see beyond the range of sight,
New earths and skies and seas around,
    And in my day the sun doth pale his light.

I will then trust the love untold
    Which not my worth nor want has bought,
Which wooed me young and woos me old,
    And to this evening hath me brought.[32]

READING THOREAU

The beginner is often puzzled about where to start reading Thoreau. Everyone should read *Walden,* but it may not be the best introduction. I shall always be grateful that I began with *The Maine Woods* on my first climb up Katahdin. It remains my conviction that Thoreau scholarship has not adequately evaluated this basic work. Too few readers tackle the fourteen-volume *Journal* now available in a reasonably priced two-volume edition by Dover. Odell Shepard's *The Heart of Thoreau's Journals* is an excellent introduction and an invitation to happy sauntering in these fields. "Civil Disobedience" is a must, but it should lead on to "Slavery in Massachusetts" and to "Life Without Principle." "Walking" and "A Winter Walk" are jewels from his *Excursions. A Week on the Concord and Merrimack Rivers* may be formidable at first, but like *Walden* it grows on one with each rereading. Many of the poems are far more significant for understanding Thoreau's religious orientation than has been generally realized. Carl Bode's *The Portable Thoreau* has been revised and is available in paperback. It is the best short anthology of his writings.

Many of the books about Thoreau have been mentioned in the notes to this book. Walter Harding's *The Days of Henry Thoreau* is the definitive biography, and his earlier *A Thoreau Handbook* is still the best guide to Thoreau scholarship. One wishes Professor Harding would update it. I consider Joseph Wood Krutch's *Henry David Thoreau* the best interpretation of Thoreau, in spite of numerous errors of fact, and Sherman Paul's *The Shores of America* a close second on a more technical level of scholarship.

The Walden or Manuscript Edition by Houghton Mifflin Company in 1906 in twenty volumes has been the standard work, but it has to all intents and purposes been unobtainable. Fortunately, the Princeton University Press is now bringing out a critical and complete edition, as described in the notes. The *Thoreau Society Bulletin,* edited by Professor Harding, keeps a bibliography in progress.

NOTES

1. Thoreau, His Interpreters, His Religion

1. *The Journal of Henry D. Thoreau,* ed. Bradford Torrey and Francis H. Allen (14 vols., 1906; 2-vol. reprint ed., New York: Dover, 1962), Book V, pp. 4-5. Italics added. Henceforth cited as J V 4-5.
2. Henry Thoreau, *Miscellanies* (Boston: Houghton Mifflin Co., 1893), p. 122.
3. Carl Bode (ed.), *Collected Poems of Henry Thoreau* (Baltimore: Johns Hopkins Press, 1965), p. 85.
4. This doctoral dissertation done at New York University in 1957 has been available only on microfilm. Carl Bode has added an epilogue to his *Portable Thoreau* (New York: Viking Press, 1972) that argues for much of Gozzi's thesis. C. Roland Wagner's "Lucky Fox at Walden," in John Hicks (ed.), *Thoreau in Our Season* (Amherst, Mass.: University of Massachusetts Press, 1962), claims that much of *Walden* expresses Thoreau's struggle for sexual identity: "We can say that Thoreau's central method for coping with his Oedipal wishes was unconsciously to submit to and unconsciously to avoid castration. The cycle of the seasons was chosen as the basic structure of Walden to allay the castration anxiety of a man who saw in nature the symbols of fulfillment with Mother" (p. 127).
5. Walter Harding (ed.), *Thoreau, Man of Concord* (New York: Holt, Rinehart & Winston, 1960), p. 190.
6. Joseph Wood Krutch, *Henry David Thoreau* (1948; reprint ed., New York: Dell, 1965), p. 180. Copyright © 1948, by William Sloane Associates, Inc. Used by permission of William Morrow & Co., Inc.
7. From *Atlantic Monthly* (June 1901), quoted in Walter Harding (ed.), *Thoreau: A Century of Criticism* (Dallas, Tex.: Southern Methodist University Press, 1954), p. 100.
8. From the New York *Tribune,* June 13, 1849, quoted in Harding, ibid., pp. 3-4, 7.
9. Krutch, op. cit., p. 192.
10. Ibid., p. 193.
11. William Bysshe Stein, "Thoreau's *A Week* and *Om* Cosmography," in John McAleer (ed.), *Artist and Citizen Thoreau* (Hartford, Conn.: Transcendental Books, 1971), p. 15.
12. Henry David Thoreau, *A Week on the Concord and Merrimack Rivers* (Boston: Houghton Mifflin Co., 1906, 1961), pp. 39-40.
13. Stein, op. cit., p. 19. The essay is immensely erudite but far-fetched. The reader becomes "disoriented" when symbolism has gone to the dogs.
14. Perry Miller (ed.), *Consciousness in Concord: The Text of Thoreau's Hitherto "Lost Journal"* (Cambridge, Mass.: Harvard University Press, 1958), pp. 33-34. Copyright © 1958 by Perry Miller. Used by permission. This book contains Thoreau's journal from July 30, 1840, to January 22, 1842, with notes and commentary.
15. J I 326-27.
16. Ibid., 327.

17. J XI 112-13.
18. Bode (ed.), *Poems*, pp. 230-33. Frank B. Sanborn, who printed the poem in the *Boston Commonwealth* in the spring of 1863, said in his 1917 biography that Sophia, Thoreau's younger sister, had handed him the poem in Thoreau's handwriting. It is impossible to date it, but it seems to have been revised out of short lines found elsewhere in his writings over a period of years. "The system" which has been overturned may refer to Puritan orthodoxy or even to the system of the older Unitarians of his day.

2. Signing Off from Organized Religion

1. *Thoreau Society Bulletin*, 120 (Summer 1972). Bibliography about Thoreau is regularly recorded in the *Bulletin*. Professor Walter Harding, State University, Geneseo, N.Y. 14454, is the secretary-treasurer of the Thoreau Society, Inc.
2. Henry David Thoreau, *Anti-Slavery and Reform Papers*, collected with an introduction by Walter Harding (Montreal: Harvest House, 1963), p. 15.
3. Carl Bode, *Collected Poems of Henry Thoreau* (Baltimore: Johns Hopkins Press, 1965), p. 391.
4. Perry Miller (ed.), *Consciousness in Concord* (Boston: Houghton Mifflin Co., 1958), pp. 210-11.
5. Edward Waldo Emerson, *Henry Thoreau as Remembered by a Young Friend* (Concord, Mass.: Thoreau Lyceum, 1968), p. 15.
6. Walter Harding, *The Days of Henry David Thoreau* (New York: Knopf, 1965), p. 27.
7. J V 58.
8. Edward Emerson, op. cit., p. 23.
9. Frank B. Sanborn, *The Life of Henry Thoreau* (Boston: Houghton Mifflin Co., 1917), p. 144. Sanborn was an eccentric and careless editor; we look forward to accurate texts of the college essays in the forthcoming volumes from the Princeton University Press.
10. Ibid., p. 148.
11. Manuscript in the Abernethy Library transcribed in Reginald Cook, *The Concord Saunterer* (Middlebury, Vt.: Middlebury College Press, 1940), pp. 60-61.
12. *Familiar Letters*, edited by Frank B. Sanborn in the Walden Edition of *The Writings of Henry David Thoreau*, volume 6 (Boston: Houghton Mifflin Co., 1906), p. 9.
13. Ralph Waldo Emerson, "Nature," p. 3, from *Selected Writings of R. W. Emerson*, edited by Brooks Atkinson (New York: Random House, 1940).
14. Quoted from p. 494 of Sanborn, *The Life of H. D. Thoreau*. Henry Seidel Canby in his *Thoreau* (Boston: Houghton Mifflin Co., 1939) writes (p. 167), "His relations with Emerson ripened slowly. There was too much veneration at first, then too much unease in the presence of the smiling serenity of the great man, who never wavered in his faith in Thoreau's genius or in his certainty of its limitations. Thoreau is always 'valiant Henry,' 'my brave Henry'—seldom, except in moments of irritation, a realized human being."
15. Emerson, "Nature," p. 6.
16. Sidney Ahlstrom, *A Religious History of the American People* (New Haven, Conn.: Yale University Press, 1972), p. 598.
17. Octavius Brooks Frothingham, *Transcendentalism in New England* (New York: Harper & Brothers, 1959), pp. 304, 355. See also William Hutchinson, *The Transcendentalist Ministers* (New Haven, Conn.: Yale University Press, 1959).

18. Henry D. Thoreau, *Excursions* (Boston: Houghton Mifflin Co., 1883), p. 56.
19. Ibid., pp. 133-34.
20. Carl Bode (ed.), *Collected Poems of Henry Thoreau* (Baltimore: Johns Hopkins Press, 1965), p. 10.
21. Henry Thoreau, *The Maine Woods*, edited by Joseph J. Moldenhauer (Princeton, N.J.: Princeton University Press, 1972), p. 122. This is the second volume to appear of *The Writings of Henry D. Thoreau* with the approval of the Center for Editions of American Authors.
22. J XI 357.
23. J III 234.
24. J XII 404.
25. J XII 407.
26. J III 21.
27. J I 309.
28. J XI 324-27.
29. J III 119.
30. J III 120.
31. J III 335-36.
32. J X 233.
33. J I 239-40.
34. J XII 419.
35. Harding, *The Days of Henry Thoreau*, p. 321.
36. J XI 438.
37. Henry Thoreau, *A Yankee in Canada* (Montreal: Harvest House, 1961), p. 24.
38. Thoreau wrote Hecker, declining an invitation to go on a pilgrimage to Rome, "I remember you, as it were, with the whole Catholic Church at your skirts—and the other day for a moment I think I understood your relation to that body, but the thought was gone again in a twinkling.... I am really sorry that the Genius will not let me go with you." Walter Harding and Carl Bode (eds.), *The Correspondence of Henry David Thoreau* (New York: New York University Press, 1958), p. 156.
39. *A Yankee in Canada*, p. 25.
40. Ralph Waldo Emerson, printed in Walter Harding (ed.), *Thoreau: A Century of Criticism* (Dallas, Tex.: Southern Methodist University Press, 1954), pp. 23-24.
41. *The Maine Woods*, p. 182.
42. Lawrence Willson, "Thoreau and Roman Catholicism," in *Catholic Historical Review* XLII (1956), pp. 160-61. Willson transcribes (p. 172) a comment from a manuscript (HM13182) in the Huntington Library: "The Catholic missionaries succeed better with savages and barbarians than the Protestant because their own religion is more savage and barbaric. Their religion is more ceremonial and interferes but little with the practices of men but is superadded to them—a superstition. The priest comes recommended to the savage by his genial social virtues."
43. J IX 283-84.
44. Harding and Bode (eds.), *Correspondence*, pp. 128-29.
45. J VIII 392.
46. J IX 188.
47. Edward Emerson, op. cit., p. 80.
48. William J. Wolf, *Lincoln's Religion* (Philadelphia: Pilgrim Press, 1970), p. 129, gives the Lincoln version of the story: "Asked then why he hadn't made a preacher, the boy smiled and said, 'I hain't got *mud* enough." The Thoreau version can be found in "Memoirs of Thoreau," *The Truth Seeker*, Nov. 20, 1897.

49. *A Yankee in Canada*, p. 26.
50. See John Aldrich Christie, *Thoreau as World Traveler* (New York: Columbia University Press, 1965), passim.
51. Bode (ed.), *Poems*, p. 27.

3. The Religions of A Week on the Concord and Merrimack Rivers

1. J I 136.
2. *Dial* III, p. 82.
3. The best analysis is Carl Hovde, "The Writing of Henry D. Thoreau's *A Week on the Concord and Merrimack Rivers:* A Study in Textual Materials and Technique," Ph.D. thesis, Princeton University, 1956, University Microfilms, Ann Arbor.
4. Henry David Thoreau, *A Week on the Concord and Merrimack Rivers* (Boston: Houghton Mifflin Co., 1906, 1961), p. 159.
5. William Jones, *Works* (London: 1807), VII, pp. 99-100.
6. *A Week*, p. 159.
7. J I 276.
8. *A Week*, pp. 145-46. Italics added.
9. Arthur Christy, *The Orient in American Transcendentalism* (New York: Columbia University Press, 1932), pp. xi and 199.
10. One of the most stimulating studies of Thoreau is Sherman Paul, *The Shores of America: Thoreau's Inward Exploration* (1958; reprint ed., Urbana, Ill.: University of Illinois, 1972). On page 217 he writes, "The *Bhagavad-Gita* was the most highly praised book in the *Week*, especially because it did complete justice to contemplation; but Thoreau, with his desire for heroic action, could not accept its counsels of passivity and fate."
11. J I 55. See also I 261, 264, 266–68, 275–80.
12. J I 151.
13. J I 263.
14. J I 275.
15. J I 277.
16. J I 18.
17. *Massachusetts Quarterly Review* (December, 1849), p. 48. Henry Seidel Canby in his *Thoreau* (Boston: Houghton Mifflin Co., 1939), p. 272, describes the *Week* as "perilously like a library of the shorter works of Henry Thoreau."
18. J I 18.
19. *A Week*, p. 12.
20. Ibid., p. 25.
21. Ibid., pp. 35-36.
22. Ibid., pp. 45, 42.
23. Ibid., pp. 55-56.
24. J I 119.
25. *A Week*, p. 61.
26. J I 391 is the 1845 *Journal* source for this interesting point: "The attribute of the one god has been infinite power, not grace, not humanity, nor love even,—wholly masculine, with no sister Juno, no Apollo, no Venus in him. I might say that the one god was not yet apotheosized, not yet become the current material of poetry."
27. *A Week*, p. 65.
28. Ibid., pp. 65-67.
29. Ibid., p. 68.
30. Ibid., p. 70.
31. Ibid., p. 71.
32. Ibid.

33. Ibid., p. 72.
34. Ibid., pp. 73-74.
35. Ibid., p. 74.
36. Ibid.
37. Ibid.
38. Ibid., p. 75.
39. Ibid., p. 78.
40. Ibid., p. 403.
41. Alexander Chalmers, *The Works of the English Poets* VI, p. 62a, quoted in Hovde's thesis, loc. cit., p. 76.
42. *A Week*, p. 79.
43. Ibid., p. 100.
44. Ibid., p. 123.
45. Ibid., p. 130.
46. Ibid., p. 135.
47. Ibid., pp. 142-43.
48. Ibid., p. 142.
49. Ibid., p. 149.
50. Ibid., pp. 141-42.
51. Ibid., pp. 146.
52. Ibid., pp. 150.
53. Arthur Christy, *The Orient in American Transcendentalism*, p. 188.
54. Although scholars universally call the Cholmondeley library "Oriental books," it should be noted that among them were a number of Christian books such as the Ante-Nicene Fathers, Hippolytus, and the Chevalier Bunson's *Christianity and Mankind*. Christianity, of course, is an Oriental religion. Among the "farther-Eastern" books were the *Rig Veda Sanhita*, the *Mandukya Upanishads*, the *Nala* and *Damyanta*, the *Vishnu Purana*, the *Institutes of Menu*, the *Sankhya Karika*, *Aphorisms of the Mimasma* and *Nayaya*, the *Bhagavat Gheeta*, *Sakoontala*, and the *Bhagavita Purana*. Although there was a manual of Buddhism, the library was not rich in this material. Many Zen classics or, for example, Lao-tzu's *Tao-Te-Ching* would have delighted Thoreau had he known them.
55. Walter Harding and Carl Bode (eds.), *The Correspondence of Henry David Thoreau* (New York: New York University Press, 1958), p. 403.
56. Ibid., p. 402.
57. J VIII 135.
58. Harding and Bode (eds.), *Correspondence*, p. 448.
59. See Albert Keiser, "Thoreau's Manuscripts on the Indians," *Journal of English and Germanic Philology* XXVII (April 1928), pp. 183-99, and *The Indian in American Literature* (New York: Oxford University Press, 1933).
60. Harding and Bode (eds.), *Correspondence*, p. 491.
61. Ibid., p. 310.
62. Walter Harding, *A Thoreau Handbook* (New York: New York University Press, 1961), p. 100. Canby in his *Thoreau* (Boston: Houghton Mifflin Co., 1939) states (p. 326), "It was too late. He had gotten what good he could extract from the Orient years before and read little in his new acquisitions."
63. *A Week*, pp. 181-82.
64. Ibid., p. 189.
65. Ibid., pp. 189-91, 193.
66. Ibid., p. 197.
67. Ibid., pp. 197-200. Italics added.
68. Hovde writes that "the whole scene on Saddle-back Mountain is the most ecstatic recognition of the realm of spirit to be found in the book" (Ph.D. thesis, loc. cit., p. 77). See also the suggestive article

by Jonathan Bishop, "The Experience of the Sacred in Thoreau's *Week*," in *Journal of English Literary History* 1966, pp. 66-91.

69. *A Week*, p. 250.
70. Ibid., p. 294.
71. Ibid., p. 281.
72. Ibid., p. 275.
73. Ibid., p. 287.
74. Ibid., p. 284.
75. Ibid., p. 285.
76. Ibid., pp. 292-93.
77. Ibid., p. 281.
78. Ibid., pp. 284-85. Italics added.
79. Ibid., p. 302.
80. Ibid., p. 303. Italics added.
81. Ibid., p. 343.
82. Ibid., p. 345.
83. Ibid., p. 362.
84. Ibid., p. 408.
85. Ibid., p. 412.
86. Ibid., p. 419.

4. A Prophet Emerges: "Civil Disobedience"

1. Henry David Thoreau, *Anti-Slavery and Reform Papers*, collected with an introduction by Walter Harding (Montreal: Harvest House, 1963), p. 15.
2. Ibid., p. 17.
3. Reprinted by permission of the University of Massachusetts Press from *Thoreau in Our Season*, John Hicks, ed., 1962, p. 13.
4. Sherman Paul (ed.), *Thoreau: A Collection of Critical Essays* (Englewood Cliffs, N.J.: Prentice-Hall, 1962), p. 130. Ethyl Seybold's interesting and helpful *Thoreau: The Quest and the Classics* (New Haven, Conn.: Yale University Press, 1951), p. 17, overstates the influence of *Antigone* on Thoreau: "From it must have come his concept of the divine law as superior to the civil law, of human right as greater than legal right." Surely Transcendentalism is the source of "his concept of the divine law," although he also saw the theme in Sophocles.
5. Paul Lauter in a perceptive essay, "Thoreau's Prophetic Testimony," in Hicks (ed.), *Thoreau in Our Season*, writes as follows (p. 82): "The prophetic book, then, becomes an embodiment of a man's search to incarnate his ultimate values in his actions and the final means by which that man would attempt to move others toward their own testimonies to such values. . . . Thoreau's works are prophetic testimonials in this sense."
6. J I 36.
7. J I 177.
8. J I 227.
9. J I 247.
10. *Anti-Slavery and Reform Papers*, p. 94.
11. J I 427.
12. *Anti-Slavery and Reform Papers*, p. 1.
13. Ibid., pp. 2-3.
14. Ibid., p. 1.
15. Ibid., p. 2.
16. Ibid., pp. 3-4.
17. Ibid., p. 7.
18. Ibid., pp. 4-5. Thoreau argues (p. 9) that the state's reluctance to reform itself brings disaster upon it. "Why is it not more apt to

anticipate and provide for reform? Why does it not cherish its wise
minority?"

19. Ibid., p. 6.
20. Ibid., p. 9.
21. Ibid., p. 11.
22. Ibid., p. 12.
23. Ibid., pp. 13-14.
24. J IV 324.
25. *Anti-Slavery and Reform Papers*, pp. 19-20.
26. Ibid., p. 20.
27. Ibid., pp. 21-22.
28. Ibid., p. 22.
29. Ibid., p. 24. Italics added.
30. Sherman Paul (*The Shores of America: Thoreau's Inward Exploration*
    [1958; reprint ed., Urbana, Ill.: University of Illinois, 1972], p. 247)
    writes, "Had he not gone to jail, *Walden* might well have been only
    an account of his spiritual rebirth; as it was, however, placed be-
    tween 'Economy' and 'Conclusion,' his experiment in renewal became
    an example of what he considered a true social reform—so much so
    that the social aspects of the book were more often remembered
    than the personal ones."
31. For further discussion of this point see William J. Wolf, *Lincoln's
    Religion* (Philadelphia: Pilgrim Press, 1970), p. 116.
32. J II 178-79.
33. J II 175.
34. J II 176.
35. J II 174.
36. J II 472.
37. J II 207-8.
38. J III 266.
39. J II 391-92.

5. The Religion of Walden

1. All Thoreau scholars are in debt to J. Lyndon Shanley for his fascinating documentary analysis of the seven versions of *Walden* in *The
   Making of Walden, with the Text of the First Version* (Chicago: University of Chicago Press, 1957).
2. Walter Harding, *The Days of Henry Thoreau* (New York: Knopf,
   1965), p. 334.
3. *Walden*, in *The Writings of Henry D. Thoreau*, edited by J. Lyndon
   Shanley (Princeton, N.J.: Princeton University Press, 1971), p. 298.
   Subsequent references to *Walden* are to this edition.
4. "Rather too much has been made of this influence, as if every hint
   of a correspondence betokened borrowing. It is near the truth to say
   that Thoreau went to the religious books of the East because of certain correspondences in him to Eastern modes of thought, than that
   these Eastern modes of thought produced correspondences in him.
   As he says himself, 'like some other preachers, I have added my
   texts—derived from the Chinese and Hindoo scriptures—long after
   my discourse was written.'" Norman Foerster in *Twentieth-Century
   Interpretations of Walden*, edited by Richard Ruland (Englewood
   Cliffs, N.J.: Prentice-Hall, 1968), p. 43.
5. *Walden*, pp. 111-12.
6. Ibid., p. 113. Italics added.
7. Ibid., pp. 224-25.
8. Ibid., p. 131. Italics added.
9. Ibid., p. 108.

10. Ibid., p. 14.
11. Ibid., pp. 14-15.
12. Ibid., pp. 90-91.
13. Ibid., pp. 75-76.
14. Ibid., p. 77.
15. Ibid., p. 78.
16. Ibid.
17. From p. 12 of Basil Willey's introduction to *Walden* (New York: Bramhall House, 1951). © 1951 W. W. Norton & Co.
18. *Walden*, p. 97.
19. Shanley, *The Making of Walden*, p. 155.
20. Ibid., p. 169.
21. *Walden*, p. 210. "Cynics may be inclined to suspect that an almost exclusive diet of rice, Indian meal, and molasses might reasonably be expected to make even woodchuck look strangely attractive to any man." Joseph Wood Krutch, *Henry David Thoreau* (1948; reprint ed., New York: Dell, 1965), p. 83. Copyright © 1948, by William Sloane Associates, Inc. Used by permission of William Morrow & Co., Inc.
22. *Walden*, p. 210.
23. Ibid., p. 212.
24. Ibid., pp. 214-15.
25. Ibid., p. 221.
26. Ibid., pp. 219-20.
27. Ibid., p. 221.
28. Ibid., p. 222.
29. Ibid., pp. 323-24.
30. Ibid., p. 327.
31. Ibid., p. 333.
32. Ibid.
33. Ibid., p. 11.
34. Ibid., p. 207.
35. Ibid., p. 129.
36. See the essay by Leo Marx in Ruland (ed.), *Twentieth-Century Interpretations of Walden*.
37. *Walden*, p. 71.
38. Ibid., pp. 317-18.
39. Henry Thoreau, *The Maine Woods*, edited by Joseph J. Moldenhauer (Princeton, N.J.: Princeton University Press, 1972), pp. 64, 70-71. Leo Stoller in *After Walden* (Stanford, Cal.: Stanford University Press, 1957) understands the shaking experience Thoreau had on Katahdin, but he unfortunately wraps it up too neatly in metaphysical categories that overintellectualize Thoreau's positions at the time (p. 45). "As if to complete the dissociation of the integrated ideology which had led him to the pond, Thoreau had what can only be described as the negation of a mystical experience, during which his essential pantheism suddenly dissolved into its component idealism and materialism and shocked him into fear and bewilderment." There is little evidence for such terms as "integrated ideology" and "essential pantheism." It is not clear that the experience represented "the negation of a mystical experience"; it might, on the other hand, be described as a deepened mystical experience.
40. *The Maine Woods*, p. 155.
41. *Walden*, p. 166.
42. Ibid., pp. 283-84.
43. Ibid., p. 332.
44. Ibid., pp. 306, 308.
45. Ibid., p. 193.

46. Ibid., pp. 195-96.
47. John B. Pickard in Ruland (ed.), *Twentieth-Century Interpretations of Walden*, p. 88.
48. *Walden*, pp. 329-30. Italics added.
49. *Anti-Slavery and Reform Papers*, collected with an introduction by Walter Harding (Montreal: Harvest House, 1963), p. 146. There is a good discussion of *Walden* and "Civil Disobedience" in their interrelationships in Stanley Cavell, *The Senses of Walden* (New York: Viking Press, 1972), chapter III.

6. "I Am a Mystic"

1. William R. Inge, *Christian Mysticism* (New York: Charles Scribner's Sons, 1899), pp. 4-5.
2. J II 150-51.
3. Alfred P. Stiernotte (ed.), *Mysticism and the Modern Mind* (New York: Bobbs-Merrill, 1959), p. 5.
4. Odell Shepard (ed.), *The Journals of Bronson Alcott* (Boston: Little, Brown, 1938), pp. 318, 350.
5. Walter Harding and Carl Bode (eds.), *The Correspondence of Henry David Thoreau* (New York: New York University Press, 1958), p. 453.
6. Ibid., p. 156.
7. Ibid., p. 251.
8. J I 279. Charles Calvin Kopp, "The Mysticism of Henry David Thoreau" (Pennsylvania State University, 1963), is an unpublished Ph.D. thesis on the subject.
9. J II 468-69.
10. Carl Bode (ed.), *Collected Poems of Henry Thoreau* (Baltimore: Johns Hopkins Press, 1965), p. 107. Emerson preferred to take his nature more gently, on his afternoon walk or in thought about nature at his study desk. Emerson commented that if God had meant for Thoreau to live in a swamp, He would have made him a frog.
11. Ibid., p. 195.
12. J II 472.
13. Bode (ed.), *Poems*, pp. 95-96. Bode comments (p. 356), " 'The Blue-birds' is notable for including the most graphic account of a mystical experience in Thoreau's poetry."
14. *A Week*, p. 408.
15. J II 140-41.
16. J VI 39.
17. Harding and Bode (eds.), *Correspondence*, p. 331.
18. J IX 246.
19. J III 71.
20. J III 253.
21. Bode (ed.), *Poems*, p. 162.
22. J IX 209.
23. Harding and Bode (eds.), *Correspondence*, p. 424.
24. W. T. Stace, *Mysticism and Philosophy* (Philadelphia: Lippincott, 1960).
25. J IV 163.
26. J III 155-56.
27. This interpretation appears full-blown in Mark Van Doren's *Henry David Thoreau: A Critical Study* (New York: Russell & Russell, 1943) and, in a modified way in Sherman Paul's *The Shores of America: Thoreau's Inward Exploration* (1958; reprint ed., Urbana, Ill.: University of Illinois Press, 1972). It draws heavily upon such entries as that of July 16, 1851 (II 306ff.), which must after all be seen in the

context of other entries that summer and of later entries like October 4, 1859 (XII 371ff.). The topic is too complicated for discussion here, but the perspective of Walter Harding's *The Days of Henry Thoreau* is well-balanced and convincing.

28. J XII 371-72. Italics added.
29. J XIV 117.
30. J II 268-69.
31. *Walden*, p. 99.
32. Ibid., p. 132.
33. Harding and Bode (eds.), *Correspondence*, pp. 257-58.
34. J IV 128.
35. J IV 284-85.
36. J XII 44-45.

7. "I Am a Transcendentalist" (Prophet)

1. J V 4.
2. Henry David Thoreau, *Anti-Slavery and Reform Papers*, collected with an introduction by Walter Harding (Montreal: Harvest House, 1963), p. 45.
3. Ibid., pp. 70-71.
4. Ibid., pp. 27-28, 30, 32, 36-37.
5. Ibid., pp. 37-38.
6. Ibid., p. 39.
7. Ibid., p. 40.
8. Ibid., p. 41.
9. *Walden*, pp. 26-27.
10. Walter Harding (ed.), *Thoreau: A Century of Criticism* (Dallas, Tex.: Southern Methodist University Press, 1954), p. 39.
11. J IX 175.
12. Walter Harding and Carl Bode (eds.), *The Correspondence of Henry David Thoreau* (New York: New York University Press, 1958), p. 496 (letter of November 16, 1857, to Blake).
13. Ibid., p. 436.
14. *Anti-Slavery and Reform Papers*, p. 43.
15. Ibid., p. 44.
16. Ibid., p. 46.
17. Ibid., p. 50.
18. Ibid.
19. Ibid., p. 63.
20. Ibid., p. 61.
21. Ibid., p. 64.
22. Ibid., p. 60.
23. Quoted from Walter Harding, *The Days of Henry Thoreau* (New York: Knopf, 1965), p. 419.
24. Quoted from Walter Harding (ed.), *Thoreau: Man of Concord* (New York: Holt, Rinehart & Winston, 1960), p. 159.
25. *Anti-Slavery and Reform Papers*, p. 70.
26. Ibid., p. 73.
27. Ibid., p. 75.
28. Harding and Bode (eds.), *Correspondence*, p. 611.
29. Frank B. Sanborn, *The Life of Henry David Thoreau* (Boston: Houghton Mifflin Co., 1917), p. 401.
30. Ibid., p. 483.
31. Quoted from William J. Wolf, *Lincoln's Religion* (Philadelphia: Pilgrim Press, 1970), pp. 119-21.
32. *Anti-Slavery and Reform Papers*, p. 71.

33. Odell Shepard (ed.), *The Journals of Bronson Alcott* (Boston: Little, Brown, 1938), p. 341.

34. William Ellery Channing, *Thoreau, Poet-Naturalist* (New York: Biblo & Tannen, 1902), p. 16.

35. J I 318.

36. J II 3.

37. J II 23-25. Leon Edel in *Henry David Thoreau* (Minneapolis, Minn.: University of Minnesota Press, 1970) to all intents and purposes charges Thoreau with arson (p. 20). "If this occurrence had in it an acting out of Thoreau's disdain for his fellowcountrymen in the community, the flames that destroyed three hundred acres of woodland also expressed Thoreau's inner rage and his malaise."

38. J III 293.

39. R. W. B. Lewis, *The American Adam: Innocence, Tragedy, and Tradition in the Nineteenth Century* (Chicago: University of Chicago Press, 1958), p. 1.

40. J II 152-53.

41. *Anti-Slavery and Reform Papers,* p. 140.

42. Carl Bode (ed.), *Collected Poems of Henry Thoreau* (Baltimore: Johns Hopkins Press, 1965), p. 186.

43. Norman Foerster, *Nature in American Literature* (New York: Macmillan, 1923), p. 132.

44. Harding and Bode (eds.), *Correspondence*, pp. 221-22.

45. J II 497.

46. J I 187-88.

47. J I 322.

48. Harding and Bode (eds.), *Correspondence*, p. 62.

49. Ibid.

50. Ibid., p. 64.

51. J I 330.

52. A MS dated August 26, 1843, quoted by Raymond W. Adams, "Thoreau and Immortality," in *Studies in Philology* XXVI (Jan. 1929), p. 65.

53. Henry Thoreau, *The Maine Woods,* edited by Joseph J. Moldenhauer (Princeton, N.J.: Princeton University Press, 1972), p. 122.

54. Raymond W. Adams presses, it seems to me, scanty evidence too far in the following conclusion (op. cit., pp. 62-63): "Though, as he says, 'The form of the soul is eternal,' yet it must abide in various bodies before it can attain perfection and rest. . . . The soul flies in the bird because it has crawled in the beast. . . . Up from the reptile to the bird, from bird to man, from man to man unto perfect harmony, and then out into nature and eternity—that is the course of the soul. That conception explains much; the peculiar sympathy of Thoreau with beasts and even with plants may be considered to have come partly from a belief that his soul had once inhabited a plant or an animal." Professor Adams has made Thoreau the holder of a metaphysical system of the progressively upward transmigration of the soul.

55. J I 302.

56. J VIII 222-23.

57. *Cape Cod,* p. 14, from *The Works of Henry David Thoreau* (New York: Thomas Y. Crowell Co., 1940).

58. Bode (ed.), *Poems,* p. 118.

8. "I Am a Natural Philosopher" (Ecologist)

1. J XIV 146-47.

2. J V 5.

3. Perry Miller (ed.), *Consciousness in Concord: The Text of Thoreau's Hitherto "Lost Journal"* (Boston: Houghton Mifflin Co., 1958), p. 185.
4. J I 320.
5. Miller, *Consciousness in Concord*, p. 193.
6. J II 245.
7. J V 225.
8. J XII 171.
9. J III 381-82.
10. J X 51.
11. J IV 482.
12. J VIII 220-21.
13. J I 306-7.
14. J V 135.
15. J I 107.
16. J IV 163.
17. J I 265.
18. J IV 445.
19. Henry D. Thoreau, *Excursions* (Boston: Houghton Mifflin Co., 1883), p. 185.
20. J VI 293-94.
21. J I 237.
22. J V 330-31.
23. J II 316-17.
24. Walter Harding and Carl Bode (eds.), *The Correspondence of Henry David Thoreau* (New York: New York University Press, 1958), p. 294.
25. J VI 294 and I 326.
26. J XI 359.
27. J I 180-81.
28. J II 468.
29. J IX 45-46.
30. J III 119.
31. Harding and Bode (eds.), *Correspondence*, p. 67.
32. J II 4.
33. J XIV 294.
34. *Walden*, p. 137. See also p. 182.
35. Walter Harding, *A Thoreau Handbook* (New York: New York University Press, 1959), p. 106. A Ph.D. dissertation by John Burns entitled "Thoreau's Use of the Bible" (University of Notre Dame, 1966) is helpful on matters of style and of statistics, as it includes a useful concordance, but it seldom discusses his "theological use" of the Bible. Burns criticizes Harding's comment quoted here, but he takes too limited a view of what constitutes "familiarity" with the King James Bible.
36. J XIII 106.
37. J VII 113.
38. J II 410.
39. Paul Elmer More, *Shelburne Essays on American Literature* (New York: Harcourt, Brace & World, 1963), pp. 225-26. A somewhat similar statement was made (p. 25) by Lawrence Willson in "The Influence of Early North American History and Legend on the Writings of H. D. Thoreau" (Ph.D. thesis, Yale University, 1944). "The impulse which sent him off to study nature in order to discover the unifying thread which binds God to man was a Puritan impulse." Quoted from p. 120 of Harding's *A Thoreau Handbook* (New York: New York University Press, 1961).
40. William Ellery Channing, *Thoreau, the Poet-Naturalist* (New York: Biblo & Tannen, 1902), p. 333.
41. Harding and Bode (eds.), *Correspondence*, p. 641.

42. Walter Harding (ed.), *Thoreau: Man of Concord* (New York: Holt, Rinehart & Winston, 1960), pp. 100-101.
43. Edward Waldo Emerson, *Henry Thoreau as Remembered by a Young Friend* (Concord, Mass.: Thoreau Lyceum, 1968), p. 118.
44. Harding (ed.), *Thoreau: Man of Concord*, p. 61.
45. Quoted from p. 462 of Harding, *The Days of Henry Thoreau* (New York: Knopf, 1965).
46. Channing, *Thoreau, the Poet-Naturalist*, p. 336.
47. Walter Harding (ed.), *Thoreau: A Century of Criticism* (Dallas, Tex.: Southern Methodist University Press, 1954), pp. 36-37.

9. Thoreau and the Religious Situation Today

1. *A Plan of Union for the Church of Christ Uniting* (Princeton, N.J.: Consultation on Church Union, 1970), p. 26.
2. J I 285.
3. Walter Harding and Carl Bode (eds.), *The Correspondence of Henry David Thoreau* (New York: New York University Press, 1958), p. 625.
4. *A Week*, p. 71.
5. Ibid., p. 79.
6. J I 386.
7. J I 326.
8. F. L. Cross (ed.), *The Oxford Dictionary of the Christian Church* (New York: Oxford University Press, 1958), p. 1010.
9. Pierre Teilhard de Chardin, *The Phenomenon of Man* (New York: Harper & Row, 1965), p. 310.
10. Henry D. Thoreau, *Excursions* (Boston: Houghton Mifflin Co., 1883), p. 204.
11. J I 150.
12. Henry Thoreau, *The Maine Woods*, edited by Joseph J. Moldenhauer (Princeton, N.J.: Princeton University Press, 1972), pp. 180-82.
13. J II 330.
14. J III 174.
15. J II 479.
16. Carl Bode (ed.), *Collected Poems of Henry Thoreau* (Baltimore: Johns Hopkins Press, 1965), p. 162.
17. Harding and Bode (eds.), *Correspondence*, pp. 257-58.
18. Ibid., p. 192.
19. Stanley Edgar Hyman from *Atlantic Monthly*, November 1946, pp. 137-46.
20. Norman Foerster, *Nature in American Literature* (New York: Macmillan, 1923), p. 142.
21. J XI 338.
22. J VI 357.
23. Henry Stephens Salt, *Life of Henry David Thoreau* (1890; Hamden, Conn.: Shoe String Press, Archon, 1968), p. 192.
24. Perry Miller (ed.), *Consciousness in Concord: The Text of Thoreau's Hitherto "Lost Journal"* (Boston: Houghton Mifflin Co., 1958), p. 156 (italics added).
25. Harding and Bode (eds.), *Correspondence*, pp. 290-91.
26. J IV 482.
27. J XI 437-38.
28. *The Maine Woods*, p. 81.
29. J II 214-15.
30. Miller (ed.), *Consciousness in Concord*, p. 173.
31. Quoted from *Thoreau Society Bulletin* 78 (Winter 1962). Used by permission. The text has been somewhat rearranged in the quotation.
32. Bode (ed.), *Poems*, pp. 231-32.

A SELECTED BIBLIOGRAPHY
ON THOREAU'S RELIGION

Adams, Raymond W. "Thoreau and Immortality." *Studies in Philology* XXVI (January 1929). Still the best on this theme.

Bhatia, Kamala. "The Mysticism of Thoreau and Its Affinity with Indian Thought." New Delhi: 1966.

Bishop, Jonathan. "The Experience of the Sacred in Thoreau's *Week*." *Journal of English Literary History* XXXIII (March 1966). Very good.

Broderick, John. "Emerson, Thoreau, and Transcendentalism." In *American Literary Scholarship,* edited by J. Robbins. Durham, N.C.: Duke University Press, 1970-72.

Burns, John. "Thoreau's Use of the Bible." Ph.D. thesis, University of Notre Dame, 1966. Helpful concordance.

Christy, Arthur. *The Orient in American Transcendentalism.* New York: Columbia University Press, 1932. Needs correction at some points, but still basic.

Cook, Reginald L. "Nature Mysticism." In *Passage to Walden.* Boston: Houghton Mifflin Co., 1949. Imaginative and helpful.

Drake, William D. "The Depth of Walden: Thoreau's Symbolism of the Divine in Nature." Ph.D. thesis, University of Arizona, 1967.

Frothingham, Octavius B. *Transcendentalism in New England.* New York: Harper & Brothers, 1959. For background.

Hart, Ray L. "The Poiesis of Place." *Journal of Religion* LIII, No. 1 (1973).

Hovde, Carl F. "The Writing of Henry D. Thoreau's *A Week on the Concord and Merrimack Rivers*: A Study in Textual Materials and Technique." Ph.D. thesis, Princeton University, 1956, University Microfilms, Ann Arbor. Comments on Thoreau's religious attitudes.

Hutchison, William R. *The Transcendentalist Ministers: Church Reform in the New England Renaissance.* New Haven, Conn.: Yale University Press, 1959. For background.

Kopp, Charles Calvin. "The Mysticism of H. D. Thoreau." Ph.D. thesis, The Pennsylvania State University, 1963. Overfreighted but useful.

Lauter, Paul. "Thoreau's Prophetic Testimony." In *Thoreau in Our Season,* edited by John H. Hicks. Amherst, Mass.: University of Massachusetts Press, 1962.

Leidecker, Kurt. "That Sad Pagan Thoreau." *Visvabharati Quarterly* (November 1951–January 1952). Pp. 218-59.

MacShane, Frank. "*Walden* and Yoga." *New England Quarterly* XXXVII (September 1964).

Miller, Perry (ed.). *The Transcendentalists; an Anthology.* Cambridge, Mass.: Harvard University Press, 1950. For background.

More, Paul Elmer. *Shelburne Essays on American Literature.* New York: Harcourt, Brace & World, 1963. Pp. 199-229. Keen insights.

Oliver, Egbert. "Thoreau and the Puritan Tradition." *Emerson Society Quarterly* XLIV, 1966.

Pickard, John B. "The Religion of 'Higher Laws.' " In *Twentieth-Century Interpretations of Walden,* edited by Richard Ruland. Englewood Cliffs, N.J.: Prentice-Hall, 1968.

Porte, Joel. "A Purely Sensuous Life." In *Henry David Thoreau: A Profile,* edited by Walter Harding. New York: Hill & Wang, 1971.

Smith, John Sylvester. "The Philosophical Naturism of H. D. Thoreau with Special Reference to Its Epistemological Presuppositions and Theological Implications." Ph.D. thesis, Drew University, 1948. An excellent analysis.

Stein, William B. "Thoreau's First Book: A Spoor of Yoga." *Emerson Society Quarterly* XLI (1965).

Stevick, Daniel. "Thoreau and Political Obligation." In *Civil Disobedience and the Christian.* New York: Seabury Press, 1969.

Thorpe, Willard. "Thoreau's Huckleberry Party." *Thoreau Society Bulletin* 40 (Summer 1952). Helpful comparison of Emerson's and Thoreau's religion.

Willson, Lawrence. "Thoreau and Roman Catholicism." *Catholic Historical Review* XLII (1956). Fine essay.

INDEX

ABOUT THE AUTHOR

William J. Wolf is Howard Chandler Robbins Professor of Theology, The Episcopal Theological School, Cambridge, Massachusetts. He is a graduate of Trinity College, The Episcopal Theological School, and Union Theological Seminary (S.T.M., Th.D.). He has made canoe and walking trips to nearly all of Thoreau's streams and mountains.

Dr. Wolf is the author of numerous publications including five previous books: *Man's Knowledge of God* (1955), *No Cross, No Crown* (1957), *The Almost Chosen People* (1959; reprinted as *Lincoln's Religion*, 1970), *A Plan of Church Union* (1965), and (with John Porter) *The Recovery of Unity: The Thought of F. D. Maurice* (1963).